About Island Press

Island Press is the only nonprofit organization in the United States whose principal purpose is the publication of books on environmental issues and natural resource management. We provide solutions-oriented information to professionals, public officials, business and community leaders, and concerned citizens who are shaping responses to environmental problems.

In 2003, Island Press celebrates its nineteenth anniversary as the leading provider of timely and practical books that take a multidisciplinary approach to critical environmental concerns. Our growing list of titles reflects our commitment to bringing the best of an expanding body of literature to the environmental community throughout North America and the world.

Support for Island Press is provided by The Nathan Cummings Foundation, Geraldine R. Dodge Foundation, Doris Duke Charitable Foundation, Educational Foundation of America, The Charles Engelhard Foundation, The Ford Foundation, The George Gund Foundation, The Vira I. Heinz Endowment, The William and Flora Hewlett Foundation, Henry Luce Foundation, The John D. and Catherine T. MacArthur Foundation, The Andrew W. Mellon Foundation, The Moriah Fund, The Curtis and Edith Munson Foundation, National Fish and Wildlife Foundation, The New-Land Foundation, Oak Foundation, The Overbrook Foundation, The David and Lucile Packard Foundation, The Pew Charitable Trusts, The Rockefeller Foundation, The Winslow Foundation, and other generous donors.

The opinions expressed in this book are those of the author(s) and do not necessarily reflect the views of these foundations.

From Conquest
to Conservation

From Conquest to Conservation

OUR PUBLIC LANDS LEGACY

Michael P. Dombeck, Christopher A. Wood,
and Jack E. Williams

Illustrations by
William Millonig

ISLAND PRESS
Washington • Covelo • London

Library of Congress Cataloging-in-Publication Data

Dombeck, Michael P.
  From conquest to conservation: our public lands legacy / Michael
P. Dombeck, Christopher A. Wood, and Jack E. Williams.
      p. cm.
Includes bibliographical references and index.
  ISBN 1-55963-955-5 (cloth : alk. paper) — ISBN 1-55963-956-3
(pbk. : alk. paper)
  1. Public lands—United States—History. 2. Land use, Rural—
Environmental aspects—United States—History. 3. Conservation of
natural resources—United States—History. 4. Nature conservation—
United States—History. 5. Sustainable development—United States—
History. I. Wood, Christopher A. II. Williams, Jack Edward. III. Title.
  HD216 .D66 2003
333.1'0973—dc21   2002015728

British Cataloguing-in-Publication Data available.

Book design by Brighid Willson
Printed on recycled, acid-free paper

Manufactured in the United States of America
10 9 8 7 6 5 4 3 2 1

We dedicate this book to all who work to promote
ecological literacy and the health of the land.

Contents

Preface

This book is not a dispassionate analysis of contemporary public land views. We admit our bias—namely, that basic wealth and quality of life flow from the lands and waters that sustain us. Consequently, the first imperative of land management should be to protect land health. The ideas for the scope of this book evolved during the heady days when protection of roadless areas seemed imminent, old-growth forest conservation likely, a coherent national fire plan possible, and dialogue about ecological sustainability commonplace.

As is so often the case, however, election cycles, political imperatives, international events, and economic pressures drive the debate over these pressing issues. Oblivious to the ongoing public policy debate is the land itself. We use the term "land" beyond the strict Webster's dictionary definition of "the solid part of the earth's surface." Our use of "land" includes the water, the watersheds, the ecosystems, the places where the physical and biological elements of nature that support our way of life, and life itself, interact—or, put more simply, the places where we all live. These places include landscapes from which our forebears carved a nation; prairies that gave way to the plow and became farms; forests that begat homes from saw and axe; and watersheds that provide water to quench our thirst and yield minerals to fuel economic growth or boom-and-bust prosperity. Fully one-third of the U.S. land base is owned by all citizens and managed in trust for the American people. With continued public interest, citizen activism, and responsible management, public lands will continue to inspire and sustain us for the next seven generations and beyond.

After working together as coeditors of *Watershed Restoration: Principles and Practices,* published in 1997, the three of us agreed to embark on a second book project—which ultimately would be delayed and shaped by job opportunities and experiences during the intervening years. We agreed that the book would be about land, especially public land, including our experiences and observations. The initial plan was nine chapters with each of us taking primary responsibility for drafting three chapters in our areas of interest or expertise and then critiquing the other chapters prior to review and comment by outside experts. As the writing progressed, we merged two of the chapters into one, leaving this volume with eight chapters.

A challenge in writing a book by more than one person is consistency of style. We hope that all the reviewing by us, outside reviewers, and editors has helped. Multiple authorship also prompted us to employ a third-person narrative style even though some of us were personally involved in specific issues such as roadless area protection. For the period between 1997 and 2001, for example, we write of the Forest Service "chief" when in fact one of us was, in traditional Forest Service lingo, "the chief."

Our philosophies stem from our lifelong love for the land enriched by a wide variety of experiences and opportunities. For childhood days as youngsters, each of us in different parts of the country, bonding with the outdoors, tromping in forests, streams, shorelines, deserts, and mountains—hunting, fishing, and the like—we thank our families and neighbors. For a wealth of opportunities, from research to field management, we are grateful to peers and mentors who supported us in our education and careers. We thank our colleagues from the agencies and other executive branch offices, Congress, academia, and the interest groups who helped sharpen our debate skills, shape our perspectives, and challenge our thinking.

This book would not have been possible without the experience and support afforded by the Forest Service, Bureau of Land Management, Fish and Wildlife Service, University of Wisconsin–Stevens Point's Global Environmental Management Education Center, Trout Unlimited, Southern Oregon University's AuCoin Institute for Ecological, Economic, and Civic Studies, and the National Wildlife Federation.

We are indebted to the many people who shared ideas, provided inspiration, and others who offered critical reviews of our writing, including: J. David Almand, Bob Armstrong, Tom Atzet, Bruce Babbitt, Carl Bond, Aimee Boulanger, Paul Brouha, Hutch Brown, Jim Clayton, Jim Deacon, Tony Dean, Hilda Diaz-Soltero, Dana Dubose, Wayne Elmore, Gloria

Flora, Harv Forsgren, George Frampton, Chris Frissell, Jim Furnish, Dan Glickman, Jesse Halsted, Kniffy Hamilton, Dave Hohler, Bob Hollingsworth, Bob House, Phil Janik, Chris Jauhola, Amelia Jenkins, Paul Johnson, Jim Karr, Jack King, Gail Kobetich, Tom Kovalicky, Danny Lee, Jim Lyons, Cal McCluskey, Jeri McGinley, Jack McIntyre, Bill Meadows, Steve Mealey, Curt Meine, W. L. Minckley, Steve Moyer, Peter Moyle, James Muhn, Bob Nelson, Joel Pagel, Francis Pandolfi, Guy Pence, Dave Perry, Phil Pister, Brooks Preston, Gordon Reeves, Bruce Rieman, Dave Rittenhouse, Don Sada, Jim Sedell, Allan Thomas, Jack Ward Thomas, Russ Thurow, Tom Tidwell, Cyd Weiland, John Whitaker, Cindy Deacon Williams, Gerry Williams, Bob Wolf, and Bob Ziemer.

Al Ferlo, Roy Menzel, and Steve Menzel deserve special thanks for taking time to review the entire manuscript. The inspiring essays written by Bruce Babbitt, Rick Bass, Mark Fuller, Steve Knick, Nina Leopold Bradley, Patricia Limerick, Curt Meine, Gaylord Nelson, Tim Palmer, David Perry, Jack Ward Thomas, and Mark Van Putten added meaningful dimensions to each chapter. We thank this diverse group for their special contributions that enrich the book immeasurably.

We express our appreciation as well to Charles Wilkinson for his thoughtful foreword. Kimberly Hoffman created the watercycle and watershed drawing in Chapter 7. The vivid illustrations by William Millonig instill mental images of the land and its many values. We thank Steve Menzel for computer formatting of the manuscript and graphics. The editorial skills of Barbara Youngblood, Laura Carrithers, and Heather Boyer at Island Press were invaluable while Barbara Dean provided overall editorial guidance and unflagging encouragement.

Most important, we thank our families for their patience throughout the writing of this book and their unwavering support throughout our careers.

MIKE DOMBECK
CHRIS WOOD
JACK WILLIAMS

Foreword

The existence of the federal public lands stands as one of the great ironics in American history. At the beginning, it was an open question whether there would be any federal-land ownership at all, as doubts sounded about whether the Constitution could allow Thomas Jefferson's historic purchase. Once that issue was resolved, the original vision for the nation's land estate was modest in the extreme: To ease the strain on a young nation's budget by paying soldiers in acres instead of dollars and by selling off land and minerals. As the westward expansion moved into high gear, the wholesale giveaway of public land, timber, and minerals, plentifully spiced with various illegal practices, became the raucous banquet that historian Vernon Parrington called "the Great Barbecue." Throughout the country's first century, the shared assumption was that the public lands—all of them, save the forts, the office-building parcels, and Yellowstone and some battlefields—would be dispensed to new states, the railroads, homesteaders, and miners.

Then the accumulated wisdom and actions of Henry David Thoreau, George Perkins Marsh, John Wesley Powell, and, more directly, Gifford Pinchot, Teddy Roosevelt, and John Muir began to take hold. Presidents and congresses made large conservation setasides. Tens of millions of acres were withdrawn from mining, national parks and national forests were established, and homesteading came to a close. By 1976 we reached a consensus, memorialized in the Federal Land Policy and Management Act, that the disposal policy no longer fit the country's needs and that the public lands should remain in the ownership of the United States. And thus today one-quarter of the world's most capitalistic nation remains the people's lands. It will always be so. It has to be. The public lands have become a cherished birthright of the citizenry, a fundamental part of what it means to be an American.

The national forests have always been the crucible for public-land policy. Those wondrous landscapes, open to the opportunities and pitfalls of multiple-use management, make up nearly one-tenth of all land in the country, more than that in the lower 48 states, more still in the American West. The national forests are an irony within the irony. They have been badly overworked since World War II, especially by high-yield logging, resulting in many wounds to species diversity, recreational opportunities, wildness, and beauty. Yet, despite the wounds, the national forests offer far greater land health than the surrounding private lands that have been overrun by the population boom of the past half century.

These pages are filled with the ideas and experiences of three career natural-resource managers who served at the apex of conservation issues during the Clinton Administration that produced, along with Teddy Roosevelt's years, one of the most dynamic and visionary eras in the long history of public-land policy. The hard results—the laws embodied in agency regulations and presidential orders—speak for themselves: roadless area protection, new national monuments, range reform, hardrock mining reform, endangered species protection, river management reform, and national forest management premised on ecological sustainability. But the progress achieved by those public servants went further than the laws. Their work was infused with an ethic, an ethic that looked to ecology, sensible human use, a passion for the land and all it can give us, and wildness.

The soul of this volume, then, is found in its many echoes of Aldo Leopold's voice. The reader sees and feels Leopold's presence in the text, the chapter titles, even the artwork. Significantly, the national forests lie at the center of his work. Leopold gave the fire of his youth to the Forest Service, gaining deep and joyful on-the-ground experience in the dry Southwest and convincing the agency to rise to one of its finest moments, the creation of the Gila Wilderness Area, the world's first government-protected wild area. During his federal service and later years in academia, he wrote on a wide array of subjects, including wildlife management, soil conservation, recreation, hunting, rangeland management, wilderness, and ethics. The books and more than a hundred articles of America's greatest conservationist owe at least as much to the national forests as to his sand county farm.

This leads to a question and a realization. The question is: Why has the

Forest Service never embraced Aldo Leopold as its guiding light? The real-ization is: The national forests will never fulfill the truest and highest national interest until the Forest Service finally begins managing according to Leopold.

At the moment this book is offered to the public, the public lands are not being managed according to Leopold's vision. Some of the laws and policies of the 1990s have been revised, and others are being ignored, all in the name of old-style extraction. But the current practices are fighting a proven public resolve and cannot prevail over time. Take public-land policy from any past date—say, 1891, 1905, 1945, 1976, or 1990—and compare it to the present. Every trend line moves steadily upward toward ecological sustainability, toward the land ethic.

I hope that many readers will, as I have, benefit from and enjoy these pages. They hold ideas that will endure.

September 2002
CHARLES WILKINSON
Distinguished University Professor
Moses Lasky Professor of Law
University of Colorado

Introduction

In the 1950s, wildlife biologists in Texas were immersed in the "doe wars," as biologists struggled to institute legal hunting of antlerless deer in response to increasing deer numbers and declining range condition. Jack Ward Thomas, former chief of the USDA Forest Service (1993–1996), tells a story from early in his career as a state biologist in Texas. An outdoor writer for the *San Antonio Light*, a local newspaper, was a persistent critic. In one article he not only criticized the intellect of promoters of antlerless deer hunting and the purposes of the policy but intimated that wildlife biologists behind the proposal were somehow being "paid off" by landowners who would profit from their actions.

That was too much for Jack. He decided to drive down to San Antonio and give the writer a piece of his mind. As a matter of courtesy, he called his boss to tell him his plans. His boss did not try to dissuade Jack but did ask him to stop by for coffee on his way. Jack did so. After he explained his intent and displayed the offending articles, his boss leaned back and said, "Hell, Jack, this guy is a sports writer. Who gives a flip about what he says? Besides, you need to come to grips with the fact that we are insignificant people in an insignificant agency dealing with insignificant things. Nobody really gives a damn about what we do." Jack was completely deflated. Then his boss continued: "But I don't think that will always be true. A time is coming when people will truly care about the management of their natural resources. You'll know when that time has come when you read about such matters on the front pages, the business pages, and the editorial pages of the major newspapers across the country."

Today stories on old-growth forests, roadless areas, energy development on federal lands, and endangered species commonly make the front pages of local and national newspapers and often dominate political discussions. Conservation issues have moved from the domain of hunters and anglers, development interests and their elected representatives, and environmental groups to the top of national polls on the issues of most concern to voters.

Just a decade ago, a few thousand comments on a proposed federal rule concerning public lands would have represented an enormous outpouring of public comment. Times have changed. Between 1999 and 2000, more than 1.6 million public comments were received on a Forest Service proposal that addressed the future of 58.5 million acres of public land. Editorials and articles about the Roadless Area Conservation Rule appeared in hundreds of newspapers and magazines across the country.

Public interest in the protection of roadless areas demonstrates that public land issues have indeed moved from the sports page to the front page. Land management officials, once viewed as infallible experts, today find their decisions scrutinized by outside experts, multiple lawsuits and courts, downstream urban residents, and rural families that have cut timber or grazed cows on public land for generations.

The multiple-use agencies, specifically the Forest Service and the Bureau of Land Management (BLM), are increasingly viewed less as experts and more as facilitators in the struggle over control of public lands. Historically the public lands that were not sold or homesteaded were the "lands nobody wanted" and by default became largely the domain of economic interests seeking to develop or produce commodities. Public land managers tried to ensure that development activities did not ruin the productive capacity of the land.

New scientific information about the value of public lands to biological diversity—as well as increasing recreation use and, perhaps most important, changing public values—has transformed the job of the Forest Service and BLM. Agency employees today spend less time as resource managers and technical experts and more time as facilitators, positioned squarely between competing interests, searching for the elusive middle ground. Inevitably, the conflicts increase. Often the only tangible result of such mediation is impasse. As a former Texas state land commissioner, Jim Hightower, once said: "There's never much in the middle of the road except dead armadillos." Many critics predict a similar future for the multiple-use agencies.

When the Bush administration and the Forest Service reopened the

Roadless Rule in July 2001 to new public comment, they asked the following question: "How can the Forest Service work effectively with individuals and groups with strongly competing views, values, and beliefs in evaluating and managing public land resources, recognizing that the agency cannot meet all of the desires of all of the parties?" This question frames the thirty-year challenge faced by multiple-use public land management agencies. That the Forest Service saw the need to ask it at all after receiving such an outpouring of public comments—the vast majority of which called for stronger roadless protection—demonstrates the challenge of implementing multiple-use management even with broad public support for conservation policy.

Although the Forest Service resides within the Department of Agriculture and the BLM within the Department of the Interior, the missions of the two agencies are nearly identical—namely, the multiple-use management of public lands for the benefit of present and future generations. Meeting this innocuous-sounding mission has proved elusive. Controversies over timber cutting, old-growth forests, mining, and grazing, for example, have dogged the agencies since the 1960s. Confounding the search for common ground over the past few decades is the fact that the complex agency bureaucracies and rigid cultures seem to find themselves out of step with public opinion. Consider Forest Service and BLM leadership over the past several decades:

- Forest Service leadership opposed passage of the Wilderness Act in 1964. Few acts of Congress are more charitable to posterity or demonstrate more hope for the future than the recognition that some of our lands and waters ought to remain "untrammeled . . . where man himself is a visitor who does not remain." The Wilderness Bill passed the House of Representatives by a vote of 374-1.
- In the early 1970s, in the face of growing opposition to clearcutting—rooted largely in aesthetic concerns—it took a lawsuit by a conservation group to force the Forest Service and Congress to address the issue through passage of the National Forest Management Act. Even then, clearcutting continued as a standard agency practice well into the 1980s.
- Forest Service leadership's slowness to recognize the spotted owl as a surrogate for public demand to protect old-growth forests in the 1980s set the stage for legal challenges and subsequent injunctions that shut down the timber program in the Pacific Northwest. Thus began a significant decline in national forest timber harvest levels.
- Passage of the California Desert Protection Act in 1994 removed several million acres of public land from multiple-use stewardship of the BLM by designating it as wilderness or entrusting it to the National Park Service

because of congressional and public desire for the land to be protected—not managed as multiple-use land.

The difficulties of balancing the interests of urban and rural, East and West, are compounded by the challenge of measuring the demands of the present generation against the need to maintain land-use options for future generations. Implicit in every multiple-use decision is the complex issue of intergenerational equity. How much should be left to future generations—and at what cost to those who presently use and depend on the land?

Many local and national elected officials accountable to voters every few years demand goods and services from the land to provide short-term economic opportunities for rural communities. Downstream towns and cities oppose soil-disturbing activities that can affect water quality for hundreds of thousands of urban residents. Local people sometimes criticize public land managers for cumbersome bureaucracies and declining production of commodities that drive rural economies. Others, often from places far removed from the public lands, insist on protecting more wild places.

Even those issues upon which there is broad agreement can stimulate intense debate. Most scientists conclude that many of our forests and rangelands evolved with frequent, low-intensity fires playing a significant, if not dominant, role in defining and shaping the landscape. Decades of fire suppression and past timber and grazing management practices have dramatically altered ecological processes on many of these lands. In the absence of fire, many of these areas have become overgrown with small-diameter trees and shrubs that can act as a fuel ladder—carrying flames from the forest floor, for example, into the crowns of larger, older trees. Similarly, the native grasses and forbs of many of our western rangelands have become dominated by woody brush and exotic species that reduce productivity and biological diversity. These conditions are conducive to hotter fires that can damage soils, cause erosion, and pose grave risks to adjacent human communities.

Most fire experts and ecologists agree that reducing the level of hazardous fuels in forests and rangelands is essential to protecting adjacent human communities and restoring healthy landscapes. The agreement ends here, however, as some in the timber industry call for aggressive logging and the environmental community rejects such a plan as simply another way to increase timber cutting.

The public land manager walks a fine line. Even the most thoughtful decisions may result in legitimate criticism. If managers base their arguments on federal laws that call for the production of forage, timber, or minerals, such as the Taylor Grazing Act of 1934, the National Forest Management Act, or the 1872 Mining Law, critics counter by citing other laws that protect water and wildlife habitat such as the Clean Water Act and the Endangered Species Act. Many, such as Jack Ward Thomas, criticize the "crazy-quilt patchwork of laws" that dictate multiple-use management as unwieldy and unworkable.

No other nation enjoys the array of public parks, rangelands, forests, rivers, and wilderness as the United States. They are a tangible reminder of the frontier heritage that defined the nation's settlement. As more and more private land is developed, the debate over public land management will only intensify. This should not be deplored. Debate is a defining aspect of a healthy and thriving democracy.

Former Forest Service employee and eminent wildlife ecologist Aldo Leopold once defined the "oldest task in human history" as "to live on a piece of land without spoiling it." Difficult issues over land use do not get any easier through delay or neglect. Like a sore left too long unattended, they fester into infection that eventually cripples an organization. Helping a diverse and opinionated nation to wrestle with these challenges is the job of the public land manager.

Such challenges are made more difficult by the lack of introspection that often plagues large organizations. For example, reluctance to press Congress and the executive branch for changes to an incentive system that rewarded commodity production at the expense of land health—even in the face of significant new scientific information, most of it generated by agency scientists—contributed to a nearly 80 percent decline in the Forest Service timber sold between 1989 and 2000. Without doubt, lawsuits brought by environmental plaintiffs and strong political pressure to maintain unsustainably high harvest levels exacerbated the decline and prolonged the debate. Nonetheless, the agency responsible for signing decision documents and authorizing the sale of public assets cannot escape a strong measure of culpability.

Informed debate and public understanding are vital to the sustenance of our public land legacy. Without these essential ingredients, public lands could fall prey to a citizenry weary of battles and uninformed of consequences. And if this were to happen, elected officials might follow the lead of other nations such as New Zealand and relegate our storehouse of public lands—what historian Frederick Turner called the "greatest free gift ever bestowed on mankind"—to parks or more intensive agricultural models for timber production, mining, and livestock grazing. More valuable lands for the production of commodities would be transferred to private corporations and the less valuable—both economically and biologically—would go to parks. Such an approach would be unlikely to serve the interests of conservation.

This book addresses Forest Service management of 191 million acres of public lands and, to a somewhat lesser extent, the 272 million acres of public land administered by the BLM. The authors bring over sixty years of experience in field management, policy development, and agency leadership. Other public lands managed by federal agencies such as national parks and national wildlife refuges are addressed as well, though their treatment is secondary to Forest Service and BLM-administered lands.

Many of the subjects treated in this book are broadly applicable to management of all land, including private lands. Many of the goals of public land management—sustainability, control of exotic species, maintaining water quality, protection of endangered species—cannot be achieved without extensive cooperation and integration of public and private land management strategies. Understanding the many ecological and social benefits to society that flow from healthy lands and waters, be they public or private, is a central theme.

Although governed by different laws and regulations, public and private lands are ecologically codependent. Reductions in livestock grazing on public lands, for example, may lead a permittee to graze private lands more intensively. These lands may be valley bottoms or riparian areas that are more biologically productive than the public lands. Conversely, poorly managed private lands often lead to more restrictive management of public lands in order to minimize the cumulative ecological damage across a watershed.

The focus of this book, however, is to propose options to maintain and restore public land and water resources so they continue to provide present and future generations with social and environmental benefits. With the exception of the roadless area debate, which is described in depth, we do not delve into details of policy issues, the development of law, or political wrangling. Instead we focus on why public lands matter and why all of the nation's citizens, whether they reside in Red Lodge, Montana, or Albany, New York, should get involved in their management.

The book has eight chapters. They describe the nation's shift from viewing public lands as something to be conquered (and later disposed of), to contemporary efforts to ensure their conservation and restoration. The first chapter summarizes the history of the public domain lands and how the territories gave up their claim to the public domain as a condition of statehood. Subsequent chapters describe the transition from managing public lands as a storehouse of commodities and goods to be brought to market in the aftermath of World War II, to broad public recognition of the need to sustain basic ecological processes such as fire that make the public lands "hum and tick."

Some of the more pressing ecological concerns on public lands such as declining rangeland and aquatic health are addressed, as well, including the ecological and social dilemma of restoring fire to fire-dependent landscapes. The concluding chapters offer new and old approaches and recommendations—both policy and organizational—to ensure that multiple-use agencies are able to sustain the health, diversity, and social and ecological productivity of the public lands into the next century.

To bring in additional perspectives and expertise, we have invited some of the country's finest writers, thinkers, and scientists to prepare brief focus essays for each chapter. These essays convey a sense of place or explore a pertinent ecological or social issue in greater depth.

It is our hope that this book will stimulate informed debate among those who care most about the future of public lands while motivating a new constituency of citizens to become engaged in their management. Since the nation was formed, these lands have been jointly owned by every citizen. They would not be ours, nor in such relative good health, if not for the sacrifices and commitment of our predecessors. In much the same way, we owe it to those who will follow to engage in their management, advocate for their protection, remain open to new ideas, and be willing to institute overdue changes.

In every large organization there is an impulse to maintain the status quo. No matter how necessary, cogent, or overdue, real change is generally viewed with suspicion. Without question the Forest Service and BLM have undergone profound changes over the past decade. The rate and inexorability of change, and the ensuing uncertainty that change has wrought, cause immense discomfort to many inside and outside the public land management agencies.

But those who make a living working on public lands—civil servants, recreationists, industry users, environmentalists—can either wring their hands in dismay or find a common cause in developing a new consensus for public land management. Such a consensus, we suggest, should be based on maintaining and restoring the health, diversity, and productivity of the lands and waters that sustain us all. Identifying the challenges, and offering solutions, is the purpose of this book.

Chapter 1

All the People's Land:
The Wealth of the Nation

There was nothing but Land: not a country at all, but the material out of which Countries are made.

Willa Cather, *My Ántonia* (1918)

Early in 1994, the newly appointed head of the BLM made the customary courtesy call to meet the newly elected governor of a western state. The first and only real question the governor asked was, "When are you going to give us our land back?" He was not joking. With a high level of discomfort the unwelcome answer was delivered: "Governor, the land can't be given back, because it was never yours to begin with. When your territory petitioned for statehood and the Congress admitted it to the union, your state agreed to cede all claims to unappropriated public domain lands. Public ownership of these lands is rooted in the union of the original thirteen colonies." The governor's comments exemplify a fundamental and widespread misunderstanding about the law and history of the western United States.

When the Declaration of Independence was signed, the colonies of Connecticut, Georgia, Massachusetts, New York, North Carolina, South

9

Carolina, and Virginia held claims to the land between the Appalachian Mountains and the Mississippi River. Maryland's legislators contended that "the lands claimed by the British Crown . . . if secured by blood and treasure of all, ought in reason, justice, and policy . . . be considered a common stock." Maryland had good reason to argue that this land ought to be "common stock" since Maryland had no land claims outside its boundary. Fearing that states with land claims to the west would have an unfair political and economic advantage, Maryland refused to sign the Articles of Confederation.

In 1780, New York ceded its lands west of the Appalachian Mountains. Maryland reciprocated by signing the Articles of Confederation. By 1802, all of the "land claim" states had ceded their western lands.[1] Land claim states such as Virginia and Georgia ceded their claims under the proviso that new states formed out of the western lands would receive the same privileges as the original states. As the western territories entered the Union, lands not specifically titled to individuals or corporations by the federal government generally remained under public ownership. In exchange for extensive land grants within their territories, prospective states relinquished claims to the unappropriated lands inside their boundaries. Congress required that these agreements be reflected in each new state's constitution as "ordinances irrevocable."

Those who want the federal government to give the public lands "back" would have to get in line behind the descendants of the Native Americans and the land claim colonies such as New York and Georgia and perhaps others who ceded or lost their claims through war or treaty. As recently as the 1990s, the "Wise Use Movement" and state's rights advocates litigated their right to take over public lands. The Supreme Court has never ruled in their favor, however, and has allowed U.S. citizen ownership of public land to stand. The concept of public land, public domain, or land belonging to all the citizens of the United States is a concept basic to the formation of the Union itself.[2] The public lands belong to all the people.

The United States encompasses a diverse 2.3 billion acres of land. The fifty states range in size from Rhode Island's 677,120 acres to Alaska's 365 million acres. Historically 1.8 billion of these acres were public domain lands belonging to all citizens of the United States. All acquisitions and cessions after the formation of the Union were part of the public domain. The peoples' land stretched from the Appalachian Mountains to the Pacific plus Alaska.

Land: The Wealth of the Nation

To the fledgling nation, the seemingly endless western lands represented wealth. Under the leadership of such visionaries as President Thomas Jeffer-

Table 1-1. The Building of Manifest Destiny

ACQUISITION	TOTAL ACRES	% OF TOTAL U.S. LAND	COST ($)
State cessions (1781–1802)	236,825,600	10.2	6,200,000
Louisiana Purchase (1803)	529,911,680	22.9	23,213,568
Red River Basin (1782–1817)	29,601,920	1.3	
Cession from Spain (1819)	46,144,640	2.0	6,674,057
Oregon Compromise (1846)	183,386,240	7.9	
Mexican Cession (1848)	388,680,960	14.6	16,295,149
Purchase from Texas (1850)	78,926,720	3.4	15,496,448
Gadsden Purchase (1853)	18,988,800	0.8	10,000,000
Alaska Purchase (1867)	378,242,560	16.3	7,200,000
Total public domain	1,840,709,120	79.4	$85,079,222

Source: USDI Bureau of Land Management, 1999.

son, the nation's land base grew rapidly during the early years. The first major addition to the public domain was the Louisiana Purchase in 1803, when 529 million acres between the Mississippi and the Rocky Mountains were added to the Union. By the 1850s, Manifest Destiny, the dream of spanning the continent from the Atlantic to the Pacific, was realized. The capstone of our public domain was the purchase of Alaska, the "northern ice-box," from the tsar of Russia in 1867. Known at the time as "Seward's Folly," referring to the secretary of state, this purchase of 365 million acres cost $7.2 million, or 2 cents per acre. Table 1-1 and Figure 1-1 summarize the acquisition of the public domain.

Cash was scarce and land was plentiful in the formative years of the United States. The first major land policy was the Land Ordinance of 1785 that established the rectangular land survey system still employed today. The measure also called for the orderly settlement of public land. Early leaders agreed that public land should be sold to raise revenue and to reward soldiers and sailors for their service. Early surveys set aside land to be granted to soldiers. An army private who fought in the Revolutionary War was granted 100 acres of land while a major general was granted 1100 acres.[3]

Public land policy debates extended to the earliest years of the Union. Thomas Jefferson wanted land sold to small farmers as the foundation to build a self-sufficient nation. Alexander Hamilton, then secretary of the treasury, wanted the government to sell land at wholesale prices to "the rich, the able, and the well-born," arguing that this would build a strong economic base for the nation.[4] Subsequent laws allowed for both points of view. Wealthy speculators who often realized great profits from land resale or

Figure 1-1. Acquisition of the public domain, 1781–1867.

development purchased the best and most productive land, particularly in the East. Auctioning off the public domain favored rich businesspeople who had cash in hand. In later years, many settlers obtained land at little or no cost. Most of them cleared the land for agriculture and farming.

The Land Rush and Land Grants

The 1800s marked the great American land rush. Local land offices were established, and by 1805 hundreds of thousands of acres were sold. The sale of public land increased so rapidly that, in 1812, Congress established the General Land Office to "superintend, execute, and perform all such acts and things touching the public lands of the U.S."[5] Within a few years the General Land Office commissioner was viewed as one of the most prestigious assignments in government. In 1849, Abraham Lincoln sought the commissioner's post and was reportedly deeply disappointed when he did not get the job.[6]

Various laws and policies regulating the disposal and price of public land were enacted and modified. In the 1820s, tracts as small as 80 acres could be purchased for $1.25 an acre. The debate over offering free land to settlers gained support in the 1840s. The Armed Occupation Law of 1842 provided

160 acres of land to each person willing to fight the Indians in Florida with the caveat that they occupy and cultivate the land for five years. In the 1850s, Congress offered 320 acres to each man and 640 acres to each couple willing to settle in the "Oregon country." The Homestead Act was passed in 1862 and provided free land—160 acres—to single persons over twenty-one, heads of households, or widows if they lived on the land and cultivated it for five years. During its existence from 1812 to 1946 the General Land Office disposed of over 1 billion acres of land. Thus was the idiom "land office business" permanently etched into the American language.

The first land grants authorized by the Land Ordinance of 1785 were for national defense and education. Military service was rewarded with title to land. Section 16 of each township was reserved for the states to finance education through the sale of land. This amount was increased in 1848 when states were granted two sections per township, later to four sections with the admission of Utah, Arizona, and New Mexico into the Union. In 1841, states were granted 500,000 acres of land for internal improvements such as canals and roads.[7]

The idea of land grants as an incentive to encourage settlement and conquer the frontier prevailed beyond the Civil War. In 1862, Congress granted the Central Pacific and Union Pacific railroads alternate sections of public land 10 miles on each side of every completed mile of the transcontinental railroad. The largest railroad grant, 39 million acres extending from Lake Superior to Puget Sound, went to the Northern Pacific Railroad. Settlers complained that the railroads were given a monopoly to the western lands however, and railroad grants were curtailed after 1871. The granting of alternate sections of land resulted in the checkerboard land ownership pattern that often confounds public land management today. Railroad grants between 1862 and 1871 amounted to nearly 132 million acres. This is a land area equivalent to Pennsylvania and California combined.[8]

The Enduring Legacy of Early Land Laws

Both enacted policies and the absence of policy can lead to problems. The Land Ordinance of 1785 reserved for the federal government a one-third interest in gold, silver, lead, and other minerals taken from the public domain. But other than the War Department's interest in lead for ammunition, there was little concern over public domain minerals. That changed in 1849 with the California gold rush. In the absence of national policy, miners and prospectors developed their own rules about how to stake and title claims.

A gold or silver find in the West often followed a general pattern with rumors of wealth enticing the adventurous to leave a job and start prospecting. The following characterization describes what many mining camps may have been like:

> If minerals were discovered, a fairly stable mining camp emerged. This was usually followed by an influx of shifty-eyed bartenders, hurdy-gurdy girls, untrained lawyers, the wildest outlaws imaginable, and peripatetic preachers, all (or most) of whom sought to prey on the miner. The lawless element eventually produced the vigilante committee. Order was usually restored about the time the mines were worked out.[9]

Miners established mining districts and miners' courts to enforce their own rules. When the first mining law was legislated in 1866, it favored miners' interests by declaring that "mineral lands of the public domain . . . be free and open to exploration and occupation." Royalties and other taxes were not assessed on hard-rock minerals removed from public domain lands. Federal mining law was amended in 1872, adding that "valuable" mineral deposits be free and open to exploitation and purchase for as little as $2.50 per acre.[10]

The 1872 Mining Law remains the law of the land. After failing in his attempt to update the measure, Secretary of the Interior Stewart Udall left office in 1969 proclaiming that mining law reform was one of the major unfinished pieces of natural resource policy. In 1993, Interior Secretary Bruce Babbitt and the 103rd Congress nearly succeeded in crafting a reform that would have eliminated provisions allowing mining companies to privatize public land, given public land managers the ability to say no to mining in sensitive watersheds and landscapes, and exacted a royalty on minerals taken from public lands. With agreement reached on most issues, they ran out of time when the Congress adjourned. The new congressional leadership of the 104th Congress, however, had little desire to take up mining law reform. The antiquated 1872 Mining Law remains in effect today—and the need for its reform is as crucial as ever.

By the Civil War, problems resulting from a lack of policy to guide public domain timberlands began to surface. Theft of public timber increased and land fraud was rampant. For example, members of the 1879 Public Land Commission visited California's redwood region and reported:

> Little huts or kennels built of shakes that were totally unfit for human habitations, and always had been, which were

the sole improvements made under the homestead and pre-emption laws, and by means of which large areas of red-wood forests, possessing great value, had been taken under pretenses of settlement and cultivation, which were the purest fictions, never having any real existence in fact, but of which due proof had been made under laws.[11]

By the 1870s, the General Land Office's primary thrust was dealing with the large-scale abuse associated with public land. Congressional legislation continued to favor development and commodity extraction. The Timber and Stone Act of 1873 authorized the sale of nontillable public timberland for personal use for $2.50 per acre. The Free Timber Act of 1878 gave miners the right to cut timber on public domain mineral claims for mining and domestic purposes.[12]

With much of the eastern United States settled by the end of the Civil War, the frontier expanded westward. Land, the prospect of cheap land, remained the currency to entice settlers west. Much of the western landscape, however, included desert lands much less hospitable than those in the East. Under the erroneous presumption that trees prompted rainfall, Congress passed the Timber Culture Act in 1873. Citizens would be given 160-acre parcels of land provided they planted 40 acres into trees spaced no farther than 12 feet apart and kept them growing for ten years.

Many citizens believed the West to be a vast garden land where eastern farming practices, which depended on adequate rainfall, could flourish. A series of wet years following the Civil War compounded commonly held beliefs that "rain would follow the plow." Farmers cultivated the semiarid rangelands west of Kansas and Nebraska.

During the 1870s, one of the West's preeminent explorers and surveyors, John Wesley Powell, began to speak of the West as largely semiarid. On April 1, 1878, Powell presented Interior Secretary Carl Schurz with his "Report on the Lands of the Arid Region of the West."[13] Powell was among the first to suggest that farming practices in the West would require irrigation and that fundamental reforms to common practices of land development such as homesteading were needed. Powell argued that while individual farmers could irrigate small tracts by diverting water from nearby creeks, a larger government presence was needed to build large dams and coordinate major irrigation projects.

American politics and policies of the time did not reflect Powell's view. The Desert Land Act of 1877 enabled settlers to buy 640 acres of desert land for $1.25 per acre if they constructed irrigation systems. Although the

Desert Land Act was more successful than the Timber Culture Act, only 65,000 of the 260,000 entries were successfully patented. Sadly the net effect of these policies was to lead land-hungry settlers into an impossible task only to experience failure.[14]

Tragedy of the Commons

Manifest Destiny was largely achieved by the end of the nineteenth century. In the eastern United States, where virtually all land was in private owner-ship, recognition of the need for a change in national policy was building. East of the Mississippi River, forests had been cleared by settlers for fuel and agriculture or by timber companies for railroad ties and lumber. The nation's prime hardwood forests of the Appalachians and the great white pine forests of the Northeast and Midwest had been clearcut with no effort to reforest cutover lands. Often forest fires were intentionally set on the cutover lands to eliminate slash. Many of these fires blazed out of control, however, some taking human lives and burning thousands of acres of forest and all vegeta-tion along with valuable topsoil. When rains came, the result was serious soil erosion and flooding.

The 1871 Peshtigo Fire in northeastern Wisconsin, the most devastating forest fire in U.S. history, killed 1500 people and burned 1.28 million acres. Other fires in Michigan, again the legacy of timber cutting, burned another 2.5 million acres that same year. Forest cover was destroyed and topsoil was either turned to ash or washed away once the forests were burned. The land lost its resilience to dampen floods or temper drought. Watershed func-tion—the basic ability to catch, store, and release water over time—was lost on millions of acres of land. It would take decades, if not centuries, to restore the landscape. By 1900, some 80 million acres of charred and decimated stump-lands lay east of the Mississippi.[15]

Settlers used the land as they wished—generally with little knowledge or concern for the long-term health of natural resources. Rivers and streams were dredged for gold and other precious metals. The waters of many west-ern rivers were diverted from their channels and put to the "beneficial use" of irrigation on the land or canals for barge traffic, leaving previously peren-nial streams dry during critical times of the year. Complex water rights laws were passed by many western states that asserted ownership of water separate from the land. Rivers were dammed and waters were impounded for various purposes. Diversions dramatically altered riparian function, blocked fish pas-sage, and changed natural river dynamics. Soil erosion and watershed degra-dation affected millions of acres.

Barbed wire was strung across public domain lands, yet livestock trespass was common. By the 1870s, federal rangelands were greatly overgrazed. In Colorado, 3 million acres of public land were fenced and range wars erupted. In 1887, a severe winter, coupled with malnutrition, killed millions of stressed livestock, bankrupting many cattle companies that were involved in land-damaging and speculative grazing practices. Vicious grazing wars between cattlemen and sheepherders broke out over water supplies. As the turn of the century neared, western rangelands were severely degraded. Concerns continued to grow that mining, timber, and grazing interests had monopolized the frontier.[16]

Seeds of Change

The seeds of change that led to the first American conservation movement were well under way by 1850. It did not reach its climax, however, until the presidency of Theodore Roosevelt. Like most major changes in national sentiment, a gradual awakening was punctuated by rapid spurts of change triggered by specific events. When colonists first arrived, the huge trees and dense forests were as foreign as this new continent itself. There was fear of attack by Indians and fear of wolves lurking in the forests. The dense forest around settlements needed to be cut down for human safety and to enable farming and grazing. After the Revolutionary War, Americans believed that the frontier needed to be conquered and that the seemingly endless land represented unlimited wealth. By the mid-1800s, with Manifest Destiny being realized, sentiments favoring the aesthetic value of the land began to grow. Americans began to appreciate the scenic beauty of the landscape and call for conservation.

The Lewis and Clark Expedition of 1804–1806 demonstrated the vastness of the West and highlighted the grandeur and beauty of the landscape, as well as the abundance and variety of plants and animals. Nonetheless, there remained little recognition of the need to conserve these and other natural resources until Vermont Congressman George Perkins Marsh's seminal speech in 1847, in which he advocated a conservationist approach to the management of forest lands by calling attention to the destructive impact of deforestation. A year later, the American Association for the Advancement of Science was organized—bringing a new focus to the need for scientific inquiry and acquisition of new knowledge.

The Department of the Interior was established in 1849. In the same year, the New York Association for the Protection of Game was founded, perhaps the earliest wildlife conservation organization in the United States.

In the 1850 *Report of the Commissioner of Patents,* Commissioner Thomas Ewing said: "The waste of valuable timber in the U.S. . . . will hardly be appreciated until our population reaches 50 million. Then the folly and shortsightedness of this age will meet with a degree of censure and reproach not pleasant to contemplate." Ewing went on to warn that "the vast multitudes of bisons [*sic*] slain yearly, the ceaseless war carried out against them, if continued, threatens their extermination, and must hereafter cause deep regret. . . . It should never be said that the noblest of American indigenous ruminants have become extinct." Concerns regarding the long-term harm of deforestation appeared in government reports from 1850 through 1880. Devastation of the Appalachian and Lake States' forests prompted many of these early conservation efforts.[17]

By the mid-1800s, American and European romantic literature, art, periodicals, and books began to extol the virtues of "nature appreciation." Photographs and lithographs of American scenery, especially in the West, stimulated wide interest and appreciation for the scenic and wilderness qualities of the landscape. Henry David Thoreau's address to the Concord, Massachusetts, Lyceum declared that "in wildness is the preservation of the world." In 1854 Thoreau published the famous *Walden or Life in the Woods.* Near the end of the Civil War George Perkins Marsh published the seminal *Man and Nature; or, Physical Geography as Modified by Human Action* (revised in 1874 as *The Earth as Modified by Human Action*)—the first systematic analysis of the human impact on the environment.[18]

Artist Frederick Edwin Church in 1860 painted the masterpiece *Twilight in the Wilderness,* which inspired numerous artists of the Hudson River school to capture the awesome beauty of the American landscape. John Muir promoted the need for government protection of forests in his 1876 article "God's First Temples: How Shall We Preserve Our Forests?" published in the *Sacramento Record-Union.* In the twentieth century, Ansel Adams carried that tradition into his famous photography that even today retains its popularity.

The First National Preserves

In his 1864 book *The Maine Woods,* Thoreau called for the establishment of "national preserves" of virgin forests, "not for idle sport or food, but for inspiration and our own true recreation."[19] That same year, President Lincoln signed legislation granting Yosemite Valley and the Mariposa Big Tree Grove to the state of California to hold these lands forever "for public use, resort, and recreation." In 1906 these lands became the core of Yosemite National Park.

The concept of setting aside land for aesthetic and recreational values was reaffirmed in 1872, ironically the same year that the General Mining Law was passed. In that year, Congress established Yellowstone National Park, the first in the United States indeed and the world, as a "public park or pleasuring-ground" for the benefit and enjoyment of the people. In August of 1873, Dr. Franklin B. Hough, an army surgeon who became very interested in forestry, presented a paper at the American Association for the Advancement of Science meeting in Portland, Maine. His paper was titled "On the Duty of Governments in the Preservation of Forests." The next day, the association began a successful effort to petition Congress to appoint a forestry expert in the federal government.

Three years later, Congress funded Dr. Hough and placed him in the Department of Agriculture. He was the first federal forestry employee in what would become, in 1905, the Forest Service. In 1873, *Forest and Stream* magazine was first published. With George Bird Grinnell, friend of Theodore Roosevelt, as publisher and editor from 1880 to 1911, *Forest and Stream* became a favorite sportsman's magazine and a force in the conservation movement.

In 1885, New York State established the Adirondack Forest Preserve that "shall be kept forever as wild forest lands." Recreation pursuits, including hunting, fishing, and travel became more popular. By 1887, Theodore Roosevelt's influence on conservation had become apparent. In December he invited a number of prominent sportsmen friends including Grinnell to dinner in Manhattan to discuss the creation of a hunting organization. The next month the Boone and Crockett Club was established with Roosevelt as its first president. The organization played a major role in associating big-game hunting and the conservation movement. With Roosevelt's energetic leadership the club later published volumes on hunting and conservation, including *American Big Game in Its Haunts*.[20]

Carl Schurz, interior secretary from 1877 to 1881, became the first cabinet member with an active interest in the conservation of natural resources. He advocated the creation of forest reserves and a federal forest service. Schurz's goals were partly realized in 1881 with the appointment of Dr. Franklin B. Hough as head of the Division of Forestry within the Department of Agriculture.

In 1885, six bills were introduced in Congress to create public forest reserves. None of them passed. Similar bills failed to pass in 1888, 1889, and 1890.[21] Finally, on March 3, 1891, the Forest Reserve "Creative" Act passed, empowering the president to create "forest reserves" by withdrawing forestlands from the public domain. On March 30, President Harrison issued Presidential Proclamation 17 creating the nation's first forest reservation— the 1.2-million-acre Yellowstone Park Timber Land Reservation lying just south of Yellowstone National Park in what is now primarily the Shoshone National Forest. Before his term ended, President Harrison proclaimed another 13 million acres of forest reserves in the West. The foundation for a National Forest System was laid. The reserves were little more than lines drawn on a map without managers, regulations, or a budget.[22]

Interest in the application of science-based forest management continued to grow. The National Academy of Sciences established a National Forestry Commission in 1896 with Gifford Pinchot as its youngest member. The commission issued a report that became the blueprint for the establishment of forest policy. This report emphasized that the forest reserves belonged to, and should be managed for, all the people, not just a particular class: "Steep-sloped lands should not be cleared, the grazing of sheep should be regulated, miners should not be allowed to burn land over willfully, lands better suited for agriculture or mining should be eliminated from the reserves, mature timber should be cut and sold, and settlers and miners should be allowed to cut only such timber as they need."[23]

The National Forestry Commission toured the West during the summer of 1896 and recommended the creation of an additional 21 million acres of forest reserves, an idea that was quickly approved by President Grover Cleveland. Fearing federal intervention, the western states decried the creation of reserves and pushed their congressional delegations to abolish the whole system. Undeterred, the commission called for passage of the Forest Management Act, or Organic Act, of 1897. The act specified that the forest reserves were "to improve and protect the forest, or for the purpose of securing favorable conditions of water flows, and to furnish a continuous supply of timber for the use and necessities of citizens of the U.S." The act also provided for the forest reserves to be managed by the General Land Office and to be surveyed and mapped by the U.S. Geological Survey with the assistance of forestry specialists.

As the nineteenth century came to a close, four trends signaled the need for change in the management of the public domain: growing western communities increasingly demanding dependable water supplies; growing public distrust of large timber companies; sustainable timber supplies needed to replace cutover forest of the Great Lakes region; and the general demand for timber products.[24]

A Conservation Ethic Emerges

The presidency of Theodore Roosevelt from 1901 to 1909 thrust the nation into its first conservation movement. Roosevelt acted energetically to expand federal forest reserves and establish the first national wildlife refuges and national monuments under the Preservation of American Antiquities Act of 1906.

The Second American Forest Congress recommended in 1905 that all federal forest programs be unified in the Department of Agriculture. Congress acted on the recommendation with the passage of the Transfer Act in 1905. With Forester Gifford Pinchot at the helm, the USDA Forest Service was established. Western members of Congress were so opposed to the concept of federal forest reserves that in a subsection of the 1907 Agriculture Appropriations Act they took away the president's authority to enlarge or create additional reserves in six western states.

With a stroke of political ingenuity and boldness, Roosevelt designated 16 million acres of forest reserves known as "midnight reserves" immediately before signing the legislation revoking his authority to make such designations. Embedded in the same legislation was a subsection that renamed forest reserves as "national forests."[25] In 1906, Roosevelt created the first wildlife refuge on Pelican Island, Florida. In 1908, the president called the first Governors' Conference on Conservation organized by Roosevelt confidant Gifford Pinchot. In 1909, Roosevelt convened the North American Conservation Conference involving Mexico and Canada. The conservation achievements of the Roosevelt administration were unprecedented. Its utilitarian theme was straightforward: the "greatest good, for the greatest number, for the longest time."[26]

Focus Essay

Public Lands: An American Birthright

JACK WARD THOMAS*

I was born, raised, and received much of my education in Texas. I worked for the first ten years of my career as a wildlife biologist for the Texas Parks and Wildlife Department, working with private landowners to benefit wildlife—with particular attention to hunting species. Over the years, paying for the privilege of hunting and fishing on private lands became more and more prevalent. The key to success in these efforts at commercialization of wildlife was the landowner's control of access. In other words, stepping

---

*Jack Ward Thomas is Chief Emeritus of the Forest Service and Boone & Crocket Professor of Wildlife Conservation at the University of Montana.

onto private land without permission of the owner was, and is, considered "trespassing"—a punishable transgression of law.

I grew up trailing my grandfather, father, and uncles as they hunted quail, squirrels, and rabbits. As was customary, I received a .22 rifle on my twelfth birthday and was allowed to hunt on my own. My grandfather's farm was soon too small to contain my ambitions as hunter and fisherman. I gained access to other farms and ranches through two methods—begging permission and, if permission was denied, sneaking in without detection or, at least, without getting caught. I became proficient in both approaches but never appreciated either. Upon being employed by the state, I gave up sneaking and was reduced to reliance on the largesse of landowners.

After ten years I joined the research division of the Forest Service. Our study areas included the Monongahela National Forest in West Virginia. This was my first exposure to public land—of which, as a citizen of the United States, I was part owner. And, to my delight, there was not a "no trespassing" sign anywhere to be seen. This was land over which I could wander without a thought of asking permission. So long as I had the appropriate license, I could hunt and fish without a by-your-leave from anyone. It seemed a wonder! It still does.

I had a right to be there—a right that ownership ensured. This was, after all, my land. So far as I could determine, this legacy of vast stretches of public land open to all was unique in all the world. I would never be rich enough to own thousands or hundreds or even tens of acres. But as part owner of hundreds of millions of acres of public lands, I was born wealthy.

I was privileged to serve the people of the United States for thirty years in the Forest Service and spent time on national forests from Florida to New Hampshire, from Pennsylvania to Oregon, from California to Alaska. These forests were all different but, in one critical sense, they were all the same. They belonged to me, to my children, and to all the American people for today, tomorrow, and forever—unless, somehow, we allow this incredible birthright to be stolen or frittered away.

For the last three years of my Forest Service career, I occupied the chief's chair in Washington, D.C. One of the duties of that job was to testify before Congress. In one such hearing, there was discussion of the "disposal" of at least some public land into private ownership or transferal to the states. The chairman asked, "Chief, what is your opinion on the matter of the disposal of public lands?"

I told him the story related earlier and concluded as follows: "Mr. Chairman, as an American citizen I am not willing to see my birthright in the public lands diminished. In fact, I would like to see those holdings strategically increased. I believe that I can speak for my two sons who were raised with national forests literally at their back door. They would be adamantly opposed to any loss of their public land heritage. I will even venture to speak for grandchildren who are not yet able to speak at all. Collectively we are not, now or ever, willing to see our heritage in the public lands sold, given away, or transferred to other ownership. These are our lands. They are probably all the lands we will ever own outside of our house lots. These lands are our birthright to be treasured and handed down, enhanced if possible, to our progeny so long as this nation exists."

The chairman replied, "Chief, if I understand your answer, it is not only 'no,' it is 'hell no!'"

"Well stated," I replied.

As the population of the United States grows and the ratio of land to people inexorably decreases and the value of land increases, there will be repeated attempts to divest "we the people" of our public lands. These efforts will never cease. Such efforts have been turned back— time after time. Yet only eternal vigilance will assure the maintenance of the American people's birthright in public land. It is a vigil worth keeping.

The conservation activism of the Theodore Roosevelt administration was followed by decades of a more custodial approach to public land management. The legacy of Roosevelt, however, prompted other notable conservation laws. The 1911 Weeks Act authorized the purchase of degraded private lands in the East for the purpose of watershed protection. The ultimate result was the establishment of an additional 24 million acres of national forests.

The National Park Service Act of 1916 established the National Park Service in the Department of the Interior with Stephen Mather as the first director. The establishment of the National Park Service marked the end of Pinchot's failed campaign to place the national parks under Forest Service management. The campaign focused on a split in the conservation movement: John Muir, who died in 1914, promoted the preservationist approach to retain the "natural" state while Pinchot advocated the sustainable use of natural resources for human benefit.[27]

The huge unemployment problem of the Great Depression and the New Deal era of President Franklin Roosevelt further expanded federal efforts in conservation. The establishment of the Office of Emergency Conservation, more commonly known as the Civilian Conservation Corps (CCC), employed by mid-1933 some 275,000 young men building roads, trails, campgrounds, and other public land improvements. By the end of the CCC era in 1942, over 3 million men had served the nation as CCC employees.[28] The Dust Bowl era of the 1930s, exacerbated by the poor condition of western rangelands, prompted the passage of the Taylor Grazing Act in 1934. This act created the Grazing Service, which in 1946 merged with the General Land Office to become the Bureau of Land Management with responsibilities for grazing on public rangeland and the management of the remaining public domain. These lands were referred to as the "lands nobody wanted" as they generally comprised the public domain lands not otherwise identified as parks, refuges, monuments, or national forests.[29]

New Emphasis on Commodities

With the need to provide raw materials for World War II, followed by the postwar wave of prosperity, great energy was focused on production of minerals and timber from public lands. Timber production from national forests increased along with a road network needed to move trees out of the woods and to the mills. Silvicultural practices and economics favored large block clearcut harvesting on a massive scale. Amenities and values such as wilderness, aesthetics, wildlife, and recreation were regarded as little more than constraints on the production of minerals, timber, and forage.

Despite the increased pressures for timber harvest and mining, the conservation movement remained alive. In 1946, the Soil Conservation Society was founded. With postwar prosperity came increased demands for outdoor recreation and the public lands increasingly became America's playground. But at the same time, the postwar prosperity continued to accelerate demand for timber, energy, and minerals. Conservationists raised concerns that public lands were being pushed beyond the limits of sustainability. Congress responded by passing the Multiple-Use Sustained Yield Act of 1960. In Section 2, this measure directed the Forest Service to manage national forests "for multiple use and sustained yield of the several products and services obtained therefrom." The act placed outdoor recreation, range, timber, water, and wildlife and fish on an equal footing—the first of a series of forward-thinking conservation laws that would follow during the next two decades.[30]

Chapter 2

Controversy Comes to the Public Lands

I truly believe that we in this generation must come to terms with nature, and I think we're challenged as mankind has never been challenged before to prove our maturity and our mastery, not of nature, but of ourselves.

—Rachel Carson, interview in CBS documentary (1963)

The evolving land ethic is perhaps best embodied in a one-time Forest Service employee's work and writings. In 1947 Aldo Leopold wrote: "The practice of conservation must spring from a conviction of what is ethically right and aesthetically right, as well as what is economically expedient. A thing is right only when it tends to preserve the integrity, stability and beauty of the community, and the community includes the soil, waters, fauna, and flora, as well as people."[1] Leopold's seminal work, *A Sand County Almanac,* was published in 1949, the year after he died fighting a fire on a neighbor's farm in Wisconsin.

Leopold's work influenced the thinking and writings of a Fish and Wildlife Service employee named Rachel Carson. Her 1962 treatise, *Silent Spring,* made millions of citizens aware of the prevalence and effects of toxic chemicals on human health and the environment and brought to focus the practical aspects of Leopold's land ethic.[2] *Silent Spring* demonstrated that conservation entails more than providing for sustained use over time, as Pinchot argued, or for the preservation of amenity and aesthetic values of nature appreciated by Emerson, Thoreau, Muir, and others. In vivid words and images, Carson made clear the inextricable link among the quality of our lands and waters and human health.

When *Silent Spring* was published, approximately 11,500 American troops were in Vietnam. Over the next decade, more than 58,000 Americans would die in a war that became the focal point for many citizens' disillusionment with the federal government. Popular opposition to the war intensified over the years, as antiwar protestors teamed with civil rights and human rights activists and led teach-ins and sit-ins at college campuses across the country. In the spring of 1970, U.S. Senator Gaylord Nelson of Wisconsin initiated the first Earth Day as a nationwide teach-in on the environment. An estimated 20 million people participated in demonstrations. Ten thousand grade schools and high schools, two thousand colleges, and one thousand communities were involved.[3]

Public distrust of government generally, and the executive branch specifically, crystallized during the Watergate scandal in 1973. Through this period Congress passed numerous laws exerting legislative direction over matters historically left to the discretion of the executive branch. Many of these laws were designed to protect the environment while opening federal land management to greater public participation and scrutiny.

The National Environmental Policy Act (NEPA) required public disclosure and citizen involvement in federal land management actions. The Clean Water, Safe Drinking Water, and Clean Air acts were intended to ensure basic protection for the nation's water and air resources. The Endangered Species Act was amended to ensure protection of rare and imperiled species and the habitats on which they depend.

The two principal federal land management laws passed by Congress during this period were the Federal Land Policy and Management Act of 1976 (FLPMA) and the National Forest Management Act of 1976 (NFMA). The Forest Service had operated under its own legislation since 1897. Now FLPMA provided the BLM with its own organic act and multiple-use mandate. Because of its roots and fragmented landownership patterns, BLM evolved as a decentralized organization with strong ties to local communities. Historically far less public attention was paid to BLM-managed public lands than that received by national forests, parks, and refuges. Passage of FLPMA, although of enormous importance to the concept of public land conservation and management, was greeted with little fanfare outside of local grazing and mining interests (and the BLM itself). FLPMA, however, represented the first recognition by Congress that remaining public domain land should remain in public ownership unless otherwise provided through agency planning. Until passage of FLPMA, the BLM-managed land was still being "disposed of" by the federal government and homesteading continued in Alaska.

NFMA, by contrast, was subject to intense lobbying and debate by national interest groups and Congress. Its passage was in direct response to a legal challenge that threatened to sharply curtail the national forest timber sale program. The roots of the controversy date to national forest management following World War II.

Postwar Changes

Prior to World War II, the Forest Service had openly criticized management of private timberlands and warned of a coming shortage of timber due to unsustainable logging practices. After the war, the agency renewed efforts begun in the 1930s to federally regulate private timberlands. The agency's public education campaigns focused on the need for fire prevention, replanting, and proper timber cutting practices. The timber industry vehemently opposed the Forest Service's drafted legislative proposals to place federal restrictions on management of private timberlands.

Upon election of President Dwight D. Eisenhower in 1952—and his opposition to "federal domination of the people through federal domination of their resources"—the issue of federal regulation of private timberlands was dropped. After twenty years of intense debate, the Forest Service and the timber industry were united through the common goals of providing wood fiber to build new homes, employing returning servicemen, and reconstructing war-torn Europe.[4] Access to the national forests was limited, however, and the Forest Service asked Congress for federal appropriations to construct new roads to get to the timber in uncut forests.

In 1952, the chief of the Forest Service, Richard McArdle, testified to Congress that without appropriated funds to build new roads, many areas with valuable timber would remain undeveloped.[5] McArdle argued that when a timber sale operator built a road, construction costs were deducted from the gross value paid for the timber. Thus publicly financed roads would allow timber to be sold at higher prices than when loggers were required to build the road themselves. The Forest Service's position was that timber sales accessed by publicly financed roads would return the same amount of revenue as sales where roads were built by the timber purchasers.

Initially the timber industry opposed efforts to publicly subsidize the cost of building new logging roads. Part of their argument involved control of access to national forest timber. At that time, the Department of Agriculture considered these roads to belong to the timber companies that built them. Thus if a timber company built a road to access a timber sale, they could maintain control over future sales in the area by blocking others' use of their road.

Soon Congress began financing the construction of new roads in the national forests with taxpayer money. The issue over who controlled access to the national forest road system was not resolved however, until Attorney General Robert F. Kennedy ruled in 1962 that the secretary of agriculture had the right to require that timber companies give the United States reciprocal access to roads built across the national forests.[6] Subsequent judicial decisions have confirmed this right.

For the next thirty years the agency began intensive development of a road system to facilitate timber harvest. The national forest road system grew from 107,000 miles in 1950 to nearly 200,000 by 1970. The increased road access that allowed for timber harvest also fostered greater recreational use of the national forests. Between 1950 and 1971, timber sales increased from 3.4 to 10.6 billion board feet per year. During the same period recreational use increased from 27 to 178 million recreation visitor-days per year.[7]

After World War II, the Forest Service's timber sale program increasingly became the linchpin of the agency's approach to multiple-use management. Timber receipts meant jobs and income for rural communities. A larger timber sale program enabled the agency to retain more timber receipts through its trust funds and ensured that congressional representatives from western states would keep agency budgets high. Roads to timber sales also meant access for people to hunt and fish in the national forests. The agency argued that clearcuts provided openings and "edge habitats" within the forest that were good for growing many species of big game such as elk and deer.

As more and more people began using national forests for recreation, those who drew little distinction between national forests and national parks were surprised at what they found. As forest historian Harold Steen has noted:

> Couched in terms of timber famine and devastation, decades of propagation by the Forest Service to justify federal regulation of logging had created the popular image of rangers protecting forests against rampaging, greedy lumbermen. Now the postwar public came to the forests—camping, fishing, hiking—and "discovered" logging in the national forests. . . . Implementation of long-term timber

management plans collided with the results of an extremely effective public relations program against "destructive" logging. As a result, the public felt deceived.[8]

A more urban and mobile population that had more free time and discretionary income increasingly came to national forests to hike, bird watch, camp, and "drive for pleasure." And though some foresters and wildlife biologists will argue that clearcuts provide benefits to certain wildlife species, few people drive forest roads for the pleasure of seeing large swaths of land stripped of trees.

In 1960, Congress passed the Multiple-Use Sustained Yield Act, a law that recognized range, wildlife, recreation, and minerals as designated uses of national forests. The agency had long managed for these uses, yet the Organic Act of 1897 mentioned only timber and water specifically. A system of "land zoning" was applied in an effort to ensure the continued flow of multiple-use outputs such as timber, forage for grazing, mining, and recreation. The Multiple-Use Sustained Yield Act recognized that "establishment and maintenance of areas of wilderness are consistent" with multiple use. Nonetheless, recreation and environmental interests lobbied Congress for permanent legislative wilderness protection—culminating in the passage of the Wilderness Act in 1964. Although the Forest Service had long advocated administrative protection of wilderness areas, a growing number of organized environmental groups and recreation interests sought more permanent, congressional recognition of wilderness areas.

Clearcutting

The Forest Service had become known as a superstar agency: an efficient organization with a decentralized field staff committed to a single and clear mission—in short, a model bureaucracy.[9] The Forest Service was motivated by the same mixture of congressional funding, sense of public purpose, and focused mission that led to the "engineering miracles" in the Columbia River basin and other parts of the western United States by the Corps of Engineers and the Bureau of Reclamation—massive dams and water projects that provided water and electricity to far-flung communities.

With the combination of a can-do attitude and scientific forest management, the Forest Service found almost no obstacle insurmountable. If commercially valuable timber was inaccessible, build a road. If harvested forest on south-facing slopes resisted regeneration, terrace the mountainside. If soil fertility was lacking, fertilize the area. If pests or fire threatened forest stands, apply pesticides and marshal all hands to combat fire. If people grew unhappy with the site of large clearcuts, leave "beauty strips" of trees along roadways to block timber harvest units from view.

Forests were managed less as interconnected ecological systems and more as complicated machines that demanded engineering skills and technological mastery. So long as enough "inputs" were delivered in the form of roads, fertilizer, reforestation, cultivation of poorly stocked lands, thinning, and protection from fire and pests, outputs would flow in the form of billions of board feet of timber.

As timber demand grew, clearcutting—the practice of cutting all the trees in a given area—became the preferred method of timber production. Historically the Forest Service had decried such practices on private timberlands and advocated more selective cutting methods. In 1935, for example, C. J. Buck, the regional forester responsible for the national forests of Oregon and Washington, whose opposition later in his career to the creation of Olympic National Park so offended President Franklin D. Roosevelt that he was reassigned to the Washington, D.C., office, stated:

> Clearcutting has always been questionable because of its tremendous losses in forest productivity, partly because of its attendant extreme fire hazard, frequently resulting in reburns and forest devastation, also because of the low degree of timber utilization. It is concluded that clearcutting practices on national forest lands should be abandoned if possible and systems of selective logging devised and substituted.[10]

Upon touring the Pacific Northwest in 1937, Gifford Pinchot wrote to Buck: "One of the things that struck me most was your wisdom in preferring the high forest selection system as against clearcutting. What I saw in the line convinced me completely that what you are doing is not only the right thing for the forest but also very much the right thing in its effect on public sentiment."[11]

In the late 1940s and early 1950s, demand for wood fiber, economic efficiencies, and the desire to facilitate replanting and regeneration led to replacing more selective logging methods with more economically efficient clearcutting. The timber industry supported clearcutting as more profitable than other methods that targeted certain species or age classes of trees. The sight of large clearcuts and erosion-prone terraced slopes, however, caused a growing number of citizens and interest groups to criticize the Forest Service's stewardship. Robert Wolf, a senior fellow at the Society of American Foresters and a congressional staffperson involved in drafting numerous Forest Service laws, recounts the time in 1968 when he engaged a United Airlines pilot in conversation while waiting for a flight. Wolf recalls: "When I said I was a forester, he launched into a diatribe against clearcutting. He said that wherever he flew, the forest landscape was beginning to look like the face of someone who had a terrible case of chicken pox. We foresters simply didn't see the storm clouds forming because we thought we were right."[12]

The Forest Service initiated several internal studies that recommended changes in the agency's timber management. In 1970, a University of Montana review of Bitterroot National Forest management in Montana resulted in a scathing indictment of the agency's practice of clearcutting an area, terracing, and then replanting it. The Bolle Report, as it became known after its principal author Professor Arnold Bolle, said that "multiple use management, in fact, does not exist as the governing principle on the Bitterroot National Forest."[13] The Bolle Report charged:

> The heavy timber orientation is built in by legislative action and control, by executive direction and by budgetary restriction It is further reinforced by the agency's own hiring and promotion policies and it is rationalized in the doctrines of its professional expertise. . . . The rigid system developed during the expanded effort to meet the national housing post-war boom. It continues to exist in the face of a considerable change in our value system—a rising public concern with environmental quality. While the national demand for timber harvest has abated considerably, the major emphasis on timber production continues.[14]

In the wake of the Bolle Report, the Forest Service adopted guidelines relative to timber harvest levels, clearcutting, and timber sale contracts. Then the BLM adopted the guidelines for use on its productive timberlands in western Oregon and Washington. But the controversy was far from resolved. Even as external pressure was growing for changes in timber management practices, market prices for softwood lumber and plywood were increasing—creating greater demand for timber from national forests. The price of softwood lumber rose about 37 percent over an eighteen-month period during 1967–1968. This price increase coincided with the congressional goal of doubling the number of housing units constructed over the previous ten years.[15]

The Forest Service told Congress that with more investments, they could increase timber production by two-thirds in the more productive regions. The chief of the agency, Edward Cliff, testified that in national forests in the Douglas-fir region, for example, allowable cuts could be increased by shortening rotations. However, much of such increase from shorter rotations would be derived merely from faster liquidation of the residual old growth timber accompanied by falloff in levels of annual cut at the end of the rotation. . . . There are some measures [that] are essential to support increases in allowable cut. These include better utilization, more thinning, cultural treatments of young growth, reforestation of non-stocked land, better protection, and more complete salvage.[16]

Sensing that sufficient appropriations for intensive forestry could translate to increased timber harvests, the timber industry argued for passage of the National Timber Supply Act of 1969, a bill that would have allowed the Forest Service to retain timber receipts for future timber harvest.[17] Although the Timber Supply Act failed to pass Congress, other "trust funds," not subject to annual congressional appropriations, such as the Brush Disposal Fund of 1916, the Knutson-Vandenberg Fund of 1930, and the salvage provisions of NFMA, still enable the agency to retain millions of dollars of timber receipts outside of the annual congressional appropriations process.

The shortfall between agency objectives and annual appropriations led to passage of the Forest and Rangeland Renewable Resources Planning Act of 1974 in order to align congressional appropriations and Forest Service management objectives. The Resources Planning Act required the agency to prepare ten-year assessments describing the nation's forest and rangeland renewable resources, prepare a five-year planning document assessing objectives over a forty-five-year time frame, and submit an annual report.

Focus Essay

Birds and Battlefields and Humor: Things Could Be a Lot Worse

Patricia Nelson Limerick*

John Wesley Powell, famous in environmental circles as an advocate for wisdom and foresight in the use of natural resources, lost his right arm in the

*Patricia Nelson Limerick is professor of history at the University of Colorado and the author of several books on western United States history.

Civil War. In *A River Running West,* Donald Worster quotes an eyewitness description of the battle in which Powell received his wound. While the battle raged and hundreds died, an infantryman reported, "the little birds were singing in the green trees over our heads!"

People turn to nature, according to a persistent belief, to escape strife. Like many long-held articles of faith, this one requires a certain willingness to suspend disbelief. As in the occasion of Powell's war injury, nature has provided plenty of cheerful and appealing settings in which humans have displayed their worst tendencies.

Just as important, nature and its wealth have provided a lot for humans to fight over. From water to minerals, from logs to scenic views, nature has placed before humanity an enormous set of opportunities for arguing, asserting, claiming, disputing, quarreling, stealing, contesting, fighting, and suing. Those who have found, from time to time, peace in nature should be aware of the novelty of their experience.

Political disagreement has always been a presence in public land issues. Consider these colorful descriptions of the Forest Reserve system from a century ago collected by the historian Michael McCarthy: The reserves were "a program designed to harass and annoy"; "crackpot schemes of politicians in Washington"; "as nefarious a scheme as ever disgraced the nation"; "the dude design for an outdoor museum and menagerie"; "a reckless exercise of power"; "rank imbecility"; "obnoxious measures of Eastern visionaries"; "intolerable usurpations of power"; and "a system paralyzing progress."

For suggesting other genres and styles (besides invective and denunciation) in which we could express our various positions on public land management, perhaps the most inspirational example from our forebears is this memorable verse from a Colorado agricultural publication in 1907:

> On the forest reserve please bury me not,
> For I never would then be free;
> A forest ranger would dig me up,
> In order to collect his fee.

More doggerel verse, more songs with humorously rewritten lyrics, more clever jokes and witty parodies: what an element of unexpected joy and pleasure this line of expression could bring to our twenty-first-century controversies! Might it be that a shift in this direction could lead to better understanding and even to some discoveries of common ground? Who knows? But the first environmental group that declares a competition for humorous, merry, good-hearted defenses of wilderness will get my largest contribution.

In the meantime, we are left with the old customs of arguing, asserting, claiming, disputing, quarreling, contesting, fighting, and suing. Oddly, those environmentalists who have found their personal peace in a retreat to nature have turned out to be some of our most aggressive fighters when it comes to kicking up a fuss and pushing for their preferences. The same person who, off by himself on a trail with a backpack, may reach heights of contemplative peace and transcendent tranquility, can return to civilization, put down the backpack, take off the gloves, and start swinging: at local extractors of resources, at federal officials judged to be inadequate in their defense and protection of those resources, and even at other environmentalists convicted of being insufficiently pure by the demanding yardstick that measures true devotion to nature. For many Americans today, having the soul restored by an interlude in a natural landscape can leave the beneficiary very angry and very feisty when that opportunity for restoration begins to look threatened.

Historians are the ultimate armchair quarterbacks—watching the struggle over rights to nature and finding the plays and players fascinating. From our angle as couch potatoes, the intensity of the current fight is comparatively easy to understand. What is at stake is a reversal in the direction of "progress." For the nation's first century, that meant expansion, development, and resource use. The federal government was an essential ally of progress. Over the last century, the term has been betraying its previous owners and reversing its direction. For more and more Americans, progress has come to mean repair, restoration, remediation, reintroduction, recovery, and rehabilitation: the rescue of nature from despoiling uses.

Which definition of "progress" will the federal government and its land management agencies finally choose? With this question hanging in the air, every policy modification, every administrative act, every official statement for the public record gets worked over as another clue to the answer. These are serious issues. Livelihoods, worldviews, and ecosystems rest on the answer. No wonder the heat of the controversy is set at "high."

And yet, if we think back to the war that took Major Powell's right arm, our conclusion has to be this: Things could be, and have been, a lot worse.

The National Forest Management Act

In 1973, the West Virginia chapter of the Izaak Walton League of America, concerned about the effects of clearcutting on turkey and other wildlife habitat in the Monongahela National Forest in West Virginia, sued the Forest

Service.[18] This high-profile lawsuit began a decades-long trend of litigation and judicial review of management of national forests. The Monongahela lawsuit alleged that the Forest Service was ignoring a section of the Organic Act of 1897 that allowed the agency to sell only dead, mature, or "large growth of trees" that were clearly "marked before sale." The plaintiffs argued that clearcutting and other silvicultural prescriptions that allowed other than dead and mature trees to be harvested were a clear contradiction of the law.

In 1975, the Appeals Court agreed with a lower court's decision that clearcutting expressly violated the Organic Act. The decision stated:

> We are not insensitive to the fact that our reading of the [Organic] Act will have serious and far reaching consequences, and it may well be that this legislation enacted over 75 years ago is an anachronism that no longer serves the public interest. However, the appropriate forum to resolve this complex and controversial issue is not the courts, but the Congress.[19]

The Department of Justice declined to seek Supreme Court review of the decision by the Court of Appeals. Fearing the decision would be followed by other courts in more timber-oriented areas of the country—possibly bringing harvest on national forests to a halt—the Forest Service proposed a legislative solution to the provisions of the Organic Act. In response, Congress drafted legislation that allowed the use of various timber harvest methods including clearcutting. The passage of the NFMA in 1976 avoided a shutdown of the timber program.

Notable among the NFMA provisions that were signed into law by President Gerald Ford were sections requiring the Forest Service to develop integrated land and resource management plans for each national forest and grassland every ten to fifteen years, identify lands "suitable" for timber production, and monitor the effects of management. NFMA required the Forest Service to develop these land management plans through extensive public involvement in hopes of developing a shared national vision for the national forests and grasslands. The NMFA reinforced some provisions of NEPA—most notably the requirements for public participation and interdisciplinary analysis of issues. NFMA was not prescriptive legislation. The secretary of agriculture was vested with broad management discretion. Though the passage of NFMA was directly related to dissatisfaction with public forest management practices, especially clearcutting, it did not specifically limit clearcutting. A committee of scientists made recommendations to the Forest Service, and regulations to implement this new law were finalized in 1982. Included in the regulations was the provision that the agency would maintain well-distributed, viable populations of all native vertebrates in national forests and grasslands.

The forest planning process resulted in the hiring of hundreds of biologists, soils scientists, hydrologists, and professionals from other disciplines and brought about an improved understanding of forest resources. It also brought greater recognition of wildlife, water, and wilderness values and increased citizen involvement in the management of public lands. Through its forest plan, each national forest calculated the sale quantities of timber that with funding could be provided within the plan's lifespan of ten to fifteen years. Other multiple-use resources and values such as water, wildlife, and recreation were often modeled as constraints against the ability to meet desired logging levels. Sometimes faulty data and optimistic assumptions in the agencies' modeling caused higher timber forecasts than could be achieved regardless of funding levels. During the Reagan administration, there was intense political pressure to increase timber harvest. Even as public controversy mounted, timber offered for sale from national forests remained stable at 11 to 12 billion board feet a year.

Throughout the 1970s and 1980s, other contentious issues—such as below-cost timber sales, the economic and ecological costs of road construction, and harvest of old growth forests in the Pacific Northwest—continued to plague the Forest Service. Nor was the BLM immune to the effects of growing public concern over environmental quality. A lawsuit brought by the Natural Resources Defense Council forced the BLM to initiate environmental analysis in an open public process as required by NEPA. Rather than use a single generic "programmatic" analysis to support public land grazing, the BLM was required to complete site-specific environmental analyses for hundreds of livestock grazing allotments.

In national forests, road development and associated timber harvest rolled on unabated. The forest road system, for example, grew from approximately 206,000 miles in 1974 to 360,000 miles by 1989. Through the mid-1980s, bowing to timber industry lobbying, Congress began assigning "timber targets" as a condition of agency budgets. Agency managers found it nearly impossible to meet the timber targets if they were also to meet new forest plan requirements for species diversity, scenic quality, water quality, and recreation.

Meanwhile, concerned citizens were turning to administrative appeals and litigation to try to stop below-cost timber sales, clearcutting, and harvest of old-growth trees. Local activists and citizens began acts of civil disobedience, chaining themselves to trees and across roads in the Pacific Northwest, the source of nearly half of the nation's timber sale program. Some activists threatened acts of violence, such as driving spikes deep into trees, potentially endangering the safety of loggers and mill workers.

In 1982, John Crowell, the Department of Agriculture undersecretary responsible for oversight of the Forest Service (and a former executive with the timber company Louisiana Pacific), said: "One of my major initiatives has been to speed up harvest of the slow-growing or decadent, overmature timber stands in the Pacific Northwest, the old growth."[20] The chief of the Forest Service, Max Peterson, issued a memo to regional foresters in 1987 directing that in finalizing draft forest plans, the agency should "achieve the RPA program multiple purpose high bound targets tempered by local issues, concerns, and conditions."[21] The long-term planning document cited in Peterson's memo included, among other goals and objectives, increases in timber sales of 30 percent by 2000 and nearly 20 billion board feet by 2030—nearly double the then timber cutting levels.

In 1989, more than sixty forest supervisors and line officers sent a letter to Peterson's successor, Chief of the Forest Service Dale Robertson, expressing their dissatisfaction with the status quo and declaring that the agency was cutting too much timber, too fast. For a hierarchical, get-with-the-program organization such as the Forest Service, the letter was extraordinary. The supervisors told the chief: "Many members of the public and many of our employees no longer view us as leaders in environmental conservation. . . . Public challenges to the timber program cannot be overcome by additional funding to timber management, nor by simply improving documentation of the NEPA process."[22]

In the late 1980s and early 1990s, Forest Service leadership tried to respond to these calls for change by implementing programs such as New Perspectives and ecosystem management and through national policies on clearcutting and old growth. Although signifying an important new direction, the programs did not immediately change agency policy or timber cutting levels—for example, the agency offered 11 billion board feet of timber for sale in 1990. With internal and external pressure mounting, change was imminent. It came in the inauspicious guise of a reclusive owl in the Pacific Northwest.

The Spotted Owl

In 1972, Eric Forsman, a student at Oregon State University, found that northern spotted owls were most commonly found in old-growth forests— the same forests that were targeted for cutting by the Forest Service and

BLM because of their large and valuable old trees.[23] Forsman's adviser, Howard Wight, shared these findings with the Forest Service. Chief John McGuire wrote back that he would suggest that the Pacific Northwest regional office of the Forest Service work with other agencies to "improve or develop interim guidelines for location and protection of the spotted owl's habitat until more complete information is available regarding the owl's habitat needs."[24]

The Oregon Endangered Species Task Force was commissioned to respond to the nascent federal Endangered Species Act of 1973 and the potential "spotted owl problem." At the first meeting of the task force, the BLM representative made it clear that "all old growth forest on BLM lands will be harvested in less than 30 years." For its part, the Forest Service said, "a similar situation exists on national forest lands."[25] The agencies also agreed to provide a map of old growth on Forest Service and BLM lands in the region by the task force's next meeting—a job that would ultimately take well more than a decade to complete.

Over the next fifteen years or more, the Forest Service and the BLM would consult with other federal and state agencies and private industry in the Pacific Northwest to study northern spotted owls and their habitat needs. When recommendations were made to protect the owl, agency leaders, if they acted at all, would adopt the bare minimum proposals. Steven Yaffee, a writer who has studied the agencies' response to the spotted owl, notes that throughout this period the agency response was to "muddle through: do the minimum possible, maintain control by keeping decision making within normal agency operating procedures. . . . Ironically, by not taking steps to provide minimal protection for owl habitat at a time when neither the scientific information nor the environmental groups were particularly demanding, agency leaders missed their best chance for resolving the controversy without major impacts on their missions."[26] The scientific information would soon become more compelling, however, and environmental groups more demanding.

Home to broad expanses of old-growth ponderosa pine on the east side of the Cascade Mountains and old-growth Douglas-fir on the west side, the Pacific Northwest had become the breadbasket of the Forest Service timber program—supplying about half of all timber harvested from the National Forest System and nearly all of the timber harvested from BLM-managed lands. Considerable Forest Service and BLM resources were committed to northern spotted owl research. Yet timber harvest levels on public lands in the Pacific Northwest remained steady or even increased through the 1970s and 1980s. Throughout this period, the Forest Service pressed for more "studies" of northern spotted owl habitat—either as a way of seeking a scientific solution that validated their timber management objectives or a way of delaying an ultimate reckoning so that harvest of old-growth forests could continue unabated.

After a set of Forest Service "regional guides" for northern spotted owl protection were rejected by the timber industry and environmentalists alike, the Forest Service in 1985 initiated a new supplemental environmental impact statement (EIS) in what would prove to be the agency's last chance to exert control over the spotted owl issue. This effort was constrained by direction from the chief's office that the final decision must not affect allowable timber sales in the region by more than 5 percent.[27]

In 1988, the states of Oregon and Washington listed the spotted owl as "threatened" and "endangered" under state laws, respectively. The two states' decision had no immediate effect on public land management. But it did place pressure on the U.S. Fish and Wildlife Service to list the species for protection under the federal Endangered Species Act. After the Forest Service's supplemental EIS was released (and publicly repudiated), an Interagency Scientific Committee was established to develop a "scientifically credible" conservation strategy for the northern spotted owl.

In October 1989, Congress entered the fray. It tried to ameliorate the conflict by legislating a slightly lower harvest level than planned by the agencies, insulating Forest Service timber sales from litigation, while also protecting certain known spotted owl habitats. Neither environmentalists nor the timber industry were ultimately satisfied by the congressional intervention. Nor was the Forest Service. For it was becoming increasingly clear that the agency was losing its grip on the northern spotted owl issue.

The Interagency Scientific Committee, chaired by a well-respected wildlife biologist and future chief of the Forest Service, Jack Ward Thomas, released its report in April 1990. Rather than trying to protect known spotted owl nesting sites—the preferred approach in the past—the Thomas Report, as the committee's work became known, called for protecting landscapes and eliminating timber harvest in large habitat conservation areas until silvicultural prescriptions could be adapted that would ensure the spotted owl's persistence in a managed landscape.

In June 1990, the Fish and Wildlife Service listed the owl as "threatened." Fearing the economic repercussions associated with implementing the Thomas Report, widely acknowledged as the best and most credible compilation of spotted owl research to date, the Bush administration appointed a task force to look for low-cost alternatives. Later a press release was issued saying that the Forest Service would act in a "manner not inconsistent with" the Thomas Report. The BLM would manage its Pacific Northwest forests under a separate—never reviewed or publicly released—strategy developed by its director, Cy Jamison.

On May 23, 1991, Judge William Dwyer, a federal district court judge in the state of Washington, citing a "deliberate and systematic refusal to follow the law," enjoined all timber sales in spotted owl habitat until the Forest Service and BLM demonstrated they could comply with the Endangered Species Act, the National Forest Management Act, and the National Environmental Policy Act.

BLM Director Jamison, and Interior Secretary Manual Lujan, decided to invoke a rarely used "God Squad" provision of the Endangered Species Act to move forward with forty-four of fifty-two timber sales that the Fish and Wildlife Service had determined as likely to jeopardize the spotted owl. The effort was meant to pressure Congress to amend the Endangered Species Act. Although many of the sales were allowed to proceed, promises of additional protections for owls were secured.

In April 1993, the newly elected president, William Jefferson Clinton, held true to a campaign promise and convened the Northwest Forest Summit in an effort to resolve the dispute. The summit was remarkable in many ways. It brought together environmentalists, timber workers, and community representatives. Both the president and Vice-President Al Gore attended, as well as several other cabinet members. Notably neither the Forest Service nor the BLM was invited to speak at the conference. The agencies responsible for managing the public lands in question were essentially cut out and had lost further control of the issue. At the conclusion of the summit, the president directed the agencies to come up with a legally and ecologically defensible and socially responsible plan for the Pacific Northwest forests.

Lessons Learned

It is fashionable to denounce what some believe to be a new phenomenon—the intersection of politics and public land management. The two have been close cousins, however, since Gifford Pinchot drew lines on a map and urged President Theodore Roosevelt to carve millions of acres of land from the public domain and convert them into forest reserves just hours before a congressional directive preventing such actions took effect. That political decisions influence public lands may be either good or bad, depending on how the outcome affects your interests. It is, however, not new.

The BLM and Forest Service approached the "spotted owl crisis" in decidedly different manners that reveal important differences between the two organizations. Political appointees in the Department of the Interior such as the BLM's director and former congressional aide, Cy Jamison, spearheaded the Bush administration's approach of casting the issue as a matter of owls versus jobs in an attempt to discredit the Endangered Species Act as unworkable and too costly. This approach, perhaps understandable from a political perspective, masked more serious policy issues affecting the livelihood of rural Northwest communities and timber workers. Between 1980 and 1988, the timber industry in the Northwest increased the production of finished lumber by more than 19 percent. During that same time frame, employment in the industry fell by 14 percent.[28] Mechanization and other efficiencies in the timber industry, along with the export of whole unfinished logs to foreign markets, were the real and tangible factors behind the loss of jobs. The specter of the northern spotted owl simply provided a convenient target for politicians who found it easier to rile rural timber communities rather than deal with the complex implications of industry mechanization and foreign trade.

Interior Department political appointees failed to convince the American people and Congress that the Endangered Species Act was unworkable and needed to be revised. Because Forest Service leadership, Congress, and others were slow (or unable) to make fundamental changes to logging practices in the Pacific Northwest, the agency's approach of throwing resources, people, and money into the spotted owl breach failed to prevent a court-ordered injunction.

Forest Service leaders were less involved in the politics of owls versus jobs. Rather they found themselves continually on the defensive—reacting to new information and court rulings by committing more people and resources and creating ever more committees and task forces. On the one hand, the BLM possessed a politically connected leadership and decentralized organization that maintained close ties to local economic interests and communities. On the other, the Forest Service maintained a centralized organization with unparalleled research capabilities and far more resources than the BLM. But so long as the issue remained within their control—arguably from 1973 to 1989—the Forest Service was unwilling to seriously consider solutions that would have anything more than a negligible impact on timber harvests in the Pacific Northwest.

Instead the agency fell back to the time-honored bureaucratic tactic of study, delay, then more study. Remarkably, almost three decades after the agency first promised to develop maps of old-growth forest, a comprehensive map of old growth on Forest Service lands has yet to be produced.[29] As the Forest Service delayed reckoning with the owl, however, their decision space narrowed. In time the agency's leadership completely lost control of the issue as the influence of interest groups, the Fish and Wildlife Service, Congress, and the court system grew more powerful. How did the Forest Service and BLM become so enmeshed in controversy over the spotted owl?

The Spanish philosopher José Ortega y Gasset once observed: "We have need of history in its entirety, not to fall back into it, but to see if we can escape from it."[30] Lessons do emerge from the spotted owl saga. First, agency leaders did not believe that the congressional or administration politics of the mid-1970s and 1980s impelled broad changes in direction. Public land management agencies and executive branch officials clearly failed to grasp the importance of—and the opportunities provided by—passage of NEPA, NFMA, FLPMA, and other environmental legislation of the late 1960s and early 1970s. NFMA, for example, was viewed less as a referendum on the need for new direction and more as an antidote to environmental plaintiffs' ability to exploit long-forgotten provisions of an eighty-year-old Organic Act. In much the same way, the Forest Service failed to understand that the spotted owl was to many people a surrogate for protecting old-growth forests. The Forest Service had built a remarkably effective organizational structure that for decades mirrored the majority of public sentiment. But when public values changed, the Forest Service did not. As a result, the agency increasingly found itself reacting to controversies over its standard operating procedures—and was bewildered when people failed to accept its "we know best" responses and turned to Congress, the media, and the courts to force change.

Second, implementation of NFMA affirmed the concepts of "scientific forestry" and the Progressive tradition's "gospel of efficiency." As the writer William deBuys notes: "Scientific forestry and the idea of land management developed from a view of the world that was mechanical. If a factory was a big machine, a forest was a bigger one. The same scientific principles that rendered assembly lines more productive would also make the machine of nature more efficient."[31] The same can-do spirit that drove agency employees to risk their lives fighting fires drove its management philosophy. If enough resources and technology were brought to bear, no problem was insurmountable. Such an approach was compromised, though, by biological realities and a congressional appropriations process that never provided enough resources to achieve the agency's goals. Timber output objectives did not fluctuate noticeably despite funding shortfalls. Instead, noncommodity programs that were viewed as constraints on timber production—such as wildlife and fish and wilderness—found their needs unfunded and often unmet.

Third, no amount of funding or technological innovation could overcome the public's growing desire for public forests that simply looked like forests. Science and research cannot make a clearcut look attractive. For people who happened to be flying into Seattle, Portland, and other West Coast cities, no amount of reasoned explanation could dispel the shock of aerial views of spaghetti-like road systems leading to broad swaths of clearcuts on public lands.

Fourth, reared in an insular and hierarchical organization that resisted outside interference, Forest Service leaders failed to take advantage of key provisions in NFMA, such as establishing citizen advisory groups, that might have helped the agency anticipate and adjust to changing social values. BLM's grazing advisory boards, formed after passage of the Taylor Grazing Act in 1936 and comprised almost exclusively of ranchers, helped the BLM to understand the outlook of local people. In 1994, Interior Secretary Bruce Babbitt abolished the grazing advisory boards and replaced them with new citizen councils that are balanced among a diversity of commodity and environmental interests as well as local people. These Resource Advisory Councils have helped the BLM develop rangeland health standards and guidelines for many of the public rangelands—no mean feat. Legislation passed in 2000 offers the Forest Service a chance to engage a balanced array of citizen interests in the management of national forests.[32] When demographics and social values began shifting in the 1960s and 1970s, the Forest Service increasingly found itself positioned squarely in the middle of competing interests—a situation likened to being "caught in a savage crossfire between uncritical lovers and unloving critics."[33] It is unlikely that citizen advisory councils alone would have girded the Forest Service against the dramatic shifts of the late 1980s and early 1990s, but they almost certainly would have helped agency leaders to anticipate the public momentum for a new direction.

Fifth, the incentive system on which the agencies relied, particularly the Forest Service, thwarts easy changes in direction. Upon passage of NFMA, agency leaders recognized the need for a more diverse workforce and greater expertise in wildlife, watersheds, recreation, research, and interpretive programs. But funding these programs would mean maintaining high timber harvest levels to finance the organization and satisfy members of Congress who controlled the budget and monitored agency programs. Based largely on an incentive system that rewarded continued production of often-subsidized commodity outputs, the Forest Service budget and organization grew steadily from 1960 to 1989. Maintaining organizational growth necessitated maintaining unpopular, sometimes unsustainable, logging practices.

Support for increased timber harvest began to swell in order to meet postwar needs. Even as that support waned, pressure to maintain or increase harvest levels came from members of Congress who controlled the agency's budget and from the executive branch itself. Until 2000, local communities adjacent to national forests and BLM-managed lands in the Pacific Northwest maintained a vested interest in increased timber production by virtue of a law passed in 1908 that guaranteed them 25 percent of all gross receipts generated from national forests for use on schools and roads—the vast majority of which came from timber harvest.

Changes in Priorities

Recent years have seen dramatic changes in the policy orientation of both the BLM and the Forest Service. The Northwest Forest Plan reduced timber harvest levels in the Pacific Northwest by more than 80 percent. Nationwide—in response to new information, litigation, and an improved understanding of how complex ecological systems respond to disturbance—timber harvest has dropped by more than 75 percent from the late 1980s. The Forest Service initiated major policy changes to protect roadless areas and reform management of its enormous road system in 1998. The BLM established balanced citizen advisory councils that helped the agency to implement new standards for healthy rangelands across 100 million acres of public rangeland. The BLM also created a system of national monuments and other protected lands that led some conservationists to nickname the agency the Bureau of Landscapes and Monuments as opposed to its derisive moniker of earlier years: the Bureau of Livestock and Mining.

Beginning with Chief Dale Robertson's articulation of the principles of ecosystem management and continuing through Jack Ward Thomas's implementation of the Northwest Forest Plan, the Forest Service made significant policy shifts emphasizing healthy lands and waters. The BLM placed new emphasis on the protection and conservation of special areas, national monuments, and other culturally or ecologically significant areas.

In the late 1990s, the Forest Service began to move away from incentive systems based on commodity outputs. The new emphasis was on performance measures based on land health, simpler and more accountable budgeting systems, and reform of its trust funds. Form must follow function, however. Federal spending on natural resources and the environment as a percentage of total domestic spending is half of what it was in 1962.[34] The agency's traditional reliance on timber sale receipts is driven by the reality that funding for natural resource management is rarely a congressional priority.

Chapter 3

Land Health: Broad-Scale Declines in Forest and Rangeland Conditions

> We summered our cattle on more than a million acres. . . .
> We owned it all, or so we felt. . . . And then it all went
> dead, over years, but swiftly. . . . We had reinvented our
> valley according to the most pervasive ideal given us by our
> culture, and we ended with a landscape organized like a
> machine for growing crops and fattening cattle, a machine
> that creaked a little louder each year, a dreamland gone
> wrong.
>
> —William Kittredge, *Owning It All* (1987)

William Kittredge grew up in Oregon's Warner Valley, a large wetland and rimrock area comprised of private, BLM, and National Wildlife Refuge lands. Many of the wetlands on private land have been diked and drained. The BLM has embarked on a plan to restore certain wetlands in the valley for waterfowl and native fishes, both of which have declined significantly from historic levels.

The health of our national forests and BLM public lands has been of long-standing concern to conservationists, agency managers, and scientists. Recent broad-scale assessments paint a troubling picture of land health from the Pacific Northwest to the Southeast. During the past decade, hundreds of state and federal research scientists have conducted broad assessments of public land conditions. The first of these surveys, published in 1993, focused on Northwest forests within the range of the northern spotted owl. More recently, assessments have been completed for the interior Columbia River basin, rangelands across the West, and southern forests.

Habitat fragmentation, simplification, and conversion have affected nearly every ecosystem. Disturbance regimes for wildfire, flood, drought, and disease now occur far beyond historic intensities and extent. As habitat has been degraded and disturbances become more widespread, a third factor, exotic species, has emerged as a major threat to the integrity of natural communities. Exotic species (also referred to as alien or nonnative invasive species) often thrive in disturbed habitats, displacing native species and perpetuating a cycle of decline. Numbers of state and federally listed endangered species, perhaps the best indicator of land health, have increased across many regions as habitats have become degraded and exotic species replace natives. This chapter reviews the health of national forests and BLM lands in selected regions of the country. Broad-scale assessments point to alarming declines that have been ongoing for many decades and will take decades more to correct.

Old-Growth Forests in the Pacific Northwest

On June 26, 1990, the emphasis for managing public forests in the Pacific Northwest shifted dramatically. On this date the northern spotted owl was listed for protection as a threatened species under the federal Endangered Species Act. This action not only formally recognized the decline of this old-growth-dependent species but also alerted the president and the entire nation to the unsustainable harvest of late-successional and old-growth forests in Washington, Oregon, and northern California. Ultimately, under the guise of what has become known as the Northwest Forest Plan, the primary management emphasis of the national forests and BLM lands of the region would change from timber production to restoration of old-growth forest conditions and protection of the many species that depend on these habitats.

Northern spotted owls prefer forests with late-successional and old-growth characteristics. Specifically this means that the owl's preferred nesting and roosting habitat consists of forests with moderate to high canopy closure

(60 to 80 percent), multilayer and multispecies tree stands with large overstory trees, and a high incidence of trees with irregularities such as large cavities, broken tops, mistletoe, and debris accumulations. Typically forests in the region require 150 to 200 years to attain such old-growth characteristics.[1]

It was precisely the overharvest of large trees in Pacific Northwest forests, the simplification of forests by removing large woody debris and irregularly shaped trees, and the accompanying broad-scale road-building program that caused the decline and subsequent listing of the owl. The timber programs of the Forest Service and BLM during the 1960s through the 1980s were designed to harvest large trees and thereby produce forests with little old growth and increasing amounts of younger to middle-aged trees. Such trees often grow fastest—an important characteristic if forests are managed primarily for timber production. Even with the large trees mostly removed, the excellent growing conditions in much of the Pacific Northwest allow for second-growth "reentry harvest" in as little as forty years.

Although the northern spotted owl was the focus of the old-growth debate, many other species were subsequently determined to be in decline as well. The marbled murrelet, a robin-sized seabird that nests in large trees of coastal forests, was listed as threatened on October 1, 1992. The murrelets depend on the ocean for food but must nest in large trees within a flight distance up to 50 miles of the marine environment. About this same time, too, stocks of Pacific salmon and steelhead were gaining increasing attention because of population declines and local extinctions.[2] Federal agency scientists tabulated long lists of Pacific Northwest species at risk of extinction. All told, no fewer than 482 species were considered to be of concern in the region's late-successional forests. In the early 1990s, some 162 of these were candidates for federal listing as threatened or endangered.[3]

Because of the widespread declines of the Pacific Northwest forests—indicated by the growing number of threatened and endangered species—President Clinton called for a new plan to manage national forests and BLM lands in the region. Jack Ward Thomas was called upon to create an ecosystem management plan. By July 1993, Thomas and a host of top interagency federal scientists—known as the Forest Ecosystem Management Assessment Team (FEMAT)—had assessed the situation and produced a strategy that would become known as the Northwest Forest Plan. The plan established a series of habitat conservation areas and late-successional reserves for old-growth-dependent species, a series of riparian reserves and key watersheds and strict standards and guidelines for aquatic species, and a watershed analysis procedure for understanding management problems and opportunities at broad geographic scales. Protocols were established to search for a

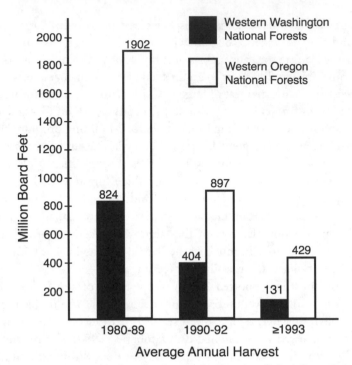

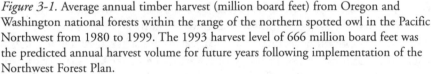

Figure 3-1. Average annual timber harvest (million board feet) from Oregon and Washington national forests within the range of the northern spotted owl in the Pacific Northwest from 1980 to 1999. The 1993 harvest level of 666 million board feet was the predicted annual harvest volume for future years following implementation of the Northwest Forest Plan.

number of lesser-known "survey and manage species." If these species were found, their habitats would be placed off limits to timber harvest.[4]

The era of high-yield, short-rotation forestry on public lands in the Pacific Northwest had come to an end. But the damage had been done. Annual average harvests of nearly 3 billion board feet of timber during the 1980s in national forests in western Oregon and western Washington, and 880 million board feet of timber from BLM lands in western Oregon, had taken their toll. (See Figure 3-1.) From the air it was clear that excessive clearcuts had produced a fragmented and patchwork forest dominated by young tree stands. As all the easy-to-get timber was cut, extensive road systems were engineered to reach the hard-to-get timber from roadless areas and other remote forests.

Large trees were clearcut from steep slopes through a series of zigzagging roads that interrupted stream flows and channeled runoff through culverts.

Landslides ripped down hillsides as heavy rains from Pacific storms fell on bare soils and jammed logging debris into culverts. These plugged culverts became time bombs waiting for heavy rains to rip them from roads and wash tons of soil and debris into streams.

Much of the forest cover was drastically simplified and quite foreign to the complex forest described earlier as favored by the northern spotted owl. Few patches of old growth remained, and those remnants were disconnected across the landscape. As the FEMAT report noted, it took nearly a century and a half to disrupt Pacific Northwest forests to this extent. It will take much longer than a mere decade or two to bring them back.

Dry Forests of the Intermountain West

As the old growth/spotted owl crisis played out in western Oregon, western Washington, and northern California, forests of the Intermountain West from northern Arizona and New Mexico to western Montana, Idaho, and northeastern Oregon had their own set of problems. During the late 1980s and 1990s, a series of wildfires swept through large portions of national forest land. Unlike the small, undergrowth fires that historically occurred in these dry ponderosa pine forests before the advent of widespread fire suppression, the new fires often burned 100,000 acres or more and killed large trees, not just the small "dog hair" tree thickets that low-intensity fires would kill.

Landscapes that evolved with high-frequency but low-intensity fires that burned smaller fuels such as grasses, shrubs, and small trees now were afflicted with large-scale, high-intensity fires. In Colorado, for example, the Buffalo Creek Fire burned vegetation and soils so completely that nothing was left to slow runoff. In 1996, rain falling on the barren soil produced flash floods that washed topsoil from the hillsides, clogged downstream water sources, reduced storage capacity of a downstream reservoir, silted spawning habitat of trout populations, and killed two people. The U.S. General Accounting Office reviewed the status of the nation's western forests and concluded in a 1999 report that the overaccumulation of trees presented a severe wildfire risk to approximately 39 million acres in the Intermountain West.[5]

Historically, small wildfires would consume grasses and small trees, leaving the thick-barked ponderosa pines and other long-needle pine species. In some areas, open, parklike stands of large pines would predominate. These patchy fires contributed to complexity in the forests by opening up new meadows—burning one area and leaving others untouched. Bark beetles and other forest insects contributed to this patchiness by concentrating in small areas.

By the 1990s, the complexity and patchiness of most forest ecosystems were mostly gone. Young Douglas-fir, grand fir, and other species formerly controlled by small fires were growing in large numbers. Meadows were disappearing. And the few remaining large pines found themselves surrounded by smaller trees that competed for water during droughts and provided fuel ladders that allowed fire to reach upper branches less protected by thick bark.

Many factors contributed to the new frequency and intensity of wildfires. Logging in the twentieth century removed many of the big pines. Livestock grazing removed native grasses that had carried fire between trees. And when fires did occur, they were quickly squelched by the traditional Smokey Bear perspective that any fire was bad news and had to be put out quickly and completely. The lack of fire allowed other species of trees to grow and create the dense "dog-hair" thickets now so common to forests of the Intermountain West. A 1991 report on forest health in Oregon's Blue Mountains summed it up thusly: "Past management practices such as fire exclusion and selective timber harvesting, though carried out with the best of intentions and using the best information of the time, have led to potentially catastrophic [conditions]."[6]

A recent assessment of national forests and BLM lands in the interior Columbia River basin documented a 25 percent increase in young trees in dry forest types such as ponderosa pine and dry grand fir/white fir associations in Idaho and western Montana. The assessment also found that ponderosa pine has been replaced by grand fir and white fir in 19 percent of its range and by Douglas-fir in another 20 percent. Open, parklike stands of ponderosa pine were estimated to be at 25 percent of their historic range while Douglas-fir and other true firs had more than tripled their range.[7]

Wildfire suppression and harvest of large pines had altered forest conditions over broad areas. Declining forest health made forests more susceptible to outbreaks of insects and disease. Defoliating insects such as western spruce budworm and Douglas-fir tussock moth increased as did *Armillaria* root disease, laminated root rot, and other tree diseases. Native insects and diseases—that at historic levels help create healthy, diverse, and complex forests—were now acting over vast landscapes to create large areas of dead and dying trees that became even more susceptible to catastrophic wildfire. Overall the report concluded that 46 percent of national forest and BLM forestlands in Idaho, western Montana, eastern Washington, and eastern Oregon had a low rating for overall ecological integrity. Most private lands in the region are in even worse condition. Of the lands classified in the report as having low ecological integrity, 61 percent of these occur on lands outside of federal management.[8]

The 2.6-million-acre Boise National Forest of southwestern Idaho typifies these problems. About 90 percent of the forested area supports ponderosa pine and Douglas-fir habitat types. As a result of past timber harvest and fire exclusion, the amount of ponderosa pine has declined by 40 percent since 1950.[9] Dense stands of Douglas-fir and grand fir, which are more susceptible to bark beetles and other defoliating insects, predominate. Tree mortality of these two species has been especially high since the mid-1980s, which has contributed to a severe fire risk. According to a forestwide risk assessment, 23 percent of the forest is classified as being at high risk to insect outbreaks and another 44 percent is considered to be at moderate risk.

Based on excessive numbers of small trees and overall fuel availability, about 31 percent of the Boise National Forest is considered to be at high to extreme risk of catastrophic fire occurring at intensities beyond the historic range of variability. At the same time, the forest has 75 (35 percent) of a total of 214 subwatersheds identified as "water quality limited" (mostly sediment problems) per Section 303(d) of the Clean Water Act. Bull trout, chinook salmon, and steelhead, all listed as endangered species, occur throughout much of the forest. The assessment concluded that 67 percent of the subwatersheds in the forest suffered from a host of problems coupled with significant endangered fish and water quality problems in the aquatic systems. The report concluded that there is no silver bullet or single management prescription that can solve the complex resource problems. Careful scientific analysis is needed to tease apart the complexity and then design appropriate restoration efforts.[10]

Rangeland Ecosystems of the West

Rangelands comprise about 70 percent of the western states, including the high deserts of the Great Basin and the lower-elevation deserts of the Southwest. Cattle and domestic sheep have grazed nearly all of this land, and much of it has been heavily grazed for a hundred or more years. Over the years, the changes seem gradual. But their cumulative effects can be staggering. Aldo Leopold recognized the extent of changes caused by livestock grazing to the American Southwest when he visited the Sierra Madre in Chihuahua in 1936. Because of unstable land policies in Mexico and periodic uprisings by Apache Indians near the turn of the century almost no livestock grazing had occurred. In 1937 Leopold offered the following contrast between the U.S. and Mexico rangelands:[11]

> It is this chain of historical accidents which enables the American conservationist to go to Chihuahua today and feast his eyes on what his own mountains were like before the Juggernaut. To my mind these live oak-dotted hills fat with side oats grama, these pine-clad mesas spangled with flowers, these lazy trout streams burbling along under great sycamores and cottonwoods, come near to being the cream of creation. But on our side of the line the grama is mostly gone, the mesas are spangled with snakeweed, the trout streams are now cobble-bars.

The degraded condition of rangelands was recognized early on in a series of government reports.[12] Overgrazing by livestock is the most pervasive threat, but other causes for concern include mining, diversion of surface and groundwaters, rapidly growing off-road vehicle use, and, more recently, the spread of noxious weeds. Moreover, domestic sheep have been the source of disease that has decimated native bighorn sheep populations.

The BLM is responsible for managing much of the rangeland in the West, including 137 million acres presently within grazing districts. Until the early 1980s, the BLM rated rangeland condition, rather simplistically, as poor, fair, good, or excellent. Since about 1982, the BLM has been using an Ecological Site Inventory process that compares existing vegetation to the potential natural vegetation community. By the year 2000, however, the BLM had measured the condition of just half of the rangelands under its jurisdiction using the newer and more scientifically sound procedures. The most recent assessment of rangeland conditions was completed in 2000 by the BLM and Forest Service's Rocky Mountain Research Station staff. For 1992, the latest date for which widespread data exist according to the 2000 assessment, the BLM reported that 5.6 percent of its rangeland was in excellent condition, 35.1 percent was good, 42.1 percent was fair, and 17.1 percent was poor.[13] Five states reported that 20 percent or more of their BLM public lands were in poor condition: Arizona (21 percent), Idaho (22 percent), Oregon (32 percent), Utah (27 percent), and Washington (28 percent).

Another indicator of rangeland health is the condition of riparian areas. Riparian areas are particularly important to overall biological diversity because they are comprised of highly complex habitats, support aquatic and terrestrial species, and often provide one of the few sources of water in arid rangelands. The BLM measures the functional condition of riparian areas by the amount of vegetation and other structure available to capture silt during high stream flows and reduce the chance of severe erosion. According to this process, riparian areas are classified as in proper functioning condition, functioning at risk, or nonfunctional. "Proper functioning condition" indicates that enough structure is present to prevent significant damage during floods. According to the 2000 assessment, the BLM classifies 41 percent of its riparian areas as in proper functioning condition, 45 percent as functioning at risk, and 14 percent as nonfunctional. Spring ecosystems are seldom considered in such assessments but have recently been recognized for their substantial contribution to biological diversity in rangelands.[14] Migratory birds, amphibians, springsnails, fishes, and small mammals are among the animal groups that depend on spring and riparian areas for their survival. But unless springs contain an endangered species and therefore receive special management attention, they are often boxed at the source and diverted into water troughs for livestock. The many benefits of springs as wetland and biological diversity sources are too often ignored.

Off-road vehicles are an increasing problem across much of the West. When confined to properly maintained roads and trails, concerns are limited. But where motorcycles and all-terrain vehicles proceed with few restrictions, damage can be severe. Allen Cooperrider, a BLM wildlife biologist for seventeen years, and David Wilcove, an ecologist with the Environmental Defense Fund, cite several types of damage caused by off-road vehicles to BLM rangelands in the Southwest: soil disturbance and erosion of sensitive soil communities; direct plant mortality; disturbance to wildlife such as pronghorn and bighorn sheep; and spread of noxious weeds.[15] As growing populations of urbanized westerners search for recreation on public lands, these problems are increasing.

Noxious weeds and other exotic plants have only recently been recognized as a significant problem for rangeland health. But their potential for damage seems virtually unlimited—especially in areas already disturbed by livestock overgrazing. The Weed Science Society of America currently classifies 2083 plant species as weeds in the United States and Canada. The Department of the Interior estimates that 17 million acres of public rangelands in the West have been invaded by noxious weeds, and their range has more than quadrupled from 1985 to 1995. By 1995, more than 10 million acres were moderately to heavily infested with species such as cheatgrass, medusahead, Russian knapweed, yellow starthistle, leafy spurge, and perennial pepperweed. The BLM estimated that by the year 2000, some 33 million acres of western lands would be infested to one degree or another with alien weeds.[16] Many exotic weeds are unpalatable or poisonous to native wildlife. Exotic plants can alter disturbance regimes and change the dynamics of entire ecosystems.

Focus Essay

Radical Changes in a Sagebrush Landscape: The Role of Exotic Cheatgrass in Disrupting a System*

STEVEN T. KNICK AND MARK R. FULLER[†]

We often think of ecological change as a slow, long-term process, a series of actions and reactions that result in a "balance of nature." In Idaho's Snake River Birds of Prey National Conservation Area (Birds of Prey NCA), however, an introduced grass has radically changed an entire landscape in little more than an ecological moment of time. Recognized over sixty years ago for their extremely high concentration of raptors, the rocky cliffs of the Snake River canyon are managed by the BLM to provide nesting areas for prairie falcons, golden eagles, and other birds of prey.

Cheatgrass appeared in the Snake River plain around the turn of the twentieth century. Aided by livestock grazing, failed agricultural practices, and drought, cheatgrass and other invasive plant species, such as tumble mustard, became well established in the system but it was not until the 1980s that they erupted. The results are staggering. Approximately 65 percent of the shrublands that existed in 1979 have been destroyed. During that time, the total grassland cover increased from just 17 percent to almost 60

---

*For further information concerning cheatgrass and its effects on sagebrush ecosystems see S. T. Knick, "Requiem for a Sagebrush Ecosystem?" *Northwest Science* 73 (1999):52–57; M. N. Kochert et al., "Effects of Fire on Golden Eagle Territory Occupancy and Reproductive Success," *Journal of Wildlife Management* 63 (1999):773–780; and U.S. Department of the Interior, "Effects of Military Training and Fire in the Snake River Birds of Prey National Conservation Area," BLM/IDARNG Final Report, U.S. Geological Survey, Snake River Field Station, Boise, Idaho, 1996.

[†]Both authors are research ecologists with the U.S. Geological Survey, Forest and Rangeland Ecosystem Science Center, Snake River Field Station, Boise, Idaho.

percent. In a relatively short time, a landscape that once was largely covered by shrublands now has been converted to cheatgrass fields.

Cheatgrass has several qualities that permit it to dominate native plants and affect the way fires burn. A shallow root system helps cheatgrass to outcompete more deeply rooted native perennials for scarce water. In addition, cheatgrass germinates in the fall and growth begins during the winter, which gives it a competitive advantage over the native perennials for nutrients. Cheatgrass cures almost a month earlier than natives and can become fuel for fires long before native plants set seed. Compared to native perennial bunchgrasses, which are patchily distributed, cheatgrass provides a continuous fuel layer that promotes fire spread. Fire was always an important part of the sagebrush steppe. But with cheatgrass, fires now are larger, more intense, and more frequent. Thus the role of fire has been changed from maintaining shrublands to one of destruction that perpetuates the cheatgrass advantage.

Concerned about the effects of habitat change on the raptors and their prey, the BLM conducted a cooperative study with the Idaho Army National Guard from 1990 to 1996 in the Birds of Prey NCA. Scientists and literally hundreds of technicians participated in the study to determine how wildfires, livestock grazing, and military training influenced the system. We studied two of the primary raptor/prey relationships: golden eagles/black-tailed jackrabbits and prairie falcons/Paiute ground squirrels.

The interval between fires averaged 27.5 years in the late 1900s compared to earlier intervals of 80.5 years. In other parts of the Snake River plain, fires now burn as frequently as every three to five years. Frequent, large fires are a problem for restoring shrubs in the landscape because sagebrush reproduces only from seed. A second fire within six to eight years of previous fires destroys any plants that sprouted from seeds already in the soil before they have a chance to produce seeds themselves. Although fire was the most visible disturbance that changed habitats, livestock grazing and military training amplified its effects by encouraging cheatgrass growth and setting up ground conditions favorable for fire.

Jackrabbits are largely associated with large patches of shrubland. They use shrubs for cover from predators, such as golden eagles, and they forage on forbs, grasses, and leaves in small openings within the shrubland. In the Birds of Prey NCA, densities of jackrabbits have been lower during each consecutive population peak in 1971, in 1979–1981, and in 1990–1992—which correlates with the steady loss of shrubland. Jackrabbits are the primary prey of golden eagles, and golden eagle reproductive success is closely tied to jackrabbit abundance. With the lower densities of jackrabbits has come a significant decline in golden eagles in the Birds of Prey NCA.

For prairie falcons, the story was different but the ultimate fate was the same. The conversion of habitat from shrubland to annual grassland actually resulted in higher densities of ground squirrels because seeds from the cheatgrass provided a huge food base. But there was a drawback. The food supply provided by cheatgrass was highly susceptible to the vagaries of climate, such as drought. Squirrel populations that depend on annual grasses crashed during droughts, especially if followed by a severe winter. As a result, prairie falcons, which depend largely on ground squirrels for food, have undergone a significant population decline. Since 1976, the number of nesting pairs has been reduced by half.

What will the future be like in the Birds of Prey NCA and surrounding public lands? Unless shrubland recovery can be conducted successfully on a large scale, we can expect jackrabbit populations to continue to decline. The golden eagles, too, will decline. The ground squirrels will continue to chirp away at intruders during the short time of the year when they are aboveground. Their populations will be characterized by boom and bust—conditions not likely to be favorable for the long-term viability of prairie falcons. If land managers are unable to break the cycle of cheatgrass and frequent fire, the reasons for which the Snake River Birds of Prey NCA was established will disappear. Perhaps most surprising of all, these changes will have occurred in a relative blink of the eye.

Pine Forests of the Southeast

While the West's forest and range health problems have gained national attention in recent years, southern forests have their own set of concerns that may be more long-lasting and even more difficult to correct. Unlike the West, where public lands comprise more than half the acreage of some states, few public lands occur in the South. For example, less than 10 percent of forested lands in the South are managed by the Forest Service. Much of the native forests have been converted to urban or agricultural uses. Of the remaining forestlands, most are privately owned and managed intensively as tree farms. Two elements that western and southern forests share, however, are rapidly growing urban populations and declining native biological diversity.[17]

Historically longleaf pine was the dominant tree in the South—the principal tree species on 60 million acres stretching from southeastern Virginia through the Carolinas, south to central Florida, and west to eastern Texas.

The species extended even farther on an additional 14.6 million acres as a codominant species with loblolly and shortleaf pines.[18] Longleaf pine was the dominant tree in an outstanding variety of habitats—from low-elevation savannas and coastal plains to rolling sandhills and mountain slopes up to 2000 feet in elevation.

Loss of longleaf pine forests began soon after the arrival of Europeans along the eastern shore. During early European settlement days, pine tar from longleaf pines was used extensively for sealing the hulls of wooden ships and preserving ropes and sails. As the country expanded, the demand for wood increased. From 1880 to 1930 great forests of longleaf pine were cleared from the Carolinas to Georgia, Florida, Alabama, and Mississippi. (See Figure 3-2.) Nearly all the old-growth forests in the South were gone by 1935.[19] Longleaf pine reestablished itself poorly because the species produces good seed crops only irregularly—and when good seed crops were in fact produced, they became a favorite food of feral hogs and other introduced species.

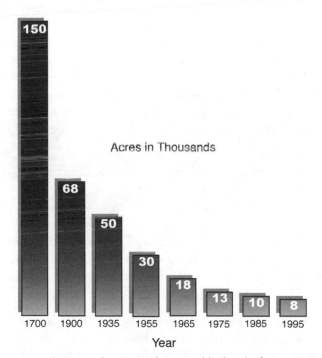

Figure 3-2. Historic change in forest area dominated by longleaf pine: 1700–1995. Based on data summarized by Kenneth Outcalt of the U.S. Forest Service's Southern Research Station.

As second-growth harvest began in the South around 1940, the remaining longleaf pine stands were mechanically cleared and replanted with loblolly pine plantations. Longleaf pine was not a preferred species in the minds of southern timbermen because of its slow growth when replanted. As a result, longleaf pine habitats have been nearly eradicated from Virginia, have declined to only 1.5 percent of their former range in Texas, and have been drastically reduced elsewhere throughout their range.

Longleaf pine forests were diverse in plant and animal associations. Although vast areas of the South were dominated by longleaf pine in the upperstory, a large variety of species occurred in the understory stands. Longleaf stands were lush with grasses, forbs, composites, legumes, and orchids. A variety of oaks and other small hardwoods occurred along with longleaf pines. Persimmon, huckleberries, blueberries, and other woody species were common in some areas. Though longleaf pine communities were dominant across much of the South, there was much variation in the types and numbers of plant species present. According to Dr. Ken Outcalt, a forest ecologist from the Forest Service in Athens, Georgia, longleaf forests were among the richest in terms of plant species of any community outside the tropics. Corresponding diversity occurred in the animal communities. Scientists estimate that approximately 10 percent of all arthropods (insects, spiders, and others) that occurred in longleaf forests were endemic to those habitats and many amphibians and reptiles preferred the same areas.[20]

Few descriptions of these historic riches remain. One of the most complete was from the explorer William Bartram, who provided the following description while traveling through a longleaf pine forest in 1773:

> We left the magnificent savanna and its delightful groves, passing through a level open, airy pine forest, the stately trees scatteringly planted by nature, arising straight and erect from the green carpet, embellished with various grasses and flowering plants. . . . We joyfully entered the borders of the level pine forest and savannas which continued for many miles, never out of sight of little lakes or ponds, environed with illumined meadows, the clear waters sparkling through the tall pines.[21]

In recent years, our understanding of the important role of longleaf pine and our concern for surviving stands have improved. Scientists from the Forest Service track remaining longleaf pine from the Carolinas to Texas. From 1985 to 1995, the amount of longleaf pine habitat stayed relatively stable in national forests but continued to decline on private lands. The largest remaining stands, about 750,000 acres, and by far the largest habitat blocks, persist in national forests in Florida. Remaining stands in Georgia seem particularly vulnerable to loss because that state has few public forests.[22]

Recent assessments project that 12 million acres of forest in the South will be lost to urbanization between 1992 and 2020. Additional native forests will be converted to plantations. Harvest of softwood timber in the region began to exceed growth rates beginning in 1997. Harvest of hardwood forests is expected to exceed growth rates within the next ten to twenty years. Although young pine plantations will help to offset the softwood timber deficit, a plantation is a poor substitute for a healthy, properly functioning forest.

The Southern Forest Resource Assessment—a combined effort of the Forest Service, Fish and Wildlife Service, EPA, Tennessee Valley Authority, and numerous state agencies—predicts that most losses of forest habitat over the next two decades will occur in the southern Appalachians, Piedmont, and Lower Atlantic and Gulf Coastal Plains.[23] Apart from outright losses owing to a growing human population, the report predicts continued simplification of forest ecosystems through expansion of pine plantations. In 1953, only 2 million acres of pine plantations existed; by 1999, plantations had expanded to 32 million acres; by the year 2040, the report predicts, pine plantations will cover 54 million acres. The growth of plantations between the year 2000 and 2040 is equivalent in area to the size of North and South Carolina combined.

As native forests are lost to urbanization or converted to tree-growing farmlands, specialized forest vegetation types are becoming increasingly rare. The Southern Forest Resource Assessment lists fourteen "critically endangered natural communities" that have lost 98 percent of their habitat since European settlement. These fourteen endangered natural communities are found in seven increasingly rare plant associations: old-growth forests; spruce/fir forests; wetlands, bogs and pocosins; bottomland and floodplain forests; glades, barrens, and prairies; longleaf pine forests; and Atlantic white-cedar swamps. Old-growth and spruce/fir forests are found largely on public lands in the South; the remaining five rare plant associations generally occur in private ownership. How private forestlands are managed will determine the future of most rare plant associations in the South and the many rare species that depend on them. Although independent third-party forest certification offers one way to encourage sustainable forest management on private land, enforceable forest practices laws are nonexistent in much of the South.

Alien Invaders

Forests and rangelands across the nation face a growing problem from the introduction, spread and establishment of exotic (nonnative) species. These so-called alien species include cheatgrass in the Great Basin, a variety of noxious weeds on rangelands and forestlands of the West, leafy spurge in the Great Plains, and kudzu in the South. Exotic species recognize no boundaries or administrative jurisdictions. Land within wilderness areas and national parks is threatened. All states suffer infestations of one sort or another, but Florida, Hawaii, and California have been particularly vulnerable.

In 1850, farmers and miners from Chile joined the gold rush that would transform the face of California. They brought Chilean alfalfa seeds to their new home, and interspersed with the alfalfa seeds were those of another Chilean species: the yellow starthistle. Yellow star thistle has thrived in the climate of California and portions of Oregon and Idaho. By 1965 it had spread to about 1 million acres of California. By 1999 the species had spread to 15 million acres, where often it is the most abundant species. In fact, yellow starthistle now has the distinction of being the most common plant species in the state. The hills of California have taken on a disturbing yellow hue.[24]

But yellow starthistle is only one of thousands of introduced species in the United States The U.S. government estimates that more than 6500 exotic species of animals, plants, and microbes have become established in the country.[25] Ecologist David Pimentel and colleagues from Cornell University estimate that exotic species cost the nation $137 billion every year.[26] This includes $32 billion damage from introduced weeds in rangelands and wildlands, $20 billion from introduced insects, and $41 billion from introduced disease-causing organisms. Introduced rats destroy $15 billion worth of grains and other food items annually.

The ecological costs, however, far exceed the dollar values. Exotic species have been implicated in the extinction of numerous native species. Some exotic species also bring in parasites and diseases. Introduced species threaten two-thirds of the endangered species in the United States and rank as the second most severe threat to biological diversity after habitat destruction.[27] The National Park Service lists invasion by exotic species as the greatest threat to our national parks. The Interior Department estimates that alien weeds are spreading and occupying approximately 1.7 million acres of the nation's wildlife habitat annually. European purple loosestrife, for example, is spreading at a rate of 284,000 acres per year and disrupting the basic structure of wetland and riparian habitats.[28] In the end, it is this disruption of entire communities and the continued homogenization of the world's plants and animals that pose the most alarming danger to land health.

No wildland habitat type or region of the country is immune to the problems caused by such exotics. In the northern Great Plains, leafy spurge contaminates more than 2.7 million acres and often forms dense stands that crowd out other vegetation. In North Dakota alone, livestock losses from leafy spurge are estimated at more than $23 million annually. Annual losses of wildlife-related recreation and agricultural production equal $144 million in the four-state area of North Dakota, South Dakota, Montana, and Wyoming. According to the North Dakota Game and Fish Department, leafy spurge is the greatest threat to wildlife in the state.[29]

The Southwest deserts have more problems from exotic plants than can be handled. Saltcedar (or *Tamarix*), first introduced as an ornamental species from Asia, now dominates many floodplains and riparian areas in California, Arizona, and New Mexico.[30] Saltcedar concentrates salt in its leaves that is later released into the soil and renders the area unsuitable for native plant species. Cottonwood trees, which used to thrive along many southwestern streams and afford valuable nesting habitat for a wide variety of bird species, are being replaced by this salt-concentrating exotic.

Once established in the United States, exotic weeds can be spread by many activities on public lands—road construction, vehicle traffic, livestock grazing, firefighting activities, timber harvest, and recreation. Dalmatian toadflax, a tall perennial plant from southeastern Europe, was recently found in the Raymond Mountain Wilderness Study Area in Wyoming. Its occurrence there was a mystery until BLM staff traced the species to a nearby phosphate mine where they found that heavy mining equipment was transporting seeds of Dalmatian toadflax from a contaminated area to the mine site.[31]

Disturbed areas and bare soils along roads, railroads, and trails offer ideal sites for establishment of weeds. Moreover, the gravel and sand that is spread onto road and trail surfaces may come from a source contaminated with weed seeds. As construction crews spread gravel along the road surface they may be spreading noxious weeds as well. Weeds often become attached to vehicle undercarriages, earthmoving equipment, or railroad cars—another source of spread. Sometimes grass mixtures and hay used for erosion control at construction sites contain weed seeds. As livestock roam large pastures or are transported by truck between pastures, they may defecate undigested weed seeds into new areas. Livestock feed, brought into forests or public rangelands, may also contain unwanted seeds. The mechanisms of dispersal for noxious weeds are numerous and, for the most part, uncontrolled.

Exotic Diseases

Alien invaders come in many forms. Not only nonnative animal and plant species but exotic diseases are changing the face of our national forests and parklands. Along the West Coast, an introduced fungal root disease is killing Port Orford cedars, which are endemic to forests in northwestern California and southwestern Oregon. The tree is widely used as an ornamental species in yards, as hedges, and for windbreaks. It is of considerable economic value and prized for its strength and pleasing appearance. As early as 1923, the root disease began killing ornamental cedar trees in a Washington state nursery and by 1952 the disease had been transferred to wild trees near Coos Bay, Oregon.[32] By 1954, the disease had spread to Port Orford cedar as far as 20 miles inland. The fungus is spread by movement of contaminated soil around potted trees as well as mud on timber harvesting machinery, off-road vehicles, ordinary passenger cars, even the boots of hikers. When contaminated mud enters a stream, the disease is transported along its course. To stop the spread, national forest and BLM access roads must be closed. Contaminated mud must be washed off boots. Any vehicle that enters a contaminated drainage must be power-washed before it enters clean areas. Public education and cooperation are key components of a successful control strategy. But as is so often the case, preventing the disease in the first place would have saved millions of dollars.

In the Intermountain and Rocky Mountain West, whitebark pine has been devastated by several interrelated factors, but principal among them is the blister rust fungus. This fungus was introduced into Canada in white pine seedlings brought over from France around 1910.[33] The disease went unnoticed until 1921 when it was detected in whitebark pine in southwestern British Columbia and adjacent northwestern Washington. By 1927 it had spread to northern Idaho. By 1945 the disease was present in the easternmost extension of the range of the whitebark pine in Yellowstone National Park, Wyoming. (See Figure 3-3.) Studies by scientists at the Forest Service Intermountain Fire Sciences Laboratory in Missoula have documented a 42 percent mortality of whitebark pine in western Montana over a twenty-year span from 1971 to 1991.[34] In some areas of Glacier National Park, mortality has exceeded 90 percent. Whitebark pines throughout their range are being hit by a one-two punch delivered by the rust fungus and subsequent attacks by mountain pine beetles that exploit the damaged trees. In addition, large-scale wildfire suppression is curtailing the pine's ability to regenerate naturally.

What is the ecological impact of the loss of whitebark pines from the Rocky Mountains? We know that the oil-rich seeds from the whitebark pine are a critical autumn food resource for many wildlife species. Clark's nut-

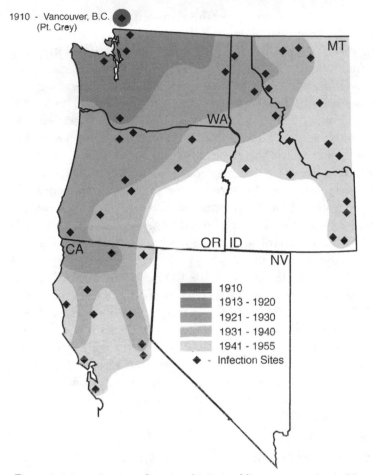

1910 - Vancouver, B.C.
(Pt. Grey)

1910
1913 - 1920
1921 - 1930
1931 - 1940
1941 - 1955
♦ - Infection Sites

Figure 3-3. Introduction of exotic white pine blister rust starting in Vancouver, British Columbia, in 1910 and subsequent spread through the West.

crackers and red squirrels are particularly adept at harvesting the seeds. We also know that cones and seeds from whitebark pine are an important food resource for black and grizzly bears. "Shocked" is how Dr. Kate Kendall, a research biologist with the National Park Service, described it when she learned of the high whitebark pine mortality in critical grizzly bear range. Loss of this high-elevation food resource in the autumn could force bears to forage beyond park boundaries and move into lower-elevation areas where bear/human conflicts would increase.

Perhaps the greatest loss to forest resources from introduced diseases has occurred in the eastern United States. American chestnut trees were once so common in eastern deciduous forests that people from New York to

Pennsylvania and south to Virginia and the Carolinas could count on finding abundant nuts from the chestnut for roasting or for stuffing their Thanksgiving turkey. Chestnuts were a dominant canopy tree throughout the eastern United States, and their wood was favored for its superior rot resistance. This all began to change when Japanese chestnut trees along with a fungal disease were introduced into New York City in 1876.[35] This fungus, known as the chestnut blight, would devastate the American chestnut during the early 1900s. Despite the best efforts of foresters, nothing has worked to control the fungus, which kills the cambium of the tree and everything above the infection site. The tree resprouts but the infection spreads. A major forest tree species was reduced to merely a multiple-stemmed shrub. Because of the historically great numbers of the American chestnut, the abundant crops of nuts, and the tree's early demise, we will probably never know the full extent of the ecological consequences of the decline. They are presumed to be substantial.

A study by Dr. Paul Opler on the vanishing biodiversity of North America offers a perspective on the interconnectedness of life and the losses to one animal group.[36] Opler found that of fifty-six moth species that fed on American chestnuts, seven species fed exclusively on the chestnut and are now extinct. The others have persisted because of broader dietary requirements. As Dr. Sandra Anagnostakis of the Connecticut Agricultural Experiment Station has noted: "We cannot undo the mistake of bringing chestnut blight into the U.S., but perhaps understanding the history of this catastrophe will make us more cautious in the future."[37]

Endangered Species: Indicators of the Health of the Land

The Endangered Species Act acknowledges that healthy ecosystems are the key to the survival of our native species. According to the act, its principal purpose is to "conserve the ecosystems upon which endangered species depend." Endangered and threatened species are good indicators of the health of our ecosystems. Healthy ecosystems contain diverse and complex habitats that are resilient to changes and support a wide variety of native species. Stressed ecosystems—such as rangelands dominated by introduced cheatgrass or forests dominated by a single tree species of one age class—support little diversity and will at the same time be subject to broad-scale disturbances beyond their historic range of variability. Catastrophic wildfire, flood, or other disturbances perpetuate the cycle of destruction.

Since the relatively recent era of endangered species management in the United States, marked by passage of the Endangered Species Act in 1973, the

Table 3-1. Number of Threatened and Endangered U.S. Species

Group	Endangered Species	Threatened Species	Total Listed Species	Percentage Listed Relative to Total Number of Species in Group
Mammals	63	9	72	17%
Birds	77	15	92	12%
Reptiles	14	22	36	13%
Amphibians	10	8	18	7%
Freshwater fishes	68	44	112	14%
Mollusks	81	19	100	Unknown
Crayfish	18	3	21	6%
Insects and spiders	36	8	44	Unknown
ANIMAL SUBTOTAL	367	128	495	
Ferns	26	2	28	5%
Conifers	2	1	3	3%
Flowering plants	565	139	704	5%
Plant subtotal	593	142	735	
GRAND TOTAL	960	270	1230	

Source: Numbers of threatened and endangered species according to U.S. Fish and Wildlife Service on April 30, 2000; see *Endangered Species Bulletin* 30(1–2) (January–April 2000). Relative rarity according to The Nature Conservancy's *1997 Species Report Card;* see B. A. Stein and S. R. Flack, *1997 Species Report Card: The State of U.S. Plants and Animals* (Arlington, Va.: The Nature Conservancy, 1997).

number of species listed as threatened or endangered has grown substantially. By April 2000, the Fish and Wildlife Service had officially listed 1230 plants and animals in the United States as endangered or threatened. (See Table 3-1.) Every state has at least some endangered and threatened species, but the highest concentrations are in the West and Southeast. (See Figure 3-4.) The highest numbers occur in California (279 species) and Hawaii (312), where habitat destruction and exotic species—the one-two punch prompting many listings—are widespread. Only five states have fewer than ten listed species: Alaska, Maine, North Dakota, Rhode Island, and Vermont.

While the Fish and Wildlife Service maintains the official list of endangered and threatened species, The Nature Conservancy and the Natural Heritage Network of state-level plant and animal tracking data centers conduct additional reviews of native species in the United States. Their 1997 Species Report Card found that nearly one-third of our native plant and

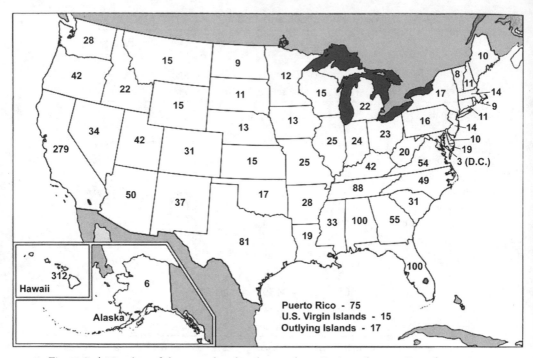

Figure 3-4. Number of threatened and endangered species in each state. Data from U.S. Fish and Wildlife Service as of September 1, 2000. Numbers are not additive because a species often occurs in several states.

animal species were in trouble. Native freshwater species (fishes, amphibians, freshwater mussels, and crayfishes) received particularly poor marks. A frighteningly high 68 percent of freshwater mussels were considered to be vulnerable, imperiled, or extinct.[38] Although little known to most people, freshwater mussels often are a critical component of the biological diversity in our stream systems, particularly in the Southeast. The report also noted that at least 110 native animal and plant species are known to be extinct and another 416 have not been found in recent years and may be extinct as well. Hawaii has had the largest number of extinctions, followed by Alabama and California.[39]

Habitat degradation and destruction is the primary problem responsible for the ever-growing list of threatened and endangered species. Next is the introduction of exotic species. Pollution is a critical problem for certain species, too, especially amphibians, mussels, and trouts and other sensitive fishes that decline or disappear in the face of poor water quality. More subtle factors may be operating as well. Many scientists have expressed concern over recent widespread declines of amphibians. Loss of wetlands and other forms of habitat destruction explain some amphibian declines, but frog species in wilderness areas and national parks also have been affected. Introduction of nonnative trout into high mountain lakes causes some declines, owing to high predation rates on tadpoles, but acid rain, metallic contaminants, and excessive ultraviolet radiation (caused by ozone layer thinning) seem to be working synergistically with diseases to cause loss and decline in many populations. A host of human-caused factors are to blame for the decline of many species.

National forests and BLM lands provide critical refuges for many species. If managed to restore and sustain land health, public lands function on a number of levels to recover threatened and endangered species. Primarily, public lands provide large blocks of high-quality habitat. Large blocks of land are critical for wide-ranging species—such as bald eagles, salmon, wolves, and grizzly bears. These large blocks of land serve as the core areas from which species disperse into neighboring areas. When peripheral populations are extirpated due to loss of habitat or other disturbance the species can be reestablished by individuals from the core area. Wilderness areas and roadless areas afford high-quality core areas. Public lands can also provide conditions favorable to native species so that exotics are not likely to be introduced or to establish themselves if introduced from adjacent lands. Healthy watersheds store and release water at rates that limit erosion and maintain good water quality. Thus nonpoint-source water pollution, especially stream sedimentation, is reduced if watersheds are managed properly.

These factors, taken together, make public lands excellent habitat for many species that have declined elsewhere. The same diversity, patchiness, and complexity of habitats that create high species richness also provide conditions less likely to experience wildfire or flood disturbance outside the range of historic variability. A landscape devoid of diversity and variability encourages disturbances to operate at larger scales and intensities. If wildfire, insect outbreak, or flood occurs in a forest dominated by small trees of a single species or grassland dominated by cheatgrass, there are few natural features to slow the spread of the disturbance. Intact ecosystems, by contrast, maintain habitat diversity and complexity that limit the impact of human or natural disturbance.

The 1990s brought an awakening to the decline of habitat conditions across much of our public and private lands. Growing lists of threatened and endangered species emphasize the declines—as do broad-scale scientific assessments of ecological conditions in the Pacific Northwest, Intermountain West, Southeast, and elsewhere. Repeated damage from wildfire, forest insects, flood, and drought on a massive scale also signaled problems with land condition. Jack Ward Thomas interpreted these declines as a clear call to action: "We don't just manage lands—we're supposed to be leaders . . . conservation leaders in protecting and improving the land."[40] As Chief Thomas and others would quickly realize, these changes would not come easily.

Chapter 4

River and Stream Health:
The Public/Private Land Connection

The effort to control the health of land has not been very successful. It is now generally understood that when soil loses fertility, or washes away faster than it forms, and when water systems exhibit abnormal floods and shortages, the land is sick.

—Aldo Leopold, *Wilderness as a Land Laboratory* (1941)

If our nation's streams and rivers were eligible for hospital care, they would be in the intensive care unit. The collective effect of dams, water diversions, pollution, habitat alteration, and exotic species is evidenced by the imperiled status of aquatic species. Nearly two-thirds of the nation's freshwater mussels, for example, are at risk of extinction and almost one in ten may already have vanished forever. About half of all crayfish species are at risk of extinction. And 35 to 40 percent of freshwater fishes and amphibians share the same gloomy prognosis.[1] Many people are at least vaguely aware of the degradation of our terrestrial environment. We see pollution on the land, witness the loss of forests, and can testify to the spread of invasive weeds. But what happens beneath the water's surface is out of sight and therefore too often out of mind.

Numerous laws and regulations, chief among them the Endangered Species Act and Clean Water Act, have sought to rectify the problem of declining watershed health and species loss. As of January 2000, sixty-eight fishes and eighty-one mollusks were listed as threatened or endangered under the Endangered Species Act. Implementation of species-level recovery plans, consultation requirements with the Fish and Wildlife Service and National Marine Fisheries Service, and other protective measures have improved conditions on public lands. Once a species is listed, the Forest Service, BLM, and other federal agencies must consult with the Fish and Wildlife Service, the National Marine Fisheries Service, or both to ensure that agency actions do not jeopardize endangered or threatened species or critical habitat. Although better scientific information and implementation of ecosystem or watershed-scale management strategies have begun to restore conditions on public lands, much work remains to be done on public lands and land managers should not get complacent.

Progress toward restoration on private lands, by contrast, has lagged far behind. In many river systems, the headwaters found on higher-elevation public lands may be in relatively good condition. But the lower-elevation valley bottoms and main-stem rivers, mostly on private lands, are in poor health. Agricultural and urban development—often occurring in valley bottom and wetland habitats—have degraded the majority of the more diverse and valuable aquatic habitats.

The recovery of many amphibian, fish, mollusk, and crayfish species depends on improving conditions on both public and private lands. Water links our landscapes. Rain and snow collect in headwater streams and make their way downstream to even larger streams and rivers. Many exotic species move freely through this water-filled transportation system. Such problems call for integration of public and private land management strategies at a scale seldom seen in this country. This chapter explores the status of various aquatic species in different regions of the United States and their dependence on public as well as private lands. We will also examine what is perhaps the greatest threat to many of our native aquatic species: the introduction and spread of nonnative species.

Salmon and Steelhead in the Pacific Northwest

Since the 1960s, biologists have monitored the return of adult salmon and steelhead to Marsh Creek, a headwater tributary of the Middle Fork of the

Salmon River in Idaho's Salmon Challis National Forest. Historically the stream was one of the most productive spawning areas for spring chinook salmon in the Snake River drainage. In the early survey years, as many as nine hundred redds—spawning nests created by female salmon for egg laying—were counted along the small stream. In 1999, biologists could not find a single redd in Marsh Creek. In 2000, twenty-seven redds were counted. Survival of salmon in Marsh Creek is tenuous. As noted by Idaho Department of Fish and Game biologist Dave Cannamela, "these fish don't have much longer."[2]

Marsh Creek is 870 miles upstream from the Pacific Ocean, and returning salmon must negotiate eight large dams between spawning grounds and the mouth of the Columbia River. Before the 1960s, only three dams stood in their path. Ironically, as numbers of returning adults have declined, habitat quality in Marsh Creek has improved. Livestock grazing has been halted along the stream to improve riparian habitat and keep water temperatures suitable for salmon spawning and rearing. The same scenario exists along Bear and Elk creeks, tributaries of the Middle Fork of the Salmon in the Boise National Forest, where reduced livestock grazing and increased attention to riparian restoration have lessened bank erosion and stream sedimentation, but salmon and steelhead numbers have declined drastically compared to pre-1970 returns.[3] With this pattern of improving headwater habitat conditions along many tributaries of the Snake River in Idaho, coupled with continuing declines in salmon and steelhead, most experts agree that downstream dams along the lower Snake and Columbia Rivers are the primary cause of decline.

Anadromous fish—that is, fish such as salmon and steelhead that migrate between fresh and salt water—returning to the Snake River drainage in Idaho, eastern Oregon, and eastern Washington must negotiate four major dams on the Columbia River and another four on the lower Snake River. From its headwaters in Yellowstone National Park to its confluence with the Columbia River 1000 miles downstream, the Snake River has twenty-five major dams along its length. When Hells Canyon Dam was completed in 1967 without provision for fish passage, more than half of the Snake River drainage was completely shut off from salmon and steelhead.[4]

While protection and restoration work has proceeded on many national forest and BLM lands in the drainage, efforts to improve habitats on private lands and to facilitate fish passage around dams have been less successful. During the 1990s, many scientists joined the voices of environmentalists in calling for breaching the lower four dams on the Snake River (Ice Harbor, Lower Monumental, Little Goose, and Lower Granite) as the single most important recovery action for Snake River salmon and steelhead. At the 1999 annual meeting of the Idaho chapter of the American Fisheries Society, more than 90 percent of the fish biologists and aquatic ecologists in attendance supported dam breaching as the single most effective management strategy for long-term survival of Snake River salmon and steelhead. A similar measure was unanimously adopted by the Oregon chapter at their annual meeting in 2000.

Various models developed by the National Marine Fisheries Service demonstrate that a three-fold increase in survival of Snake River chinook salmon is necessary to ensure their long-term survival.[5] Despite increasing evidence that dams are the single largest impediment to recovery, many politicians in the Pacific Northwest call for stream habitat improvements, "fish-friendly" turbines, and more hatcheries to solve the problem. But none of these approaches will result in the leap of increased survival necessary to avoid extinction. Russ Thurow, a Forest Service researcher who has studied salmon and steelhead in central Idaho for more than twenty years, testified in November 2000 before a U.S. Senate Committee on the flawed logic behind our failure to address the "dam problem" and insistence on focusing on freshwater habitat improvement. Thurow said:

> If freshwater habitat were the primary cause for declines, then stocks in high quality habitats should be faring substantially better than stocks in degraded habitats. The preponderance of evidence demonstrates this is not the case. Snake River chinook salmon redd counts in both wilderness and degraded habitats have similarly declined since the mid-1970s. . . . Habitat conditions in the Middle Fork Salmon River have remained the same or improved since the 1960s.[6]

The need for new watershed-level strategies to manage lands became clear during the 1980s and early 1990s. The listing of several stocks of salmon and steelhead as endangered or threatened species was a sign of poor habitat conditions and declining watershed health. The cumulative effects of timber harvest, road construction, agriculture, livestock grazing, mining, and other land uses throughout the 1900s had resulted in significant declines in freshwater habitat conditions on both public and private lands. In forested lands, perhaps the biggest single cause of increased erosion and stream sedimentation was construction of an extensive road network associated with logging.[7]

Public lands in western Oregon, western Washington, and northwestern

California contain an estimated 110,000 miles of roads with more than 250,000 stream crossings through culverts, the majority of which cannot contain more than a twenty-five-year flood event without failure.[8] Bull trout, a species that is not anadromous but is widespread in the Pacific Northwest, also was listed for protection under the Endangered Species Act, a clear indicator that freshwater habitat conditions had declined.

Long-term monitoring provided more examples of declines in habitat conditions on public lands. From 1987 to 1992, Forest Service researchers resurveyed 116 streams in the Pacific Northwest and found that the number of large deep pools had declined substantially compared to original surveys conducted between 1935 and 1945. This finding is important because deep pools provide cool-water refuges that salmon and steelhead need during summer months and drought years. Comparing the historic and recent data showed that within nonwilderness areas, the number of deep pools declined 66 percent in the Grande Ronde River drainage, 65 percent in the Clearwater River, 57 percent in the Lewis and Clark River, 54 percent in the Salmon River, and 36 percent in Asotin Creek—all because of increases in stream sediment and reductions in large wood, boulders, and other structures that help create pools.[9] During the same period, the number of deep pools actually increased 28 percent in wilderness areas of the Salmon River drainage. Overall, streams contained more riffles and fewer pools, especially deep pools, than in the past. In eastern Oregon, 80 percent of fish habitat in the upper Grande Ronde River failed to meet forest plan standards for water temperature, stream sediment, and riparian conditions. In Idaho's Clearwater National Forest, 70 percent of streams failed to meet these same criteria.[10]

For conditions to improve, the high levels of road building, logging, mining, and livestock grazing that characterized public land management from the 1950s through the 1980s had to change. Endangered species became the harbingers for this change—catalysts for the improved stewardship of Forest Service and BLM lands in the 1990s. Chief of the Forest Service Thomas and Acting BLM Director Dombeck called for strategies that would produce a "quantum leap forward" in protecting and restoring fish habitat in the Pacific Northwest. In response, public land management agency scientists and managers developed regional aquatic conservation strategies to protect the best remaining salmon, steelhead, and associated trout habitats on federal lands in the Northwest.

Thousands of distinct stocks of salmon, steelhead, and sea-run cutthroat trout occur in the Pacific Northwest. Because of local adaptation to spawning streams and the strong tendency of adults to return to the stream where they were hatched, each spawning population, or stock, is more or less genetically unique.[11] Unfortunately, many of these stocks are declining—and an alarming number already are extinct. A 1991 report by the American Fisheries Society found 214 stocks at risk of extinction and 106 stocks already extinct in California, Idaho, Oregon, and Washington.[12] Of the 214 at-risk stocks, 134 occur at least partly in national forests and 106 occur on BLM-administered lands. Among those stocks gone forever are coho salmon in Idaho's Clearwater River and fall chinook salmon that at one time extended up Snake River tributaries as far as northern Nevada. Expanding on the data available for the 1991 report, a team of federal agency scientists assessing habitat conditions within the area of the northern spotted owl (western Oregon, western Washington, and northwestern California) documented 384 stocks at varying levels of risk of extinction.[13] And 259 of the 384 occur on national forest and BLM lands.

As stocks such as the Snake River spring chinook salmon became protected pursuant to the Endangered Species Act, management decisions of the Forest Service and BLM fell under close scrutiny of the National Marine Fisheries Service, the federal agency charged with enforcement authority for salmon and steelhead. The Forest Service and BLM became increasingly proactive during the 1990s in efforts to protect and restore fish habitat in the Pacific Northwest. Development of the Northwest Forest Plan in 1993 mandated more protection and management emphasis for anadromous fish stocks within the range of the northern spotted owl. Among other protections, the Northwest Forest Plan implemented a riparian reserve system on national forest and BLM lands, created new standards and guidelines for all management activities affecting riparian reserves, and required watershed-scale analysis before reaching any major management decisions.

Outside the range of the northern spotted owl, the Forest Service and BLM implemented a strategy known as "PACFISH." This plan included many of the same provisions and emphasis on protection and restoration of riparian habitats contained in the Northwest Forest Plan.[14] The inherent logic behind managing aquatic resources in this manner, and the listing of bull trout, led to application of similar provisions on Forest Service and BLM lands in the Intermountain West through the INFISH strategy.

In many areas of the Pacific Northwest, habitat conditions on Forest Service and BLM lands are improving. These changes are due largely to addressing biodiversity concerns, and subsequent changes in public land management practices through implementation of the Northwest Forest Plan in western Oregon and western Washington, and application of the PACFISH strategy in eastern Oregon, eastern Washington, and Idaho. Protection of roadless areas and riparian habitats also plays a critical role in prescrving aquatic habitats on public lands. Roadless areas are often the last strongholds for salmon and steelhead spawning in the Columbia River system.[15] Permanent protection of such areas is our best insurance against loss of genetic diversity of anadromous fish stocks on public lands while restoration efforts move downstream to more needy habitats.

But protection of headwater habitats is no guarantee that salmon and steelhead numbers will increase. Downstream dams, water diversions, agriculture practices, livestock grazing, urbanization, pollution, overfishing, changing ocean conditions, and a host of other factors on private lands or in the ocean may prevent recovery of endangered fish stocks. Historically, the most diverse, complex, and therefore important habitats for anadromous salmonids occurred in valley bottoms—which usually are privately owned and far downstream from the lands managed by the Forest Service or BLM. The need to restore valley-bottom habitats and ensure main-stem fish passage for adults moving upstream to spawning areas and juveniles moving downstream to estuaries demonstrates the necessity of a broad-scale watershed approach to salmon and steelhead recovery.

Fishes of the Southwest Deserts

States such as Arizona and New Mexico cannot rival midwestern or eastern states in numbers of rivers and lakes or numbers of native fishes. Despite its larger size, the state of Arizona is home for only 31 native fishes whereas the state of Arkansas has 197 native fish species.[16] What makes Arizona's fewer fishes especially interesting, however, is that many of them are endemic—that is, found only in a handful of small streams or desert springs. Many of these endemic fishes of greatly restricted distribution are also uniquely specialized to life in the desert.

A small minnow called the woundfin, for instance, is adapted for life in desert streams by having specialized spiny rays in its fins that help keep fins erect during desert flash floods and by lacking an air bladder—thus keeping the fish along the bottom where drag reduces the impact of high water velocity. Like many of its desert cousins, the woundfin is listed as an endangered species pursuant to the Endangered Species Act. Of the thirty-one native Arizona fishes, only two, the speckled dace and longfin dace, are not on state, federal, or other agency lists of endangered or otherwise sensitive species.

Water is in high demand in the Southwest. Because most fishes in this region are restricted to a small number of springs or streams, their life is precarious. In most other regions of the country, when water from one river is diverted the fish there may die but at least that same species often occurs elsewhere. This is seldom the case in desert environments. The few large rivers and desert reservoirs are generally full of exotic fishes that were intentionally stocked as "game fish," released from home aquariums, or escaped from aquaculture facilities. To meet the demands of anglers, state fish and game agencies have introduced a myriad of game fishes, many of which are predators of native fishes and amphibians. Lake Mohave, for example, is a reservoir along the Arizona-Nevada border on the Colorado River where surveys have documented twenty-three introduced fish species and only six native fishes. Most of the introduced fishes, including largemouth bass, sunfish, crappie, striped bass, and trouts, prey on the few remaining natives.[17]

The threats to remaining native fish habitats of the desert Southwest are many. Numerous dams have been built across larger rivers, and water has been diverted to fast-growing cities like Phoenix, Las Vegas, and Albuquerque. Silty reservoir waters now inundate what remains of larger desert rivers such as the Colorado, Salt, and Rio Grande. Overgrazing by cattle has damaged small springs and riparian vegetation along other desert streams. Water from many desert streams has been removed for irrigation, and spring levels have been lowered by groundwater pumping.[18] And, as mentioned earlier, reservoirs are stocked with warmwater game fishes such as bass and crappie while smaller higher-elevation streams are stocked with rainbow, brown, and brook trout. None of these game fishes is native. But all prey upon, hybridize with, or otherwise crowd out the native fish.

Lands managed by the BLM and Forest Service provide most of the remaining viable habitat for native southwestern fishes. The San Pedro River and its tributaries in southeastern Arizona supply habitat for a number of desert fishes, including the longfin dace, speckled dace, desert mountain sucker, loach minnow, and spikedace. One single San Pedro tributary, Aravaipa Creek, is habitat for seven native fishes or almost 23 percent of the state's total fish fauna. The San Pedro is managed by the BLM as a national conservation area and is renowned internationally for its riparian habitats and diverse bird and mammal communities as well as its native fishes. Despite protection of public lands, groundwater withdrawal from nearby private land threatens the interconnected surface and subsurface flows in the San Pedro drainage. The city of Sierra Vista, located only 8 miles from the river, did not even exist until the 1950s, but now the Sierra Vista–Fort Huachuca area contains some 40,000 people. As BLM hydrologist Ben Lomeli notes in his report on future options for the San Pedro National Conservation Area: "Continued overdrafting (by about twice the annual recharge), between the mountain front recharge zone and the last remaining perennial reach of the river, is cause for concern."[19]

Cienega Creek, southeast of Tucson, is a largely intact desert stream system managed by the BLM. The Gila Box, a section of the Gila River managed by the BLM, protects the best remaining riparian habitat along that river system. BLM-managed springs and desert streams are keys to the survival and recovery of many desert fishes in California, Nevada, Arizona, and New Mexico.[20] But with the thirst for water from growing cities on nearby private lands, the viability of these rare and unique desert oases is uncertain. Many springs in desert environments harbor a rich but poorly known fauna. If this fauna includes an endangered species, public land managers have probably been protecting the spring. But if the spring is without any such species, it has probably been degraded by livestock (or wild horse) grazing or water diversion.

During the 1990s, Dr. Robert Hershler and colleagues from the Smithsonian Institution conducted systematic surveys of springs in the Great Basin to determine the presence of undescribed species of springsnails. As a result, Hershler and others have described more than sixty species new to science from Great Basin springs.[21] Many of these springs occur on public lands in Nevada, western Utah, and southeastern Oregon. These recent discoveries indicate our incomplete understanding of many aquatic systems—and demonstrate the care needed from public land managers and planners toward such sensitive habitats. Because of habitat modifications and the restricted range of many of these springsnails (some occur only in a single spring), many could qualify for Endangered Species Act protection. Public land managers and others should act now on this new information to restore and protect these spring systems and their faunas. Sound management should not have to depend on the Endangered Species Act to trigger protective actions.

Even if the historic range of a spring-dwelling fish is confined to a few sites on public lands, it may be necessary to manage water diversions or groundwater pumping on adjacent private lands so that habitat on public lands does not dry up. In these cases, the network of concern is primarily underground—the inhabited spring is simply the most visible component. Such was the case with the endangered Devils Hole pupfish, which was threatened by groundwater pumping for development of nearby privately owned lands. Ultimately the U.S. Supreme Court decided that the unique spring system providing the only habitat for the species should be protected from groundwater withdrawal. Most parties would agree, however, that cooperative planning and zoning measures which protect the integrity of spring flows are better than lengthy court reviews.[22] But this would mean a much higher level of coordination among federal, state, county, and municipal governments and a shared public/private responsibility that has eluded us thus far.

Two southwestern trouts, the Gila and Apache, are already protected under the Endangered Species Act. The Gila trout historically occurred in the Verde River system of Arizona and the upper Gila River system in New Mexico. Although this species has been eliminated from the Verde River drainage, five natural populations persist in headwater streams in the Gila National Forest, New Mexico. These remnant populations have been used as the source for fish to reestablish additional populations in the Gila National Forest and elsewhere. The historical range of the Apache trout included the White and Black rivers as well as headwaters of the Little Colorado River, all in eastern Arizona. When the recovery plan for the Apache trout was published in 1983, genetically pure strains of the fish persisted only in six small streams in the Apache-Sitgreaves National Forest and Fort Apache Indian Reservation.[23]

Historically both trout species occurred in headwater areas and in larger downstream rivers. As livestock grazing, clearcutting, and other types of habitat alteration occurred downstream, the fish became restricted to smaller headwater streams. Surviving headwater populations in turn were threatened by stocking of nonnative trouts. Introduced brown trout preyed on the native trouts. Introduced brook trout reproduced in such large numbers that they outcompeted the native trout. Of all the introduced trouts, hatchery rainbow trout proved to be the greatest long-term threat because they hybridize with the Gila and Apache trouts and reduce their genetic fitness.

Headwater populations, once protected from nonnative trout stocking, appeared to be secure. But their small remaining range made them susceptible to loss by wildfire, flood, or drought. Historically the native trouts occurred throughout larger stream systems where the sheer extent of interconnected habitat and the variety of stream sizes afforded population reservoirs for reestablishment after wildfire and other natural disturbances. Like the situation in the Pacific Northwest, the long-term protection of fish populations in headwater streams of national forests is problematic. Private land and public land conservation measures must be integrated to ensure that large expanses of interconnected stream habitats are accessible for these and other threatened species to recolonize.

Mississippi River and the Southeast

In both size and variety, the Mississippi River is one of the world's great rivers. Its drainage basin includes all or parts of thirty-one states stretching from the Rocky Mountains to the Appalachians and from the Great Lakes to the Gulf of Mexico. It is the center of aquatic biological diversity in North America, especially in regard to fishes and freshwater mussels. The highest numbers of native fish and mussel species occur in southeastern states. Alabama, for instance, has 306 native fish species and another 173 native mussel species. Tennessee accounts for about 297 native fish species and 127 native mussel species.[24] Small streams in the Southeast commonly contain dozens of species of minnows, darters, madtoms, and mussels. Despite research on this diverse stream fauna that spans well beyond a century, a handful of new species is described each year. What we know must always be tempered by how much we have yet to learn.

Compared to the small but well-adapted native aquatic faunas of western states, the numbers of fishes, mussels, crayfishes, and other aquatic invertebrates in the East and Southeast are staggering. Midwestern states such as Kansas, which has 131 native fish species and 44 native mussel species, cannot compare with the diversity of the Southeast. Even so, they still are part of the Mississippi River drainage and harbor a much more diverse stream fauna than found in western states. The disparity between native mussel species is even more striking between East and West. Only a handful of native mussel species occurs in western streams. Four native freshwater mussel species occur in Idaho and five in Oregon, for example, whereas southeastern states can boast a hundred or more.[25]

During the 1990s, the American Fisheries Society (AFS) reviewed the status of freshwater mussels, crayfishes, and freshwater fishes.[26] Results show alarming trends of increasing peril in the Mississippi River drainage and Southeast. Mussels, probably the most sensitive to pollution and other habitat degradation, have suffered the most. Some 33 percent of the 297 native freshwater mussels in the United States and Canada (the vast majority occurring in southeastern U.S. streams) are considered by the AFS to be endangered or possibly extinct. Another 14 percent are classified as threatened and 24 percent are of special concern. With another 5 percent in the undetermined category, this leaves only 24 percent as "currently stable." The status of crayfishes is much the same—nearly 20 percent of the species are listed as endangered or possibly extinct by the AFS. Of 662 native fishes in the southern United States, the AFS has documented that 28 percent were extinct, endangered, threatened, or vulnerable to extinction. This assessment represents a 75 percent increase in the degree of rarity among freshwater fishes in the South since the previous review was completed in 1989.

In 2000, The Nature Conservancy and the Association for Biodiversity Information published a thorough treatise on biodiversity that included an analysis of rare fish and mussel species throughout the United States.[27] They documented that the Southeast's river basins contain the lion's share of aquatic biodiversity—much of it at risk of extinction. (See Figure 4-1.) Two river systems accounted for 35 percent of all rare fish and mussel species in the United States: the Mobile River basin (in Alabama and parts of Mississippi, Georgia, and Tennessee) and the Tennessee and Cumberland river basins (in Tennessee and adjacent states). Of the rare species in these river systems, 70 percent are endemic and found nowhere else in the world.

The vast majority of rare fish, mussel, and crayfish species in the Mississippi River basin and Southeast are threatened by habitat alteration. Much of the problem can be traced to ubiquitous stream channelization, dams and impoundments, sedimentation, and changes in stream flow regimes—the same problems that plague streams and rivers throughout the country.[28] Lands in the Mississippi River basin and Southeast, however, differ from

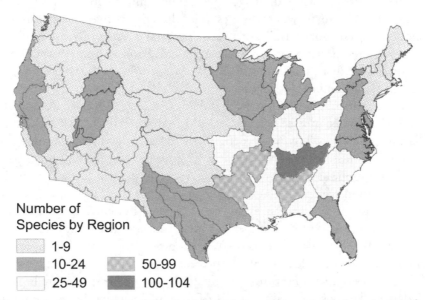

Figure 4-1. Concentrations of aquatic biological diversity in major drainage basins of the United States. Data from The Nature Conservancy and the Association for Biodiversity Information.

those in the West by at least one important attribute: few lands are in public ownership. The absence of public lands confounds traditional stream and river conservation in the Southeast. The AFS report notes that forested watersheds support most of the biologically significant creeks and rivers in the Southeast, but only 11 percent of lands in these watersheds are in public ownership. Furthermore, consistent with the nationwide pattern, most public forestland in the Southeast is at higher elevations. As a result, most rare aquatic species in the Southeast do not receive any protection through public land management.

Invaders in Our Lakes and Streams

If you cast a line into a local river, lake, or reservoir, in most parts of the country you are more likely to catch an introduced fish species than one native to the site. Not only have fishes been relocated, both intentionally and unintentionally, but exotic aquatic invertebrates and plants dominate many habitats.

Geological Survey staff at the Florida Caribbean Science Center in Gainesville track the status of aquatic species introductions throughout the country. And they are documenting a dramatically increasing number of introductions since 1831, the earliest known date of a nonnative fish introduction in the United States.[29] Between 1831 and 1950, a period of 120 years, approximately 117 fish species are known to have been introduced. But in a span of only forty-five years between 1950 and 1995, some 458 additional fish species were brought into this country. All states have been affected, but the largest number of introductions has occurred in the Southwest and portions of the Southeast. (See Figure 4-2.) More than half of these introductions were deliberate releases approved or carried out by government agencies. Some introductions were unauthorized; others were accidental. A large share of the introductions, about 44 percent, were made to expand sportfishing opportunities.[30] Another 16 percent were associated with sportfishing but were bait releases. Aquarium releases and escapes from aquaculture facilities accounted for 26 percent. Smaller percentages were accounted for by release of ship ballast water (2 percent), biological control agents (2 percent), or other purposes.

Even with the best of intentions, most of these introductions were misguided. Some have proved to be disastrous for native fishes. A good example is provided by brook trout, a native to streams in eastern Canada and the eastern United States. This trout is prized by anglers in the East and has been introduced widely into western streams and high-country lakes on public lands where the story has taken a different turn. Because of their

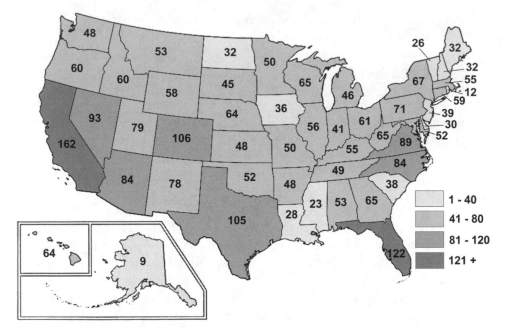

Figure 4-2. Number of nonnative fish species and subspecies introduced in each state. Data from the Florida Caribbean Science Center, Biological Resources Division of the U.S. Geological Survey.

aggressiveness and high reproductive rate, brook trout have replaced many golden trout, cutthroat trout, and redband trout native to western streams.[31] The fast-reproducing brook trout become stunted in most western streams and lakes. The result is habitats filled with 5- to 6-inch-long brook trout—not a pleasing perspective for conservationist or angler. Moreover, brook trout hybridize with the endangered bull trout of the Columbia River basin and are considered to be the greatest threat to that species aside from habitat loss.[32]

Our propensity for introducing nonnative fish despite growing evidence of the problems this causes can best be seen in the high-elevation lakes stocking programs carried out in backcountry areas of many national forests. High-elevation lakes in most national forests and some national parks commonly are stocked with nonnative trout to provide angling opportunities. Some of this stocking occurs in wilderness areas, where one might think that such practices would be prohibited. Because many high-elevation lakes were "fishless," no environmental degradation was anticipated. Recent studies have demonstrated, however, that sharp declines or even elimination of native amphibian populations in high-elevation lakes can be attributed to predation from introduced trouts.[33] Additional amphibian declines may be attributable to fungal diseases transmitted to frogs by trout from hatcheries.

In Idaho's Frank Church–River of No Return Wilderness in the Payette National Forest, 43 of 101 historically fishless lakes have been stocked with cut-throat, rainbow, and golden trout. These 43 lakes are the largest and deepest, comprising some 90 percent of the total surface acres of lakes in the wilderness. Scientists at Idaho State University are finding that not only are populations of long-toed salamanders and Columbia spotted frogs disappearing from the lakes stocked with trout, but they have been eliminated from many of the unstocked sites as well.[34] It appears that many of the remaining lakes are too small and shallow to provide suitable breeding and overwintering habitat for amphibians. Before fish stocking, salamanders and frogs could move from the larger lakes to recolonize smaller water bodies and survive quite well. In effect, the nonnative fish introductions have disconnected the high-elevation-lake network.

The story from "The Frank" Wilderness is being repeated throughout the West with similar results. As Phil Pister, rare fishes expert from California, has summarized: "The western states are collectively involved in a massive and expensive wilderness stocking program, the value of which has never been conclusively demonstrated, and which is known to be destructive to native fauna and not in accordance with generally accepted wilderness val-ues."[35] Protecting mountain lake biological diversity should be of greater concern to the Forest Service and state fish and game agencies than provid-ing dubious fishing opportunities.

Sportfish comprise only a portion of the many species of fishes released into the waters of the United States. Various species of tropical fishes such as cichlids, tilapia, loaches, mollies, and goldfish, species more commonly known to living-room aquariums than springs and streams, have nonetheless become established in natural habitats. Although these tropical species sur-vive best in southern parts of the country where temperatures are warmer, some species have become established in warm-water springs in Wyoming, Idaho, and Nevada. Some tropical fishes have escaped from aquaculture facilities, but many have been introduced intentionally by people who have given up on their own aquariums and do not realize the harm they cause by releasing aquarium fish into the wild.

Introductions of tropical fishes are a particular problem for BLM-managed public lands in the West. In Ash Meadows, Nevada, for example, Jack Rabbit Spring and Big Spring harbor endangered desert fishes but also populations of mollies, mosquitofish, and other exotics that prey on larvae of the endangered pupfish and dace.[36] Elimination of exotic species has proved nearly impossible in spring and wetland areas despite continued efforts. Where elimination of exotics seems to have succeeded, they often are back just a few months later.

The blue tilapia from Africa and the Middle East is one example of a tropical fish that has found a home in the wildlands of the United States. Staff from the Florida Caribbean Science Center have documented the introduction and establishment of blue tilapia in thirteen states, including Idaho, California, and Nevada, as well as the East Coast states of North Carolina, Georgia, and Florida.[37] In some areas of the Southeast, blue tilapia are so abundant they have consumed most of the aquatic vegetation and outcompeted native fishes for remaining habitat. In Everglades National Park, the Park Service considers the blue tilapia to be "a major threat."[38]

The Frankenstein Effect

When a species is transported from its native ecosystem to a novel environment, we seldom know how the new species will function. By moving the species into a new ecosystem, we have removed it from the environment in which it evolved and placed it in a system without all the predators and competitors that kept it in check. Because of the new environment and the new community of species, the introduced species may take on a somewhat different role than it had in its native range—or the role it played in its native range may play out differently in the new environment. Dr. Peter Moyle, a researcher at the University of California at Davis who has studied the effects of hundreds of introduced species on California's native biota, uses the term "Frankenstein Effect" to describe how many introduced species end up creating unanticipated problems of monstrous proportions.[39]

Moyle and his colleagues documented nine native fishes that have disappeared from the fish fauna of California, although they may persist elsewhere.[40] Introduced species played a significant role in many of these declines. In general there are mechanisms that allow introduced species, aquatic or terrestrial, to replace native species: predation, competition, inhibition of reproduction (by behavior or physical modification of habitat), environmental degradation, hybridization, and the introduction of parasites and diseases. When a new species is established, this presence always comes at a cost to native species. In essence, the niche of the native species has been narrowed to make room for the introduced species. If the redefined niche is too narrow, extinction may result.[41] Usually these impacts on the native species are unanticipated. Sometimes the effects are straightforward—such as introduced brown trout preying on native fishes in a stream—but sometimes they are quite convoluted.

One of the more interesting examples of this Frankenstein Effect occurred when opossum shrimp were introduced between 1968 and 1975 into the Flathead Lake drainage of Montana, outside their native range, in an effort to provide an additional food item for kokanee salmon.[42] Kokanee feed on zooplankton, tiny crustaceans like copepods and cladocerans, which in turn feed on small plant material that floats in the lake. Ironically kokanee had been introduced into Flathead Lake in 1916 and largely had replaced the native westslope cutthroat trout. Like the native cutthroat, the kokanee spawned in tributaries, including McDonald Creek, located about 60 miles upstream of Flathead Lake in Glacier National Park. Like the native cutthroat before them, the swarms of spawning kokanee attracted numerous predators and scavengers that fed on spawning kokanee, their carcasses, and kokanee eggs. In some years, more than 500 bald eagles congregated along a 2.5-mile stretch of McDonald Creek. Approximately 100,000 spawning kokanee and 639 eagles were counted along McDonald Creek in 1981. The problems started soon after the opossum shrimp introductions—and escalated in the 1980s. The introduced shrimp fed voraciously on the smaller copepods and cladocerans. Although it was assumed that kokanee would feed on the opossum shrimp, few of the shrimp appeared in the fish's diet. Ultimately researchers found that kokanee normally feed during daylight nearer the surface waters while the opossum shrimp spend daylight hours near the lake bottom and migrate to the surface to feed on the copepods and cladocerans at night. As a result, the opossum shrimp largely were unavailable to the kokanee and the populations of the usual kokanee foods declined because of predation from the shrimp. And when the kokanee runs collapsed, it triggered concomitant losses of the eagles, mergansers, gulls, waterfowl, coyotes, river otters, and grizzly bears that fed on the kokanee or their eggs. By 1989, only twenty-five eagles were counted along McDonald Creek.[43]

Focus Essay

Rivers: Lifelines of the Land

TIM PALMER*

At the time of my youth, my backyard river, the Ohio, could have been called the largest barge-floating cesspool in America. Though my grandfather and I fished for carp in some less foul backwaters, the river was mostly

*Tim Palmer is a writer and photographer and has written over a dozen books about rivers and the environment.

a wasteflow for commerce and industry, bridged but scarcely even seen through cultural filters that tinted out any sense of responsibility, or imagination, or hope.

So it was with fascination that I discovered my first healthy stream, Pine Creek, in northern Pennsylvania. River-sized and clean enough for swimming, its fishery thrived, its watershed half wild, half rural, all of it a paradise to me. Along Pine Creek I learned that everything alive needs water and that rivers are the water supply of the earth. I also learned that the land and water are inextricably connected because everything we do to a watershed is reflected in the runoff of rivers.

I was fortunate to have lived along Pine Creek during the greatest storm in its history. While the torrent crested, I zipped up my raincoat and explored the nearby country. I found one tributary running clear, even at the height of the deluge. No roads had been built near it. But a similar stream, with only one logging road in its basin, ran chocolate with silt, the stormwater gouging out ditches and slabbing off whole mudslides because the runoff had pummeled into cuts that had been knifed into the earth by the blade of a bulldozer. When scoring time rolls around for our stewardship of the earth, each stream or river is a report card on how we treat its watershed.

Before long I realized that a big difference between Pine Creek and the Ohio River was the corresponding presence and absence of public land. Like many of our national forests and other reserves, the state forests along Pine Creek had been set aside years before with the twin goals of protecting water supplies and logging with care. Much to my joy, I later discovered unspoiled western streams such as the Salmon River of Idaho. I learned that protection of national forest land there was essential to the stream's health and to its wild resonance in my heart.

Think of this as a two-way street: rivers are essential to our public land, a fact evident in the life concentrated along the streams and in the thin corridors of green that lace together the ecosystems of the West. But just as important, public land is essential to our rivers, even many miles below the boundary lines where private land begins. Consider that 90 percent of the municipal and agricultural water supplies of western America originate on federal lands. Towns, industries, farms, and ranches are all possible because the upper reaches of many streams are owned in trust as the unspoiled source of water that everyone needs. Where would San Francisco be without the snowmelt of Yosemite National Park and the Stanislaus National Forest? To describe New York without the fresh runoff of the Adirondacks and Catskills—set aside as water sources in the 1800s—is to imagine our largest city without spigots. How would virtually every irrigator in the West cultivate a livelihood without water that is generously handed down from upstream public land? Not to mention the fact that most recreation—and the economic engine it stokes—depends on water along with accessible land not marred by "keep out" signs.

Where the land has not been explicitly protected, many watersheds are polluted, developed, clearcut, overgrazed, or mined. Of course, all these impediments to river health exist in national forests and other commons. But the plague of the Ohio River is far more typical where we don't have public land—and the qualities of Pine Creek are far more common where we do.

This all seems so simple. Yet a vocal constituency in some political circles argues that land held in trust by the people is unnecessary and undesirable. Those people should try eating carp out of the Ohio River of my youth. Let them seek their rugged independence amid the suburbanizing sprawl of the Chattahoochee River near Atlanta. Let them exercise their freedom from public landownership along the Des Moines River with its toxic load of nitrates and pesticides. And then let them decide if public land is superfluous to us, to our ideals as a nation, and to the generations unborn. Without good land, properly stewarded and held in trust for all, good water will be a memory as distant as fresh air in Houston, Texas.

We know that to care for our water is to care for our land. But to feel this in our bones and to be truly motivated, a personal connection is essential. Go to the river. Breathe the moist air and smell the fertile mud. Listen to the birds and the jumping of fish. Soak your feet in the riffles of summertime, and from there, look up at the hillsides that shed their rainfall and snowmelt to make the river what it is.

Healthy Watersheds: The Public/Private Land Connection

The importance of federally administered public lands to conservation of rare or endangered species is clear from a wealth of research and observations. According to recent studies, federal lands (including Department of Defense lands) harbor more than 30 percent of populations of federally listed and otherwise imperiled species in the United States. This is more than any landowner provides, although all private lands combined do support a surprisingly high number of rare species. (See Figure 4-3.) Among federal agencies, lands managed by the Forest Service provide habitat for the greatest number of rare species.[44]

The role of private lands in conservation of biological diversity is gaining increasing attention. Private lands account for about 25 percent of all known

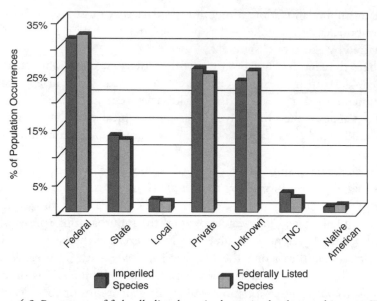

Figure 4-3. Percentage of federally listed species by major landownership type. Total percentages may exceed 100 because some species span more than one ownership type. Data from The Nature Conservancy and the Association for Biodiversity Information.

populations of federally listed or otherwise imperiled species in the United States. If only federally listed species are considered, the importance of private lands actually exceeds that of federal lands. More than 60 percent of all threatened and endangered species occur at least in part on private lands.[45] Moreover, most of the highly productive habitat of the past that now is unoccupied or is host to greatly reduced populations is privately owned. Restoration investments in these core areas would yield enormous returns.

As we have seen, the impact of federal lands in conservation is not the same across the country. Most protection occurs in the West where federal public lands are more widespread. But even in the West, conservation on federal public lands alone cannot ensure the long-term survival of most rare native fishes. There are several reasons for this: the distribution of federal lands across the landscape, the lack of attention to private land conservation, and linkages between public and private land management.

Public lands generally are located at higher elevations—especially Forest Service and National Park Service lands. Even within national forests, most designated wilderness areas, which receive the greatest ecological protection, are located along the mountain peaks and ridges. Lands managed by the BLM are mostly at mid-elevations. The bulk of private lands, however,

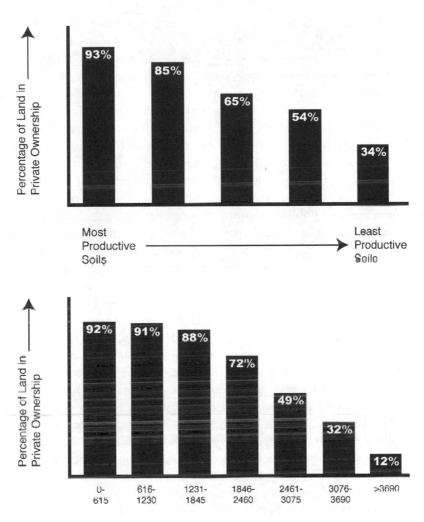

Figure 4-4. The most productive and diverse habitats historically occurred in lower-elevation valley bottoms. As indicated by these two graphs, the most productive and lower elevation habitats often are privately owned. Data for the entire United States and adopted from the work of J. Michael Scott and colleagues at the University of Idaho. (Information from Scott, J. M., R. J. F. Abbitt, and C. R. Groves, 2001 "What Are We Protecting?" *Conservation Biology in Practice* 2(1):18–19.)

are located in lower-elevation riparian and valley-bottom habitats. Private lands tend to include most of the land with highly productive soils and diverse habitat types. (See Figure 4-4.) In an article titled "What Are We Protecting?" J. Michael Scott and colleagues argue that about half of all the land dedicated to conservation in the United States is in the least productive soil types and at the highest elevations.[46] Conservation strategies for private lands represent the critical link in expanding efforts across a broad range of habitat types and ecosystems—a move that is essential to the long-term survival and eventual recovery of many of our native aquatic species.

Few attempts have been made to link the management strategies of public and private lands for conservation. Some of the best efforts are in Oregon, western Washington, and northwestern California. In Oregon and Washington, dozens of watershed councils have been formed to guide management efforts on public and private lands. These watershed councils constitute a focal point for federal agency collaboration with private landowners. The Coquille and Rogue rivers in Oregon are good examples where federal and state agencies, watershed councils, and private landowners are developing watershed-scale goals, management plans, and restoration projects jointly. The Blackfoot River in western Montana has been the site of a well-integrated watershed strategy since 1990. A similar watershed approach is being implemented in California's Mattole River basin. In addition, efforts by the BLM and Forest Service to assess proper functioning condition across much of the West have resulted in a valuable dialogue between federal land managers and livestock grazing permittees, all of whom are private landowners as well. Watershed-scale restoration and management efforts are spreading across the nation, but they are still the exception rather than the rule.[47]

Healthy rivers are products of healthy watersheds. Watersheds in good condition store and release rain and snowfall in amounts that maintain natural flow regimes. If floods occur, energy from high river flows is dispersed onto floodplains where stands of healthy riparian vegetation trap silt and dissipate energy. Water from healthy rivers connects the landscape in all directions. Healthy rivers connect laterally onto riparian areas and upland habitats. But their health depends also on proper functioning conditions in upstream headwaters. If headwaters, riparian areas, and uplands function within limits that maintain natural flow regimes, then downstream river, floodplain, and valley-bottom habitats maintain their diversity and complexity.

A truly healthy watershed—stretching from headwaters to valley bottoms, from groundwaters to surface waters, with all habitat elements in proper functioning condition—is rare. Especially rare are functional valley-bottom habitats. Over the years, most lower-elevation rivers, floodplains, and valley-bottom habitats have been simplified, fragmented, and constrained by a combination of agricultural and urban development, dams, and development of transport systems (highways and railroads along rivers). Implicit in the concept of a healthy watershed is the integrity of the continuum of lands from headwaters to the river mouth.

Intact and healthy river ecosystems in the United States are few and far between. A nationwide rivers inventory, completed more than a decade ago, found that only 2 percent of streams and rivers in the Lower 48 remained in sufficient condition to warrant their consideration for national wild or scenic status.[48] By all accounts, we must do better at managing our nation's watersheds and rivers. And this will require unprecedented integration of public and private conservation efforts.

Chapter 5

Roadless Areas: The Last Wild Places

This country has been swinging the hammer of development so long and so hard that it has forgotten the anvil of
wilderness which gave value and significance to its labors.
The momentum of our blows is so unprecedented that the
remaining remnant of wilderness will be pounded into road
dust long before we find out its values.

—Aldo Leopold, "Why the Wilderness Society" (1935)

Few public land issues have elicited as much interest as a Forest Service proposal to protect unfragmented and roadless national forest lands from new
road construction and most timber harvest. Dan Glickman, secretary of agriculture, signed the Roadless Area Conservation Rule on January 12, 2001.[1]
The rule prohibits road construction and most commercial timber harvest
on 58.5 million acres of national forests—about one third of the entire
National Forest System. (See Figure 5-1.)

The Forest Service developed a protective strategy for roadless areas over
a three-year period that involved more than six hundred local public meetings and a record-breaking 1.6 million public comments. Although the large

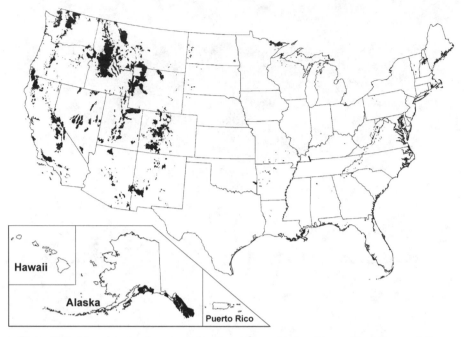

Figure 5-1. Map showing location of national forest lands with road building prohibited by the Roadless Rule.

majority of these comments took the form of postcards and form letters—and while it is true that such rules are not determined by vote counting—remarkably, more than 90 percent of public comments favored increased national protection of inventoried roadless areas.[2]

Keeping roadless areas roadless would cost less than two-tenths of 1 percent of the nation's timber demands from national forests. Oil and gas development in the entire National Forest System supplies less than one-quarter of 1 percent of the nation's energy, far less from roadless areas. Other uses such as grazing, hard-rock mining, and recreation are essentially unaffected by the rule. Although roads allow people to access public forests for recreation, only 33 miles of new roads in roadless areas were planned from 2000 to 2005 to support recreation opportunities.[3]

The economic effects of the rule, therefore, were minimal. The vast majority of roadless areas, for example, do not contain productive timberlands—only 8 or 9 million of the 58.5 million acres protected by the rule are considered "suitable for timber production" by the Forest Service, and even this amount is viewed by many as a very optimistic assessment. That a federal rule entailing such minor economic costs could generate such a huge public response demonstrates that, like so many other conservation issues, the roadless area debate has more to do with values than with environmental protection or economic prosperity.

Behind the Great Debate

Local forest plans would have allowed new road construction in about 34 million acres of the 58.5 million acres of roadless areas. Attempts to build roads or otherwise develop these areas are among the most contentious issues faced by local forest managers. Litigation over road construction and commercial timber harvest proposals within roadless areas are the norm, not the exception. Roadless areas are often found at higher elevations with steep slopes and erosive soils—where timber values are generally low and road construction and environmental analysis costs are high. The vast majority of timber sales in such remote reaches cost taxpayers far more than they generate in receipts to the Treasury.

In 1926, prompted by Arthur Carhart, a young Forest Service landscape architect who believed that the Quetico-Superior region in Minnesota and other national forests should be kept in a wild state,[4] the Forest Service inventoried all areas larger than 230,400 acres that were without roads. More than seventy-four tracts of land totaling 55 million acres were identified. Between 1924 and 1964, the Forest Service managed 9 million of these as wilderness areas.[5]

After passage of the Wilderness Act in 1964, the Forest Service began reviewing National Forest System roadless areas larger than 5000 acres to determine their suitability for inclusion in the National Wilderness Preservation System. A second review completed in 1979—known as Roadless Area Review and Evaluation II (RARE II)—resulted in another nationwide inventory that identified approximately 62 million acres of roadless areas larger than 5000 acres. Through RARE II, the Forest Service recommended that Congress add 15 million acres to the National Wilderness Preservation System, allocate 36 million acres to "nonwilderness uses," and study nearly 11 million acres for further planning.[6] Over the next twenty years, additional reviews and inventories were conducted.[7] Congress passed wilderness legislation in states such as Oregon and Washington that protected some roadless lands and included "release language" that committed the remaining roadless areas to the forest planning process.

Because roadless areas are the last reservoir of future wilderness, proposals to build roads or sell timber in these areas always generate extreme controversy. Many forest supervisors—in order to avoid negative media coverage and avoid the ire of the environmental community and some members of Congress—simply allowed staff proposals to build roads into remote areas to languish. And, as noted, building expensive road systems into remote roadless areas with low timber values generally costs more than the timber sales generated in receipts. With increasing public scrutiny leveled at below-cost timber sales, it was far easier for the agency to focus on the accessible timber.

Since the completion of RARE II in 1979, only about 2.8 million acres of the RARE II areas have had roads built within them to facilitate the harvest of timber and other extractive uses. Nonetheless, every year roadless-area timber sales would emerge—with names like Deadwood, Dome Peak, and Otter Wing that read as though they came from the title page of a Louis Lamour western novel. And every year the sales would enrage the environmental community and result in congressional intervention and negative publicity for the Forest Service. In an effort to end this cycle, Chief Jack Ward Thomas directed forest supervisors in 1995 to either remove roadless areas from the suitable timber base or commence plans for their harvest. Thomas was "convinced that continued concentration of cutting in higher site productivity lands would quickly come to a point where either timber yields would drop precipitously or the timber sale program would shift almost entirely into roadless areas identified in the 'suitable timber base' with an associated expansion of conflict."[8]

Thomas was right. The agency's timber sale program did drop precipitously in the early 1990s. His directive, however, was either ignored or failed to have the intended effect. In 1997, after years of congressional amendments to the Forest Service appropriations bill attempting to cut funding of forest roads, the House of Representatives came within a single vote of eliminating 80 percent of the Forest Service's road budget. The sponsor of the amendment cited roadless area protection as a primary reason to cut the road budget. To some Forest Service leaders, the time had come for decisive action.

Why Roadless Areas Matter

National forest roadless areas comprise only 2 percent of the nation's land base. Yet in an increasingly developed and urbanized landscape, the ecological and social value of these wild and unfragmented lands is immense. From 1978 to 1994, the proportion of private forest landowners owning less than 50 acres nearly doubled.[9] An average of 3.2 million acres per year—8700 acres per day—of forest, wetland, farmland, and open space was converted to urban uses between 1992 and 1997,[10] twice the rate of development in the previous decade. As development of remaining privately owned open spaces, forests, and rangeland increases, the value of large unroaded tracts of public land becomes ever more apparent.

Focus Essay

A Dream for Healing the Kootenai

RICK BASS*

In the nearly 1 million acres that lie north of the Kootenai River, stretching up to and over into Canada, there are but fifteen little roadless cores remaining, wild gardens, and they are all as yet unprotected for the future. The Yaak is an intensely green and wet low-elevation ecosystem, a rainforest kind of place that possesses the violent, elegant topography of the northern Rockies while being graced with the heavy snows and rains of the Pacific Northwest.

The Yaak is a land of two identities, two stories—fire next to rot, stability next to disturbance, conifers next to broadleafs. Perhaps because of this duality, the valley seems destined to be a place of conflict, though it need not be.

Year after year, the Yaak has given up more timber than any other valley in Montana. Because the Yaak grows big timber, protection for its wildlands has always been traded away at the last moment, and even now, thirty-eight years after the passage of the Wilderness Act, there is still not a single acre of designated wilderness in the Yaak—despite the fact that from a standpoint of biological diversity, the Yaak is one of the wildest places in the lower 48.

The Yaak is home, still, to a Noah's Ark population of gray wolves, grizzly bears, lynx, bull trout, west slope cutthroat trout, Coeur d'Alene salamanders, inland redband trout, fisher, caribou, great gray owls, and bald eagles. Even if a thing is rare, or extinct elsewhere in the West, it is often still possible to find that thing in the Yaak—in one of those fifteen little gardens that we have failed to protect as wilderness.

---

*Rick Bass, the author of several books, is a wilderness activist living in the Yaak Valley, Montana.

Along with other conservationists up here, I keep clinging to our little dreams of peace and justice, hoping for some solution, some permanence, within an injured system on a wounded landscape. What must it be like for the land itself, this vast sheet of mountains and jungle spilling over into Canada: a land that has been so altered, so manipulated? In the last fifty years, the Kootenai National Forest has been converted to an overstocked landscape in which two-thirds of the forest is made up of trees measuring 16 inches in diameter or smaller.

There remains a wild spirit in this land, and it is that which I hope to help preserve. It is a spirit that is still found, as well, in the human inhabitants of this valley, and even though some of them hate or fear the future, and any notion of plans, or borders and boundaries, I admire them, even as they distrust me and my dreams, for we all share a love of this place.

Here is my dream. It's neither original nor bold, and it's constructed upon a protected system of leaving the best and strongest trees and taking only the weak and the crooked, the diseased and overstocked. It will take a hundred years of such practice for us to even crawl out of the hole we've been digging for the last fifty; in that regard, if no other, the dream is strong and patient: though again, it makes too much sense, and is too moderate, to be called anything other than common sense. I am ashamed of my dream's moderation. It is not revolutionary. It is as mild and tame as this landscape is rank and wild.

The dream advances the surety of permanent protection for the Yaak's roadless cores, giving us invaluable ecological leverage into the reservoir of Canada's wildness and genetic diversity.

Because of the Kootenai's great productivity—its low-elevation lands, its high precipitation—there would still be ample opportunity for fiber extraction. It just wouldn't be the kinds of fiber that industry has long been accustomed to pulling out of the Kootenai. The dream would instead be an experiment, a new way of doing business. Because of the Kootenai's moisture regime (as well as our sparse human population), it is here, too, that a pilot program aimed at increasing the amount of prescribed burning could be conducted most safely and cost-effectively.

How ironic that our reckless mistakes of the past have conspired to present us with such eminently achievable opportunity. If this is not a definition of grace, then what is? Undeserved bounty. Unexpected opportunity.

It might be naive, but when people can work together on a specific project—raising a roof beam, digging a ditch, repairing a carburetor—they come together in that shared language of the specific that is capable of binding them more tightly in a way that abstract philosophical discussions can never approach. And in this binding, this knitting, I believe healing can occur, both on the land and in the community.

The Kootenai has always been last. Doesn't it make sense, for once, for it to be first?

Nationwide the land available for dispersed outdoor recreational opportunities such as hunting, fishing, and cross-country skiing is shrinking.[11] And it will continue to shrink as more private property is posted off-limits and development encroaches on the remaining open space. Roadless areas provide recreational opportunities in abundance—and unlike congressionally designated wilderness areas, the use of mountain bikes and other mechanized means of travel is often allowed in roadless areas unless otherwise prohibited by local agency planning. Such areas also take the pressure off heavily used designated wilderness by affording additional solitude, quiet, and dispersed recreation opportunities. Inventoried roadless areas offer other environmental benefits, too, such as clean drinking water. National forest roadless areas contain all or portions of 354 municipal watersheds contributing drinking water to millions of citizens. Maintaining these and other forested areas in an undisturbed condition saves downstream communities millions of dollars in water filtration costs.[12]

By limiting ground-disturbing activities that encourage noxious weeds and other exotic species, roadless areas serve as a bulwark against the spread of invasive species. Roadless areas also function as biological strongholds for native fish and wildlife species.[13] Research from the Interior Columbia River Basin Assessment indicates that the most intact native fish communities are often associated with roadless areas.[14] Areas with higher road densities, by contrast, are associated with declines in populations of bull trout, westslope cutthroat trout, Yellowstone cutthroat trout, and redband trout. Approximately 60 percent of roadless or low-road-density areas within the basin support strong salmonid populations. But less than 25 percent of areas with moderate road densities and 18 percent with high road densities possess strong populations of these species.[15]

Of the nation's species currently listed as threatened, endangered, or proposed for listing under the Endangered Species Act, approximately 25 percent of the animal and 13 percent of the listed plant species are likely to have habitat within national forest roadless areas. Roadless areas provide habitat for more than 280 threatened, endangered, and proposed species, including more than 65 percent of all Forest Service sensitive species.[16]

These statistics highlight the important role that roadless areas play in maintaining biodiversity. The numbers are remarkable given that roadless areas are most often found in the least biologically productive higher elevations—areas with more erosive soils and higher-gradient streams. Nonetheless, many conservation biologists believe that protection of the remaining roadless areas is the first step to reconnecting the headwater areas to the more biologically rich main-stem rivers and lower-elevation areas.[17]

The BLM is responsible for managing millions of acres of remote wild places possessing many of the same values as national forests. During the Clinton administration, Interior Secretary Bruce Babbitt established the BLM National Landscape Conservation System with the focus of preserving the social and ecological values and wildness of vast acreages of public lands. These lands, like roadless areas, were the subject of intense debate.

Focus Essay

The Heart of the West:
BLM's National Landscape Conservation System
Bruce Babbitt*

The unreserved public lands administered by the Bureau of Land Management (BLM) have always been treated as leftovers, passed over by homesteaders and then ignored by conservationists as they high-graded what they considered to be the most desirable lands into national parks, forests, and wildlife refuges.

To me, however, the characteristic BLM lands are the essential, defining landscapes of the American West. These are the matrix lands, spaces that surround and protect the boundaries of our parks and forests. BLM lands are the connective tissue that sustains seasonal wildlife migration pathways across the land and maintains complex desert ecosystems. They provide the desert setting: the silvery sage vistas in which the crown jewels of our national parks sparkle even more brightly.

In 1996 as President Clinton pondered creation of a large national monument in southern Utah, I suggested that he break with tradition by desig-

---

*Bruce Babbitt is a former secretary of the interior and fomer governor of Arizona.

nating the Grand Staircase Escalante as the first Antiquities Act monument to be administered by the BLM. He agreed, and then in the next four years he followed with another fourteen BLM monuments. They include the purple blooming ironwood forests of the Sonoran Desert, the mountain tributaries of the Grand Canyon, the last free-flowing stretches of the Missouri River, the unique species assemblage of the Klamath Siskyou, and the archaeological treasures of western Colorado and central Arizona.

Then in 1999, we gathered these monuments, together with congressionally legislated national conservation areas, into a new National Landscape Conservation System. My hope is that, by endowing the BLM with a high-profile conservation mission, the old bureaucratic mule will awaken to a new future as environmental steward right up there with the National Park Service and the National Wildlife Refuge System. The day is coming, I believe, when the BLM, so often stereotyped and dismissed as the Bureau of Livestock and Mining, will be better known as the Bureau of Landscapes and Monuments.

The BLM administers about 270 million acres of public land, of which less than 10 percent, about 15 million acres, has been designated for conservation status as monuments or as wilderness or conservation areas This is a woefully inadequate figure. The protection goal for the next generation should be to protect half the remaining undesignated lands for a round number, let's say an additional 100 million acres.

We could begin with the BLM lands that surround and protect our national parks, such as Centennial Valley alongside Yellowstone and the lands adjacent to Canyonlands, Great Basin National Park, and Carlsbad Caverns, to name just a few.

Our work in southern Utah remains unfinished. There are millions of acres yet to be protected, whether as monuments or as wilderness, in such spectacular regions as the San Rafael Swell, the Henry Mountains, the West Desert, and the Book Cliffs.

In southern Idaho, northern Nevada, and eastern Oregon the canyons of the Owyhee River and its tributaries meander across more than 5 million acres of pristine high desert country that rivals the Colorado Plateau in scenic splendor and ecological distinctiveness.

The BLM is also landlord of more than 80 percent of Alaska's North Slope—a 20-million-acre tundra plain that extends west from the Arctic Wildlife Refuge all the way to the shores of the Bering Sea within sight of Siberia. The great western caribou herd, more than 500,000 strong, the largest of all caribou herds, migrates across these plains. And it is here that the strings of sparkling tundra lakes provide summer nesting habitat for the spectacled eider, the snow goose, and myriad other species. Just offshore, packs of bowhead whales migrate each spring from the Bering Sea up into Arctic waters. This area, overshadowed by the continuing struggle over the future of the Arctic Wildlife Refuge to the east, is threatened by road building, habitat fragmentation, and oil development. These lands should be officially designated as a national Caribou Commons to be protected in perpetuity for wildlife and for the subsistence needs of native Alaskans.

Everywhere in the West the BLM lands should be inventoried, prioritized, and protected for their role in maintaining the integrity of natural grasslands and riparian corridors and desert ecosystems. The lands of southern New Mexico and in the Great Basin of Nevada and Oregon come to mind as good places to begin. The remaining BLM lands in the Great Plains east of the Rocky Mountains should be examined for the appropriate site to begin restoration of the Buffalo Commons. A true Buffalo Commons, a place to restore not only the bison but the wolf, the grizzly, elk, antelope, prairie dogs, ferrets, and all the other sadly diminished creatures that once graced the High Plains, would not be a small undertaking. It will require a vision and a commitment on the scale of the restoration of the Everglades. There are large blocks of BLM short-grass prairie and national grasslands remaining in Montana, Wyoming, and the Dakotas that could provide the nucleus for High Plains restoration.

The BLM lands are the heart of the West. With the new National Landscape Conservation System, the door has been opened to a new public lands conservation future. But we still have a long way to go and a lot of land to protect—at least another 100 million acres.

The Forest Road System

Roads allow people easy access to the public lands they love. They also provide access for fighting fires and conducting other management activities. Proper road maintenance allows for continued safe public access to national forests and minimizes environmental impacts such as soil erosion. Road maintenance can range from keeping roads smooth, repairing bridges, and keeping culverts open for proper drainage to major reconstruction such as replacing smaller culverts with bigger ones able to withstand higher flows of water and more storm debris without washing out.

Roadways may also do harm. They can disrupt the hydrological function of a watershed, increase erosion, and result in greater roadkills of mammals, reptiles, and birds.[18] Moreover, human-caused fires are far more likely to occur in roaded areas than in roadless areas. Roads also create corridors of disturbed land that accelerates the invasion and spread of noxious weeds. The effort needed to build a road is temporary. But keeping the road in functional condition and environmentally benign—particularly in high-elevation areas with erosive soils—requires a long-term commitment of resources. In the thirty-five years between 1944 and 1979, the forest road system grew by 122,000 miles—from 100,000 to 222,000 miles. In the next six years, from 1979 to 1985, the road system grew by an additional 121,000 miles to a total of 343,000 miles. To maintain the high timber harvest levels of the previous decade, the Forest Service would have had to construct roads into more and more remote locations with generally steep slopes and more fragile soils.

The extensive road system was financed in large part by timber sales. In other words, responsibility for road work was assigned to timber purchasers as part of the timber-sale contract. This strategy reflected the belief by successive administrations, by the Forest Service, and by many in Congress that road construction in national forests created a public asset. In time, however, the strategy's flaws became apparent. At the peak of the timber program between 1984 and 1990, approximately 6 million acres of forest were logged. Much of this harvest came from the Pacific Northwest, where the Forest Service and BLM sought to "fill the gap" left by earlier harvest of old-growth private forests. The agencies sold some 4 billion board feet of public timber each year. Even with these unsustainably high levels of logging, by 1989 only 47 percent of forest roads were being maintained to standard,[19] even though the Forest Service consistently requested higher road maintenance budgets than were allowed by the administration or funded by Congress.

By 1997, as harvest levels fell and timber purchasers assumed fewer and fewer road maintenance responsibilities, only 38 percent of the existing road system was maintained to the safety and environmental standards to which it was designed.[20] Even with the smaller timber program, the Forest Service had little choice but to continue to rely on timber sales to address its growing roads problem. Between 1992 and 1998, for example, more than 80 percent of all road reconstruction was financed through timber sale contracts.[21]

In hindsight, the shortcomings of this scenario are obvious. Without the ability to maintain high—unsustainably high—timber harvest levels, the Forest Service could not take care of its roads. Without adequate congressional appropriations, field managers were compelled to find other ways to maintain a deteriorating infrastructure and pay for employees and other projects. Many forest managers faced an impossible dilemma: arranging timber sales that required the buyer to attend to some of the outstanding road reconstruction needs or watching roads fall into disrepair. With easy-to-access timber already harvested, the only option to meet timber targets was to sell timber in more remote areas. The agency was trapped in a catch-22. The status quo, of course, served certain interests. Many in Congress and the Office of Management and Budget in the executive branch were happy to see timber receipts used to defray road maintenance costs, because such receipts did not count against the agency's discretionary budget.[22] For the timber industry, the status quo provided an incentive for forest managers to offer more timber sales.

The neglect of road maintenance is not simply a "timber issue." Recreation on National Forest System lands annually generates over $25 billion in total economic output.[23] Failure to maintain forest roads poses perhaps the greatest risk of losing access to public lands for public enjoyment—due to the growing maintenance backlog, for example, between 1990 and 1998 some 9200 miles of forest roads became impassable to passenger cars.[24] As road maintenance needs are increasingly unmet, the cost of repairing roads increases at an exponential rate. So, too, do safety risks. In December 2000, the Forest Service determined that only 13 percent of all forest roads were in good condition and 50 percent were in "poor condition and pose immediate threats to public safety or environmental degradation."[25]

Beyond the strong environmental benefits of protecting roadless areas, the fact that the maintenance backlog on Forest Service roads exceeded $8 billion was a very good reason to call a halt to building new roads in roadless areas. Certainly no corporate or private landowner would continue to build new roads into undeveloped areas in the face of such an immense liability.

The Natural Resource Agenda

The initial public endorsement of an end to development in roadless areas occurred on February 25, 1997, when Chief Dombeck testified before the Senate Energy and Natural Resources Committee on the health of the national forests. This testimony came in the immediate aftermath of what has become known as the "Timber Salvage Rider." Enacted as part of an emergency supplemental appropriations bill in 1995, the Salvage Rider suspended certain environmental laws and citizen appeal provisions in order to expedite the harvest of dead and dying trees following severe wildfires. The Salvage Rider created a firestorm of controversy among environmentalists, local communities, the timber industry, Congress, and the Forest Service. Testifying on the use of timber sales to promote forest health, the chief said: "The unfortunate reality is that many people do not presently trust the Forest Service to do the right thing. Until we rebuild that trust and strengthen those relationships, it is simply common sense that we avoid riparian, old growth, and roadless areas."[26]

At the time, some in Congress were debating changes in landmark environmental legislation such as the National Forest Management Act and the Endangered Species Act amid fears that the Forest Service had "lost its sense of mission." As public values shifted and the Forest Service's commodity production emphasis between 1970 and 1990 began to conflict with environmental laws protecting rare species and clean water, many argued that the agency was adrift. Retired employees lamented the loss of the Forest Service's sense of esprit de corps. Current employees complained about not knowing what their priorities should be. Some alleged that the mission of the agency was confused. They attributed this "confusion" to conflicts among environmental laws, shifts in social values, and the implementation of the Endangered Species Act.

The General Accounting Office endorsed that sentiment. At the February 1997 hearing, the General Accounting Office reported: "The Forest Service's decision-making process is broken and in need of repair." Their report went on to say that "disagreement over the Forest Service's priorities, both inside and outside the agency, has not only hampered efforts to improve the efficiency and effectiveness of its decision-making but also inhibited it in establishing the goals and performance measures needed to ensure its accountability."[27]

Some in the Forest Service did not believe that the laws needed to be amended. It was the agency's leadership, they said, that needed to clarify its priorities. One of the enduring dilemmas of multiple-use management is that it tends to create organizational functionalism—with all of the range, timber, fish and wildlife, and recreation specialists regarding their own programs as paramount. But if everything is a priority, there is no clear direction.

In the fall of 1997, the chief convened a meeting of senior agency leaders in St. Paul, Minnesota, to examine the priorities of the Forest Service. What flowed from this meeting eventually became known as the Natural Resource Agenda.[28] The agenda emphasized four topics: watershed health and restoration; ecologically sustainable forest and grassland management; recreation; and roads.

No New Roads?

Around the same time, senior policy staff in the chief's office began to discuss the idea of suspending new road construction in roadless areas until long-term road management reforms were initiated and a strategy was developed to protect roadless areas. In the face of withering congressional criticism about the lack of accountability in the Forest Service,[29] the concept of calling time-out on new road construction into roadless areas seemed obvious. How could the agency legitimize efforts to build new roads into pristine areas when it was getting less than 20 percent of the road maintenance funding it needed and carrying an $8.4 billion maintenance backlog?

In January 1998, the chief proposed suspending new road construction into most roadless areas, and assigned a team to oversee scientific and social analyses. The temporary suspension of new road construction was finalized in February 1999.[30] The new policy prohibited new road construction into inventoried roadless areas for eighteen months with the exception of forests that had recently revised forest management plans such as Alaska's Tongass National Forest and Pacific Northwest forests amended by the Northwest Forest Plan. Although the exemption of the Tongass and the Northwest Forest Plan drew harsh criticism from environmentalists, the moratorium was praised by others.[31] The response of some in Congress was less sanguine. In the context of a letter known to Forest Service employees as "the salvo of the Four Horsemen of the Apocalypse," Senators Frank Murkowski (R–Alaska) and Larry Craig (R–Idaho) and Representatives Don Young (R–Alaska) and Helen Chenoweth (R–Idaho) threatened to cut the agency's budget to a "custodial" level because the Forest Service was not harvesting as much timber as they liked and seemed "bent on producing fewer and fewer results from the national forests at rapidly increasing costs."[32]

Although the "Four Horsemen" letter was criticized as a "triumph of irrationality"[33] and a "schoolyard threat to take their football and go home,"[34] it demonstrated the frustration of those who represented commodity interests. With Congress unable to pass new legislation or otherwise resolve the controversy, with litigation determining more and more how national forests would be managed, Forest Service leaders believed it was up to them to resolve the issue.

A New Road Policy—or Long-Term Protection?

The road moratorium was designed to provide a time-out while a new long-term forest road policy was developed. The Forest Service received 119,000 public comments on the moratorium—at the time, the second largest in the agency's history—the vast majority of which called for the Forest Service to ensure "permanent protection" of inventoried roadless areas.

The road moratorium energized the environmental community. Accustomed to fighting agency projects, they found the roadless issue brought together local and national conservation groups in common cause: the long-term protection of roadless areas. Polls demonstrated nationwide support for roadless protection, and ad campaigns charged the chief and the president to develop a regulation that not only addressed the Forest Service's road problems but also protected roadless areas permanently.[35]

Moderate Republicans involved in the annual budget debates over forest roads in Congress also weighed in. Congressman John Porter (R–Illinois), the sponsor of the House appropriations amendment that came within a vote of cutting 80 percent of the forest road budget back in 1997, now expressed his "pleasure" that the Forest Service "is presently working on a forest road reform effort that I hope will obviate the need for future such debates in Congress." Anticipating the roadless issue, Porter suggested that the Forest Service "severely curtail new road construction in roadless areas system-wide until they have a better understanding of the ecological consequences and can afford to better manage the existing road system."[36] After the moratorium the agency's road budget, reversing years of decline, began to increase. The moratorium separated the issues of roadless area protection from the need to reform management of the 386,000-mile road system.

Agency leaders debated whether to focus the long-term road policy exclusively on road management or to combine road management issues and roadless area protection. Telegraphing the agency's direction, on July 1, 1998, the hundred-year anniversary of Gifford Pinchot's first day as a public servant, Chief Dombeck sent a letter to all employees on conservation leadership:

> To me, a conservation leader is someone who consistently
> errs on the side of maintaining and restoring healthy and
> diverse ecosystems even when—no, especially when—such
> decisions are not expedient or politically popular. . . . For
> example, our proposed suspension of road construction in
> roadless areas will help us develop not only a science-based
> long-term road policy but one that also reflects the values
> that society places on wild places, old growth, wilderness,
> and on intact and unfragmented landscapes. . . . We need
> to do a better job talking about, and managing for, the

values that are so important to so many people. Values such
as wilderness and roadless areas, clean water, protection of
rare species, old growth forests, naturalness—these are the
reasons most Americans cherish their public lands.[37]

After the road moratorium was finalized in February 1999, the chief's
office and White House staff discussed long-term options for protecting
roadless areas and the agency's desire to resolve the seemingly intractable
debate. Such meetings angered some in the Republican majority on Capi-
tol Hill—prompting numerous congressional information requests of
meeting notes, diaries, e-mail and other correspondence, and hearings and
investigations over the "inappropriate White House interference in the
roadless issue."[38] The Society of American Foresters went so far as to inform
the chief that his continued membership in their organization would
depend on the outcome of their "ethics investigation" into his involvement
in the roadless area issue. None of these investigations discovered any
infractions of law or ethics.

But not everyone was happy within the Forest Service, either. In 1998,
some five hundred employees, mostly field level, signed a letter asking the
chief to protect roadless areas. Others in leadership positions, however, were
uncomfortable with both the trajectory of the policy and the chief's relationship with the administration. Typical of these concerns was a letter to the
chief from a recently retired forest supervisor that said: "You are coming
across like the purist [sic] of pawns of this Administration, and not a leader
of a longstanding natural resource agency who's [sic] guidance has been provided by Congress. Past leaders understood the role of working with an
Administration and not being rolled over by it." The letter went on to chas-
tise the chief for "not emphasizing and leading the Forest Service in a mandated multiple use fashion."

The charge the chief's office worked too closely with the executive branch
was somewhat ironic. The first chief of the Forest Service, Gifford Pinchot,
enjoyed a personal and professional relationship with President Theodore
Roosevelt that led to a dramatic expansion of the forest reserves—a move
that was widely criticized by western congressmen at the time. Nearly a century later, the fact that the administration of George Herbert Bush ignored
findings of the Interagency Scientific Committee (headed by Jack Ward
Thomas) findings urging the protection of northern spotted owls and the
old-growth ecosystems on which they depend, turned the issue into a political football for those seeking to overturn the Endangered Species Act and

others seeking to use it to shut down the timber sale program in the Pacific Northwest.

F. Dale Robertson, chief of the Forest Service (1987–1993) throughout the spotted owl controversy, offers a unique perspective on utilizing the president's bully pulpit to advance public lands conservation. As President Bush was preparing to address an international environmental conference in Rio de Janeiro in 1992, Robertson received a series of anxious phone calls from William Reilly, then head of the Environmental Protection Agency and a former leader of the World Wildlife Fund. Reilly was concerned that the United States would be embarrassed in Rio by complaints from environmentalists and Democratic senators that clearcutting remained standard practice on public forest land in the United States. Robertson, who perhaps unfairly has borne the brunt of criticism for the Forest Service's response to the northern spotted owl/old-growth forest imbroglio in the Pacific Northwest, wrote a policy statement for the president announcing that clearcutting would be phased out as a standard practice. "Ecosystem management" would be the new objective for national forests. The announcement headlined the national news the next day. Later in an interview, Robertson said:

> [After the announcement was made] my phone was ringing again from industry, "what in the world are you doing, Chief?" Of course, I caught them by surprise. I caught everybody by surprise. But it was my one chance to get a major policy decision with the President's signature and settle all the debate. So Bush went down there and incorporated [the policy statement] into his speech in Rio, that we're changing major policies in managing our national forests.[39]

Years later, senior staff in the chief's office argued similarly for presidential involvement in helping to split the protection of inventoried roadless areas from development of a road management policy. Meetings were held with the White House to discuss the issue. At every decision meeting with the chief and his senior policy advisers, the chairman of the Council on Environmental Quality, George Frampton, and when present, White House Chief of Staff, John Podesta, would begin by asking: "How does the Forest Service want to proceed?"

There are distinct advantages and disadvantages to presidential involvement in an agency initiative. Bureaucratic infighting and process delays are part and parcel of all federal rulemaking. With White House support, however, they are quickly moved aside. Key issues in the Roadless Rule, for example, were discussed with an interagency group that included the Fish and Wildlife Service, the Environmental Protection Agency, the Small Business Association, the Office of Management and Budget, and other federal agencies.[40] These meetings sped up a White House clearance process that could have resulted in interminable delays. But Presidential involvement also heightened the political stakes dramatically—and hence opposition from those who opposed the president for political or personal reasons.

Federal agencies routinely undertake initiatives that drag on for years, even decades. With the White House investing significant political capital in its success, not completing the Roadless Rule was never an option for the Forest Service. One thing is certain. Without the active interest of the president and his staff, the roadless issue would no doubt have languished in controversy—flummoxing field managers and stalling completion of other priorities.

The Roadless Rule

On October 13, 1999, a crystal clear day with the George Washington National Forest's Reddish Knob roadless area as a backdrop, President Clinton spoke to the nation about the value of roadless areas. The president said: "Within our national forests there are large parcels of land that don't contain roads of any kind. . . . These areas represent some of the last, best, unprotected wildland anywhere in our nation." Then the president directed the Forest Service to develop options for protecting roadless areas:

> I have determined that it is in the best interest of our Nation . . . to provide strong and lasting protection for these forests. . . . Specifically, I direct the Forest Service to develop, and propose for public comment, regulations to provide appropriate long-term protection for most or all of these currently inventoried "roadless" areas.[41]

Within days of the president's announcement, the Forest Service initiated the process to begin development of the regulation. More than 16,000 people attended 187 "scoping" meetings that elicited more than 517,000 responses and helped the Forest Service to determine what issues should be analyzed to develop a final rule. Opponents of the effort faulted the agency because maps detailing all of the inventoried roadless areas were not immediately available, and hundreds of requests for an extension of the comment period were received. The Forest Service opted not to grant an extension, however, because opportunities for public comment would follow release of a draft plan in subsequent months. Moreover, at the time the Forest Service did not know what areas would be included because it had yet to develop any alternatives for public review. Once the alternatives were drafted and the analysis was released for comment, maps of all roadless areas were posted on a Website and made available to the public.

A team of Forest Service employees led by a forest supervisor was brought in to conduct the analysis required for the environmental impact statement. Wishing to avoid unnecessary bureaucratic delays, the analysis team was structured under the Incident Command System—a scheme used to manage large wildfires. At the group's first meeting a decision-making structure was developed that ensured all policy decisions would be quickly reviewed and answered by the deputy chief for National Forest Systems, the associate chief for natural resources, and the senior policy adviser to the chief. Decisions needing the chief's or Secretary Glickman's involvement were not allowed to languish. Critics allege that typical agency rulemaking takes many years to complete—if indeed ever it reaches fruition—and that the Roadless Rule was developed at top speed simply to have it completed before the 2000 presidential elections. In fact, this was not an insignificant factor for Forest Service leaders. Clearly the Clinton administration wanted the rule to be finished under the president's watch, as it was he who directed its initiation.

The Forest Service team retained control of the rulemaking process by working directly with the chief's office for decisions and the precise wording of the rule. They were assisted with comments from those associated with the project, upper agency management, and the agency's regulations and directives office. This separation of the rule writing from the socioeconomic and environmental analyses helped to maintain the team's objectivity by insulating them from the political debates and extensive staff work that accompany such controversial issues.[42] The team, many of them away from home for extended periods, conducted a detailed analysis and review in a short time—dispelling the notion that large-scale conservation initiatives inevitably result in endless study and review.

Public debate moved quickly from the issue of roads in roadless areas to the protection of roadless areas for their inherent values. This became clear when the Forest Service released its draft environmental analysis and proposed to end new road construction in roadless areas but did not address logging and application of the rule to Alaska's Tongass National Forest. Under the proposed rule, a decision on the Tongass was postponed until the regularly scheduled forest plan review in 2004. Environmentalists were angered that timber harvest was not banned from roadless areas and that the Tongass was not included in the proposal. Off-road vehicle users were concerned that a provision of the proposed rule calling for identification of roadless values could block their access and use of roadless areas. The timber industry argued that roads were needed for forest health. Each interest put its own "spin" on the issue.

Public comment on the proposed rule was overwhelming. More than a million comments were received—most on pre-addressed, printed postcards from environmental groups. Although the majority of citizen comments from every state except Idaho favored increased protection of roadless areas,[43] the response from state governments depended on demographics. Officials representing rural counties adjacent to public lands generally thought they should be able to build roads or harvest timber for either commodity production or forest health reasons. Officials from urban areas wanted to see roadless areas protected for their values as unfragmented landscapes, scenic beauty, recreation opportunities, or sources of drinking water. The comments from elected officials in the state of Washington are representative of this trend. The governor of the state, as well as King and Spokane counties and the Seattle City Council, all called for increased protection of roadless areas while rural areas such as Stevens County, the City of Forks, and the City of Port Angeles were opposed.[44]

Concerns were raised about the effect of the proposed rule on public access, forest health, energy supplies, and fire management. In response, the final rule guaranteed legal access to state and private inholdings. No existing roads would be closed. Existing off-road vehicle access was ensured, and future decisions on public access were left to the forest planning process. Exemptions were provided allowing road construction for human safety reasons and for firefighting. And, in response to concerns about energy supplies, roadless areas presently under lease to oil and gas companies were essentially exempt. The two thorniest issues were timber harvest and whether the rule applied to the Tongass National Forest. Public comment was overwhelmingly in support of including the Tongass and applying the strictest protections possible to roadless areas. Surveys conducted by Republican pollsters affirmed that public comment broadly reflected public sentiment.[45]

Politically, the Tongass was vexing. Alaska's powerful congressional delegation—including Ted Stevens (R), chairman of the Senate Appropriations Committee, Frank Murkowski (R), chairman of the Energy and Natural Resources Committee, and Don Young (R), chairman of the House Resources Committee—was strongly opposed to the Roadless Rule. Moreover, the Tongass had recently begun implementation of an expensive new forest plan that had taken more than a decade to complete. From a substantive perspective, however, the Tongass was the easier of the two issues. The Tongass contains nearly one-quarter of the world's intact temperate rainforests. The Forest Service could not reasonably call for protection of fragmented roadless areas in the lower 48 while leaving unprotected the one national forest where they existed in abundance—especially while other nations were being criticized for cutting rainforests. Not only that but the Tongass road system was in notoriously poor condition. A joint Forest Service and Alaska Fish and Game study reviewed the condition of 60 percent of the permanent roads in the Tongass and found that "sixty-six percent of the culverts across anadromous streams (Forest Service Class I streams) are assumed not to be adequate for fish passage. Eighty-five percent of the culverts across resident fish streams (Forest Service Class II streams that naturally do not support anadromous fish) are assumed not to be adequate for fish passage."[46]

Fiscally, the Tongass fared little better. In fiscal year 1998, for example, due to costs associated with logging and road building in the remote forest, the Tongass lost nearly $30 million in selling public timber—about 30 percent of the money lost on the entire national-forest timber sale program that year.[47] That timber sales cost more to prepare than they generate in revenues is not always inappropriate. Sometimes the sales can be used to accomplish broader stewardship objectives. In such cases, the timber sale is simply a means to achieving a larger management goal. In the Tongass, however, all of the timber sales are "commodity purpose," that is, their primary purpose is to sell public timber (in this case, at a loss) for private profit.

Whether or not to prohibit timber harvests, struck at the core of the Forest Service. Since the proposed road moratorium, in light of the $8.4 billion road maintenance backlog, the fiscal arguments for ending new road construction in roadless areas had begun to take hold within the agency. Limiting timber harvest, however, as countless public comments called for, compromised strong beliefs among many forest supervisors and field managers that they themselves should retain maximum discretion in planning timber sales. Moreover, some agency personnel disputed the roadless initiative's apparent intent to override locally developed forest plans. Several of the agency's regional foresters said that in light of the public response, the new rule should address timber harvest in some form, otherwise people would regard the public comment period as a sham. However, no regional foresters supported an alternative that would prohibit all forms of vegetative management and timber harvest in roadless areas. Intense pressure was brought to bear on the Clinton administration by the environmental community— many of whom wanted roadless areas left untouched so they might qualify for future wilderness designation. On the other side, the timber industry argued that without timber sales, roadless areas would be subject to insect and disease outbreaks and catastrophic wildfires due to decades of fire suppression.

The Forest Service's senior leadership believed that banning all timber harvest would eliminate management tools that could be used to restore forest ecosystem health and lessen the risk of unnaturally intense fires. This rationale did not apply to road construction, however, because it made little sense to trade a potential remedy for one liability—building roads to facilitate forest thinning—in a way that would certainly increase another liability: the road maintenance backlog.

The priority for fuel reduction, however, was not remote roadless areas. It was in places where communities and forests intersect. And these, by definition, are not typically remote roadless areas. Thus the agency decided to allow the harvest of "generally small-diameter" trees for clearly defined circumstances. Permissible under the rule were forest thinning projects to reduce fuel loads so long as they did not require new road construction. Similarly, the cutting or removal of small-diameter trees was permitted if it was essential for recovery or conservation of threatened, endangered, proposed, or sensitive species. In all cases, the rule made it clear that cutting, selling, or removing small-diameter trees would be rare and consistent with preserving the ecological values of roadless areas.

Upon taking office in January 2001, the new Bush administration suspended implementation of the Roadless Rule and a series of other federal environmental measures that had recently taken effect. Later, the administration's unwillingness to defend the rule against lawsuits brought by industry users and several western states prompted the Forest Service chief to express his disappointment with the lackluster legal defense of the Agriculture and Justice departments. Chief Dombeck wrote:

> The Forest Service recently concluded nearly two years of analysis and public process, involving over 600 public meetings and 1.6 million comments—over 90 percent of which supported roadless area protection. I understand that the Department may have political motives for not supporting the protection of roadless areas. I hope, however, it would have the integrity to act in a more open and forthright manner than that displayed by the Administration's legal filings last week.[48]

Days later, Dombeck stepped down as head of the Forest Service. Eventually the Roadless Rule was enjoined by a district court in Idaho and appealed to the Ninth Circuit by environmental groups and others. The administration did not defend against lawsuits or appeal the injunction. The new chief of the Forest Service, Dale Bosworth, serving under President Bush, opted to make all decisions to build roads or harvest timber in roadless areas subject to his or a regional forester's approval. Once forest plans are amended or revised, the fate of roadless areas would once again be determined on a local basis through forest planning.

Critics may disagree with the Roadless Rule because it deviates from their own values. But, unlike some past efforts, in this case the public process was not used to forestall or obfuscate. Instead the Forest Service allowed public sentiment and sound science to shape the outcome of the rule—and in the process affirmed the value of public opinion in management of public lands. Many critics allege that the Roadless Rule illegally circumvented the NFMA planning process. Ultimately the courts or the political appointees that oversee the Forest Service may well determine that the rulemaking process was flawed. But such determinations will not diminish the national desire to keep these last undeveloped areas intact.

The Roadless Rule was part of a conscious effort to demonstrate that the Forest Service would not shy away from such controversies as clearcutting or northern spotted owl/old-growth protection that have dogged, and come to define the agency for many people. Regardless of legal and political wrangling, the era of road building in the Forest Service has come to an end. The Roadless Rule publicly formalized what had become a reality—a reality that some still refuse to accept, however, despite overwhelming public support and economic and scientific rationale.

Decades of controversy over such issues has bred a culture of cynicism regarding public land management—a mistrust that pervades Congress, public land managers, local communities, the media, and interest groups. One reason for protecting roadless areas was to end the cycle of contention, distrust, and litigation that had plagued multiple-use management of public lands for two decades or more. The Bitterroot and Monongahela clearcutting controversies and the northern spotted owl imbroglio make it clear that allowing long-standing contentious issues to simmer ends up limiting policy options and narrowing the decision space for agency leaders.

A willingness to exert leadership over festering national controversies and rebuild public trust is essential to breaking the cycle of controversy that has beset the Forest Service and BLM for decades. As Undersecretary James Lyons said: "In the absence of adequately addressing the roadless issue, it is questionable whether the public would support other actions needed to restore healthy, diverse, resilient, and productive national forests and grasslands."[49] Perhaps the most painful lesson the Forest Service learned between 1970 and 2000 is that thorny issues such as old growth, clearcutting, and roadless areas do not get any easier through delay or by forcing local managers to attempt to resolve national controversies on a forest-by-forest or project-by-project basis.

The Roadless Rule offered a rare opportunity to mesh a science-based solution that was good for the land with overwhelming public support for protection. For natural resources with national significance such as roadless areas, the forest planning process (and the inescapable political pressures built into it) is often an inadequate tool for balancing the national interest against local demands. Political elections occur every four years or so. But roadless areas—and their wildlife and fish habitats, their clean drinking water, and their opportunities for an urbanized nation to reconnect with nature—transcend such time frames. As the writer Ian McTaggert Cowan once said: "In our militant enthusiasm to throw back the wilderness and open up this continent for man, we have been so far successful that we are about to destroy a part of us that is as indispensable as it is irreplaceable."[50]

Innovation and development helped make this nation great. In the final analysis, however, it is respect for our lands and waters—the sort of humility that allows roadless areas to persist—that will sustain us and allow us to endure.

Chapter 6

Restoration: Healing the Land and Healing Ourselves

Restoration work . . . is accepting an abandoned responsibility. It is a humble and often joyful mending of biological ties, with the hope clearly recognized, that working from this foundation we might, too, begin to mend human society.

—Barry Lopez, *An Introduction to Environmental Restoration* (1991)

Society needs a renewed commitment to restore the health of our lands and waters. Whether the issue is the decline of salmon in the Columbia River, the invasion of exotic weeds, unnaturally intense fires in the West, declining aquatic species in the Great Lakes, loss of longleaf pine forests in the Southeast, or protecting the integrity of roadless areas, we are increasingly reminded of the need to live within the limits of the land. Countless benefits from the land sustain us daily, but often we take them for granted. If future generations are to enjoy benefits we take for granted—clean water, stable and productive soils, healthy forests and grasslands, diverse fish and wildlife populations—a restoration ethic must be nurtured. Not only do our livelihood and quality of life depend on a sustainable relationship with the land, but restoring the land's health is a moral responsibility. Making the transition from a consumptive culture bent on resource exploitation to one that embraces restoration and a sustainable land ethic is the foremost challenge facing not only public land managers but our nation as a whole.

Technology, Ecology, and Land Health

Space travel brought us the first photographic images of our own planet—a stark reminder that there truly are limits to the land, that the earth is finite. Through the 1960s and 1970s, this realization of the limits of our planet was affirmed by problems such as air pollution in Los Angeles that sickened and hospitalized thousands, the burning of the polluted Cuyahoga River in Cleveland, Ohio, and the decline of the bald eagle, our national symbol. Today we recognize that the soil, air, and water are our life support system and improved stewardship of the land is critical to our long-term survival.

For all but the last few centuries, human life, particularly in the Americas, depended entirely on natural systems. These systems supplied food, air, and water of sufficient quantity and quality to sustain human life. Waste products for the most part remained within ecological limits and were naturally processed and recycled. Only in the last century have the combination of human population and technological prowess put new global-scale stresses on the planet.

Focus Essay

The Once and Future Land Ethic
CURT MEINE AND NINA LEOPOLD BRADLEY*

When Aldo Leopold's *A Sand County Almanac* appeared in 1949, few foresaw the impact that the book, and especially its capstone essay "The Land Ethic," would have. Conservation science, policy, and practice have contin-

*Curt Meine is director of conservation programs with the Wisconsin Academy of Sciences, Arts, and Letters and a biographer of Aldo Leopold. Nina Leopold Bradley, a noted naturalist and botanist, is the daughter of Aldo Leopold.

ued to respond to Leopold's call to see land as "a community to which we belong." Yet Leopold understood the land ethic, not as one individual's effort, but as "a product of social evolution" forming "in the minds of a thinking community." And "evolution never stops."

Perhaps Leopold recognized the contingent nature of the land ethic because the idea itself evolved continually in his own thinking and in widely varied landscapes. In his work to conserve private lands (including his own), Leopold came to appreciate the key role played by individual responsibility for land health. In his efforts to conserve public lands, Leopold came to appreciate the challenge of managing land in the long-term public interest. "The Land Ethic" was Leopold's final effort to synthesize these lessons of individual and social responsibility in conservation.

But, following Leopold's lead, we know that synthesis does not cease. How must the land ethic evolve in order to thrive and guide conservation in the new century? There are, of course, innumerable answers to this question. We can, however, recognize at least some of the overarching challenges facing conservation philosophy and practice.

The land ethic will need to embrace, and be embraced by, new constituencies. Leopold's land ethic reflected the social realities of his time and place. How do we encourage the land ethic within constantly changing human communities with diverse traditions and varied relationships to land?

The land ethic will need to respond to emerging scientific insights and shifting scientific foundations. Leopold's land ethic rested on a solid foundation of integrated natural science subject to continuing intellectual evolution. How can we ensure that the land ethic will continue to absorb, reflect, and adapt to the insights that flow from the natural sciences?

The land ethic will need to extend across—and recognize connections within—the entire landscape. Leopold's land ethic focused on the health of wild, semiwild, and rural lands across the broad spectrum of conservation interests. Since Leopold's day, conservation's constituency has suffered fragmentation, reflected especially in the increased polarization among urban and suburban environmentalists and rural people who own and work land. How can we revive and strengthen bonds of common interest within the landscape and within conservation?

The land ethic will need to reach into the marine realm. Leopold did not address issues of marine conservation except by implication. Only in the 1990s did conservation biologists begin to devote serious attention to the conservation of marine biodiversity and the functions of the oceans as a community. How can we extend the land ethic to embrace and encourage an "ocean ethic"?

The land ethic will need to confront directly the challenges posed by human population growth and contribute to the shaping of a parallel "consumption ethic." This remains one of conservation's most politically and economically vexing topics. How can the land ethic help to address the issue of population growth responsibly, respectfully, and effectively? Will we recognize—and act upon—the inescapable connections between ecosystem health and resource consumption?

The land ethic will need to help redefine the traditional economic worldview to include conservation concerns in a fundamental way. Conservation has had a hard time getting a full hearing by the dominant schools of neoclassical economics. Can the land ethic have deep and meaningful impact on the human economic enterprise?

The land ethic will need to engage—and find acceptance within—diverse professions. We cannot achieve our conservation goals if only biologists and resource managers are working in their behalf. An effective land ethic will require commitment from a range of professions. How can we speed this process and encourage innovative thinking among, for example, engineers, planners, manufacturers, journalists, educators, and health care professionals?

The land ethic will need to encourage awareness and critical thinking among the young. Environmental education has made great strides in recent decades. How will changes in education and in society affect the next generation's sense of personal engagement? We also face a more specific challenge: how do we sustain traditions and historical awareness of our conservation legacy during times of such rapid social and cultural change?

The land ethic will need to build the foundations for vastly expanded community-based conservation projects. Conservation has always reflected our inherent tension between top-down centralized approaches and bottom-up grassroot approaches. But this can be a creative tension. How can we evoke a sense of local responsibility for the full spectrum of land values while stimulating cooperative measures to restore and sustain land health?

Finally, the land ethic will need to recognize its strong roots in the American experience while encouraging its adoption in other settings. A thriving land ethic will draw on expressions of stewardship from diverse cultural sources. We must continue to explore these varied traditions and forge new links that can contribute to a more robust conservation vision. That process has a long history not only on this continent but around the world. It began long before Aldo Leopold wrote his "tentative summary." It will last as long as we care about people, land, and the connections between them.

The agricultural and industrial revolutions enabled human numbers to increase and concentrate in cities and towns. Human population levels continued to grow, and consequently human society became dependent on a support system that is both natural and technological. Today the natural support system alone can no longer sustain our population or our lifestyle. From food production to water systems and sewage disposal in big cities, we now rely on advanced technology to assist ecological processes and sustain human life on the planet. Now we have the added responsibility of maintaining the integrity of our natural support system, our technological support system, and the balance between the two.[1]

The land provides our basic biological needs of food, water, and shelter. As a society we tend to take many of these ecosystem services for granted. We are most familiar with the commodities that are bought and sold in the marketplace. Items such as agricultural crops, timber, commercial fish products, and pharmaceuticals have specific values that are widely publicized and understood in economic markets. Many vitally important ecosystem services are often considered "free" because they are not bought and sold in the marketplace and their monetary value is not obvious. Yet countless ecological services create an invisible foundation that supports life, societies, and economies.[2]

Here are some examples of ecosystem services that support life and enhance human society:

- Capture and conversion of solar energy into biomass for food and shelter.
- Decomposition of waste and sewage.
- Regeneration of nutrients essential to plant growth (nitrogen fixation).
- Storage, purification, and distribution of water.
- Creation and maintenance of soils.
- Control of insect pests by animals such as birds and bats.
- Preservation of the genetic library for development of new food and drugs by selective breeding and bioengineering.
- Maintenance of air quality.
- Control of micro- and macroclimates.
- Capacity for recovering from natural stresses such as floods, fire, pestilence.
- Pollination of plants, including agricultural crops, by insects, bats, and others.
- Aesthetic enrichment, recreation, inspiration.

We tend to undervalue these ecosystem services. Behind all the commodities and commercial products that have an obvious market value are well-organized constituencies to influence policy. There are lobbies for logging, mining, and livestock grazing, even lobbies for roadside billboard signs.

Few lobbies exist for rebuilding topsoils. Yet soils moderate the water cycle, provide physical support for plants, shelter seeds, regulate element cycles such as carbon and nitrogen, and recycle wastes into plant nutrients. Nearly 140 billion tons of dead organic material and waste are processed and recycled by the soil. Of this volume, about 30 percent is generated by humans.[3]

Forests are widely valued for their supply of wood for paper and building materials. Yet we scarcely hear about the many ecosystem services that technology cannot replicate, particularly at the landscape scale. Studies by Cornell University ecologist David Pimentel have documented the critical role of forest vegetation in holding topsoil on the land. He found that under normal conditions an acre of land loses less than 100 pounds of soil to erosion each year—less than what is added through soil-building processes, resulting in a net gain of topsoil each year. Lands recently used for logging, grazing, or crop production in the United States and Europe, by contrast, had erosion rates of about 7 tons per acre every year and 12 to 16 tons in Asia, Africa, and South America. On the most severely degraded lands, erosion can be as high as 40 tons per acre a year.[4] This is a massive loss of topsoil.

The value of forests as a source of high-quality water is often overlooked. Forests make up some 760 million acres or one-third of the U.S. land base but supply about two-thirds of the runoff. The 192 million acres of national forests make up 8 percent of the land base but provide about 14 percent of the runoff. In the state of California, the 20 million acres of national forests make up about 20 percent of the land base but provide over 50 percent of that state's water supply.[5] National forest watersheds supply drinking water for an estimated 60 million people. Given the increasing scarcity of clean water, it may well be the most valuable forest product.

Urban forestry researcher Greg McPherson analyzed the value associated with one large front yard tree in the San Joaquin Valley of California:[6]

- It saves $29 in summertime air conditioning costs or about 9 percent of the annual cost.
- It absorbs 10 pounds of air pollutants, including 4 pounds of ozone and 3 pounds of particulates. This is worth $45 in emission reduction credits.
- The nitrogen oxide emissions (NO_x) uptake of 1.07 pounds is equivalent to the emission of an average car driven 188 miles.
- It intercepts 750 gallons of rainfall, reducing polluted runoff and flooding at an estimated $6 annually.
- It cleans (sequesters) 330 pounds of carbon dioxide and 90 pounds of carbon from the atmosphere.

McPherson's research demonstrates that even one big tree can provide substantial ecosystem services on a local scale. In the Southeast, researchers

Linda Anderson and Ken Cordell reported that a single large tree in the yard adds about 1 percent to the sale price of the property.[7] Our appreciation of the services we get from lands and waters, and the complexity of their underpinning processes, are intrinsic to understanding the value of land health.

Though our understanding of ecology today is better than ever, a comprehensive definition of land health remains elusive. Aldo Leopold defined it as the "capacity for self-renewal in the biota."[8] This is consistent with the Webster's Dictionary definition of health as "optimal functioning." Jane Abramovitz, senior researcher at the Worldwatch Institute, refers to self-regulating processes as the mechanisms that keep ecosystems and the biosphere stable and resilient: "The ability to withstand disturbances like fires, floods, diseases, and droughts, and to rebound from the shocks these events inflict, is essential to keeping the life-support system operating."[9] The interaction of vegetation, soil, water, and air is basic to good land health, as are the concepts of self-renewal, function, sustainability, and resilience.

Why is it so much easier to describe an unhealthy ecosystem than one that is healthy? We can improve our understanding of land health by considering problems associated with "unhealthy land." General symptoms of ecological decline include loss of species diversity and habitat complexity, abundance of invasive species reducing native species, waning in productivity, and disruption of energy.[10] Table 6-1 lists a few symptoms of dysfunction in terrestrial, riparian-wetland, and lake and river systems.

It is important not to confuse degraded land health with short-term natural occurrences such as wildfire, flood, and insect infestation. Change is the one constant in nature. From the repeated "100-year" flood events on our larger rivers we have learned that no matter how we ditch, dike, levee, or

Table 6-1. Signs of Unhealthy Land Condition in Terrestrial, Riparian-Wetland, and Lake and Rivers Systems

TERRESTRIAL SYSTEMS	RIPARIAN-WETLAND SYSTEMS	LAKE AND RIVER SYSTEMS
Accelerated runoff	Reduced ability to moderate floods	Bank erosion and altered channel morphology
Accelerated rates of soil loss	Altered vegetation and soil condition	Water temperature, sediment load, and nutrients beyond expected range
Change in fire frequency and intensity	Reduced ability to filter sediments	Increased municipal water filtration costs
Reduced ability to recover from drought	Reduced water-holding capacity	Decline in water quality

dam a river it will eventually find its floodplain. Similarly, we have learned from increasingly intense wildfires on fire-dependent landscapes that no matter how many resources we deploy to suppress wildfire, fire-dependent forests, rangelands, and chaparral will burn.

The Concept of Restoration

Ecosystem restoration focuses on the recovery of unhealthy lands and waters. Restoration implies reestablishment of the structure and function of an ecosystem, including its natural diversity.[11] "Structure" includes the native species diversity, both plant and animal. "Function" refers to an ecosystem's productivity (growth of plant biomass is the basis of food webs) and the interaction of soil, water, and vegetation in a manner that sustains the system itself. Conceptually, restoration may be viewed as reversing the decline and improving degraded lands and waters. Simply recreating the form of an ecosystem without its function—or creating the functions in some artificial

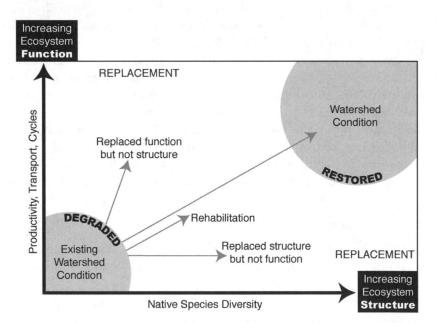

Figure 6-1. Redirecting the trajectory of a degraded ecosystem—a primary goal in restoration. This redirection applies both to its structure (species complexity) and its function (biomass and nutrients). Trajectories away from its original structure and function result in further degradation, partial rehabilitation, or novel conditions. Modified from A. D. Bradshaw, "Ecological Principles and Land Reclamation Practice," *Landscape Planning* 11 (1984):35–84.

way—does not constitute restoration. As depicted in Figure 6-1, the goal of restoration is to redirect the trajectory of a degraded ecosystem toward historic conditions.[12] The structure and function of an ecosystem are restored when ecological processes and the biological components are healthy and functioning.

Rehabilitation, reclamation, habitat recreation, or mitigation can be achieved through manipulation of site-specific or isolated problems and elements of ecosystems. But true restoration is a more complex and integrated undertaking. Successful restoration means that ecosystem structure and function are repaired and that natural ecosystem processes occur. These distinctions between restoration and such concepts as rehabilitation or reclamation may seem subtle, but they are fundamental to defining and achieving successful watershed restoration.

Restoration means taking the long view. It is a rigorous, comprehensive, and adaptive process. It is not site or problem specific. A striking example of a series of unsuccessful piecemeal fixes is the attempt to reverse salmon declines in the Columbia River basin through improved technology while ignoring the health of the rivers and watersheds themselves. Fish ladders were constructed around many of the large dams to permit passage of salmon during their upstream spawning migration. Little thought, however, was given to the downstream migration of salmon smolts. Subsequent actions included barging smolts downstream around dams, instituting bounties on predators such as pikeminnow, releasing hatchery-reared fish, and artificial attempts to mimic higher spring flows. Habitat management was improved; harvest was curtailed. To date, billions have been spent to "restore" the salmon of the Columbia River basin. But our collective unwillingness to address the fundamental problem of monolithic dams on the Columbia River basin and the Snake River, dams that serve limited public purpose, almost ensures the extinction of many native runs of salmon and steelhead.

Restoration must take into consideration the historic conditions of watersheds—including an understanding of how human and natural disturbances have shaped the system. Historically we have applied simple solutions and technological quick fixes to complex problems and then react with surprise when they fail. During the 1950s and 1960s, for example, logjams and woody debris were removed from Pacific coastal streams to improve fish passage. Then stream and watershed managers began to recognize the critical value of wood in streams as food for insects and structure in creating pools. More recently, large quantities of wood have been put back into coastal rivers.[13] Restoration must treat the *primary* causes of degradation—thereby setting the stage for a dysfunctional ecosystem to heal itself. As a result of actions taken in the 1990s, many forested riparian zones are now managed to allow trees to mature and fall naturally into the rivers.[14]

Restoration requires a constituency. Rivers cannot be divorced from the uplands. Watersheds cannot be managed apart from their communities. Communities of interest and communities of place must work together to develop long-term objectives. They must ask the basic questions: What do we want the land to look like? What will future generations need from the land in fifty or a hundred years? We must learn the limits of the land and be willing to live within those limits. And there is another basic question that must be asked: Is restoration succeeding? Restoration requires continuous monitoring, learning, and evaluation of progress. Although no single model can guarantee success, a basic conceptual framework for restoration is outlined in Figure 6-2.[15]

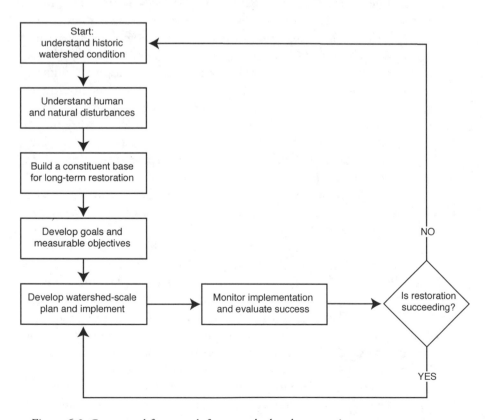

Figure 6-2. Conceptual framework for watershed-scale restoration.

The Paradox of Smokey Bear

The history of wildfire in the United States and our attempt to control it offers many lessons that can guide restoration of the land. A century ago wildfire was considered the number one enemy of the forest, a dangerous force that had to be "snuffed out cold." Public opinion—that all wildfire is bad—was shaped by destructive fires that ravaged the West and Midwest in the late 1800s and early 1900s following the "cut and run" logging era. The combination of leftover slash and drought produced huge uncontrollable wildfires that Americans had never before experienced. The 1871 Peshtigo Fire in northeastern Wisconsin, where some 1500 people died and over 1.2 million acres burned, remains the single most tragic wildfire in our history.[16] Ironically the great Chicago Fire that instilled such fear into urban dwellers, apocryphally started by Mrs. Brown's cow that kicked over a lantern, was burning at the same time as the Peshtigo Fire. The serious fires of 1910 focused the populace on declaring war on wildfires. By the 1930s the Forest Service had developed the most effective wildfire fighting capability in the world. Indeed, firefighting became the agency's top priority. In 1935 the "all fires out by 10 AM" policy was formally adopted.[17]

The slogan "remember only you can prevent forest fires" with Smokey Bear as the mascot was perhaps the most successful conservation campaign ever. In 1968, a national advertising research report noted that Smokey was the most popular symbol in the United States—better known than the president.[18] The "all wildfire is bad" perception became as American as baseball. The National Interagency Fire Center was established in Boise, Idaho, in the 1960s as the wildfire fighting command center and soon became a model of government agency cooperation.

The huge 1988 wildfires in and around Yellowstone National Park initiated a public reawakening to the fact that fire is not always bad. The 1988 wildfires helped people understand that even with fire's short-term and potentially destructive social costs, wildfire plays an important role in maintaining land health. Throughout the 1990s and again in 2000, in 2001, and in 2002 the exceptional severity and magnitude of the fires in the West served as a constant reminder that fire is a natural force that cannot be completely controlled. In 1994, fourteen firefighters died tragically on Colorado's Storm King Mountain. That year a total of thirty-four people died fighting wildfire. In 2000, wildfires were front-page news from May to September—starting with the loss of over two hundred homes in the Cerro Grande fire in Los Alamos, New Mexico, and continuing with a series of huge fires in Montana and Idaho. The severity of the fires that year even attracted the attention of the president. Bill Clinton was perhaps the first president in history to tour a wildfire, visiting the Burgdorff Junction fire camp in Idaho. In 2002, President George W. Bush toured the wildfires in Arizona and Oregon. The years 1988, 1994, 2000, and 2002 were clarion calls that society's century-long attempt to control fire in the fire-adapted ecosystems of the West was not working. With advanced technology and the skill of fire fighters, 98 percent of wildfires are snuffed out in an initial attack. Despite these advances the total acres burned have generally been mounting since the mid-1980s.[19]

We now realize, more than ever, that fire is as much a part of nature as wind and rain. Our zealous and successful effort to suppress all fire was a major reason behind the severity of these recent wildfires. The exclusion of fire allows the continued accumulation of fuels—so when wildfires do occur, they are more intense. Human intervention in this natural process has actually skewed the intensity of wildfire toward catastrophic. Most of the forest and grassland ecosystems of the interior West are "short-interval" fire-adapted ecosystems. They evolved the ability to thrive with frequent low-intensity fires. Periodic low-intensity burning enhances nutrient recycling, reduces fuels and the encroachment of competing vegetation, and contributes to overall land health.

Burning was commonly practiced by Native Americans. By the late 1800s, curtailment of this practice began to alter the composition, structure, and function of ecosystems. Fire-tolerant species such as ponderosa pine began to be replaced by fire-intolerant species such as Douglas-fir. Cattle and sheep grazing and forests cleared for agriculture altered many long-standing natural processes and cultural practices. A typical fire-adapted forest ecosystem in the Intermountain West may once have had fifty large ponderosa pine per acre, a fire-tolerant species. Without the culling effects of fire, shade-tolerant seedlings filled in beneath old-growth ponderosa pine. The open parklike forest became a dense tangle of flammable vegetation. Gradually the structure changed to a forest of perhaps 300 to 500, mostly small, fire-intolerant trees per acre. This increased density of trees and brush provides more fuels. So when fire does occur it burns much hotter, often burning into the crowns of the remaining large old-growth trees, killing the trees and destroying topsoil as well. In many areas, harvest of the old-growth overstory and clearcutting practices in combination with suppression of natural fire further compounded the fire risk. Scientific assessments indicate that in the upper Columbia River basin, prior to European settlement, about 6 million acres burned every year. With the recent campaign of intense fire suppression, fewer than half a million acres burned each year.[20]

Today, some fifteen years after the awesome 1988 Yellowstone fires, the park has bounced back and its overall ecological function is improved. Ecosystems such as our western forests evolved with fire and are shaped by fire. Despite a century of fire suppression, we have learned that it is not *if* they will burn, but when and where and with what intensity. The role of natural wildfire in ecosystems clearly demonstrates the interconnectedness of natural processes in maintaining land health. A century of widespread suppression of fire has resulted in altered ecosystems and much more serious fires during unusually dry years. In many cases, it is our interruption of natural processes that led to the land's inability to heal itself—resulting in even more serious problems. And because public land issues are more social than technical, fire has become the golden calf for those who advocate a return to higher logging levels on public lands by "fireproofing" forests through logging. Consider the position taken by two prominent national newspapers in 2002 in response to the 135,000-acre Hayman Fire in Colorado, which was caused by humans. The *Wall Street Journal* had this to say:

> How did one of America's great resources come to such a pass? Look no further than the greens who trouped into power with the last Administration. Senior officials adopted an untested philosophy known as "ecosystem management," a bourgeois bohemian plan to return forests to their "natural" state. The Clintonites cut back timber harvesting by 80 percent and used laws and lawsuits to put swaths of land off-limits to commercial use.[21]

Nine days later the *New York Times* published the following editorial in response:

> That is, of course, a preposterous reading of nature and history, not to mention of Mr. Clinton. Ecosystem management—managing the forests to protect watersheds and the wildlife and humans who depend on them, rather than commercial interests alone—took root in the first Bush administration. That is also when logging began to decline, largely as a result of Judge William Dwyer's landmark decision to protect huge swaths of spotted owl habitat in the Pacific Northwest from clear-cutting. The notion that environmental lawsuits have hindered fire-prevention projects is equally absurd. According to a federal study last summer, fewer than one percent of 1,671 fire-prevention projects had been appealed. A greater obstacle to fire prevention

may have been the governors themselves, some of whom
have resisted the Forest Service's proven strategy of preventing larger fires with smaller, controlled burns.[22]

The fire debate—certain to arise whenever drought, wind, and bad luck
coincide—should not be a clash of titans, a battle between rapacious industries and environmental pantheists. It should be about correcting decades of
fire suppression and timber and grazing practices that have left fire-dependent landscapes susceptible to unnaturally intense fires. The priority for
restoration should be the places where forests and communities intersect. It
should include thinning of small trees and removal of brush followed by the
careful use of prescribed fire. Building roads and cutting trees in remote
roadless areas, far from human communities, makes neither ecological nor
economic sense. Political rhetoric will not help threatened communities or
ailing forests and rangelands.

Some Principles of Successful Restoration

Restoration must take into account the land, the biotic community, and
social values. Each watershed, each ecosystem, and each community presents
its own set of unique challenges and opportunities. Numerous case studies
of restoration efforts, such as those in *Watershed Restoration: Principles and
Practices*,[23] provide important lessons that can help expand and improve
future restoration efforts.

Watersheds are dynamic and complex.

Watersheds exist in a landscape that is constantly changing. Natural disturbances, such as floods, drought, wildfire, and insect and disease infestations,
shape watersheds. Attempts to lock a watershed into its current state usually
meet with failure. In healthy watersheds, most natural events are beneficial to
long-term ecosystem structure and function. Fire reduces fuels, thins trees and
vegetation naturally, recycles nutrients, promotes plant vigor, and can eliminate undesired nonnative species. Floodwaters flush sediment from spawning
gravel, scour pools, and deposit fertile silts on riparian areas and valley floors.

Reestablish structure and function on the largest possible scale.

Restoration efforts should encourage natural processes and conditions.
Greater habitat complexity generally results in greater biological diversity.

And this in turn leads to ecosystem stability and resilience to natural and human disturbances. In river habitats, deep pools, riffles, runs, and glides may be important to one species or another or to one life-history stage or another. Managing wetlands primarily as duck farms or managing forests as deer reserves may result in a short-term increase in numbers of the desired species. But in time the system that supports them will weaken and eventually collapse.

Focus on the health and integrity of the watershed.

Healthy watersheds support a broad range of native plant and animal species. They are more resistant to disturbances and bounce back quickly when they occur. Noted stream ecologist Jim Karr at the University of Washington calls the ability of a habitat to support an intact and adaptive natural community its "biological integrity." Certain species of plants and animals are key indicators of ecosystem health.

Treat the primary causes of degradation, not just the symptoms.

In the past, many restoration projects sought to stop erosion at the sites where it appeared most severe. Despite good intentions, these projects often failed because the primary source of the problem—poor land management within the watershed—was not addressed. Restoration should focus on improving land management practices that directly affect watershed health—such as livestock grazing, roads, logging, exotic species, and unmanaged off-road vehicle use. Soil erosion is merely the symptom of improper management.

Protect the best remaining habitats.

The first priority for restoration is to do no harm to the remaining high-quality habitats such as old-growth forests, roadless areas, and wilderness study areas. Often these places often provide the core areas for restoration and sources for species recolonization. The first steps to restoration are to protect and expand areas that remain in good health.

Watershed restoration takes a long-term commitment.

The eminent stream ecologist H. N. B. Hynes said that we "cannot divorce a stream from its valley." In other words, we cannot manage a stream outside the context of its watershed. Large watersheds are made up of smaller watersheds. Rivers are influenced by smaller streams. The condition of each tributary is determined by the overall health of the uplands in the watershed. To be successful, restoration must occur at both the local level and the watershed scale. Even the most technically proficient restorations cannot endure if local people do not support the restoration itself and the long-term maintenance that will be needed.[24] Working at large scales brings together the community of interests and the community of place, including landowners and managers and government agencies. Watershed damage typically occurs over decades. Better land and water management can immediately improve habitats and ecological processes. Restoration, however, requires a long-term sustained commitment.

Grassroots efforts work.

Community-based watershed councils and other coalitions of stakeholders increase the effectiveness of restoration efforts and promote citizen support. They bring together diverse groups of people—environmentalists, industry representatives, community leaders, landowners—under the common goal of restoring watershed health. These coalitions can be formally structured or loosely organized. But they must be diverse and balanced and create clear lines of communication among all interests, especially competing interests.

Maintain effective communication and education.

Successful watershed restoration, whether on private land or public land, is usually the result of effective communication and education. In the 85 percent privately owned Mattole watershed in northwestern California, for example, scientists from Redwood National Park taught mapping and aerial photography techniques to local citizens so they could locate erosion sources and find solutions. In the 70 percent privately owned Coquille watershed in Oregon, the Coquille Watershed Association helped to tier restoration efforts from public land to concerned private landowners. Working with community leaders and those whose opinions are widely respected is essential. There is no more important task than to ensure that the average citizen understands the benefits of restoration and the consequences of degradation. All the money and technical expertise in the world cannot overcome disinterest in—or, worse, distrust of—restoration efforts.

Find common ground among interested parties.

Too often conservation and commodity interests allow their differences to define them. Restoration requires temporarily setting aside divisive issues and finding areas of agreement. Few would argue with the need for clean water, less soil erosion, higher biological diversity, and better fish and wildlife habitat. The key is to build on early successes based on areas of agreement. As mutual trust improves, the divisive issues become opportunities.

Focus time and resources on areas of agreement.

Perhaps the key ingredient in collaborative restoration is for the community of interests to agree on common goals. There are always areas of disagreement. Rarely will a group of people agree completely on everything. Take, for example, the dispute over Henrys Fork in Idaho and Wyoming in the early 1990s.[25] The adversaries were typical of many land-use conflicts in the West. A coalition of local and nonresident anglers wanted river water for the large rainbow trout well known in the region; seed potato farmers needed much of the same water for irrigation. When the Henrys Fork Watershed Council was formed, it provided a platform for open communication and led to areas of agreement. Former adversaries now worked in a collaborative spirit to promote cooperation in watershed planning, to prioritize proposed watershed projects, to explore for research and monitoring, and to educate people about the importance of clean water and watershed health. Above all, energy and resources must be directed to the achievement of common goals, not wasted on disagreements. Environmentalists and public-land ranchers, for example, disagree on grazing fees. But both agree on the need to maintain large unfragmented tracts of land in the West and keep family ranches intact without subdivision. Imagine the possibilities if the collective energy of the community of interests was focused on maintaining large tracts of healthy land.

Monitor restoration actions and modify tactics as needed.

Ecosystems are complex—and because of this complexity we need to remain humble and learn as we go. The concepts of adaptive management and listening to the land are described later in Chapter 7, but their importance here cannot be underestimated. Monitoring is the primary means of evaluating the success of restoration efforts. *Implementation* monitoring addresses the question of whether restoration efforts were implemented as planned. *Effec-tiveness* monitoring addresses the question of whether the actions achieved the desired results. Once collected, monitoring information should be ana-lyzed and the findings summarized and communicated regularly to all part-ners. Future management should then be adjusted accordingly. Understand-ing failures—what didn't work—can be just as important as celebrating successes.

Stemming the Tide of Alien Invasions

Controlling exotic species is—like restoring endangered salmon or restoring forest health—clearly among the greatest challenges in restoring the health of our land and water. To be successful in the long term, control of alien species requires a philosophical approach that is ecosystem-based, collabora-tive, and integrated across multiple agency and private land ownerships. As we have seen, we need solutions that restore the health and proper function of the whole ecosystem.

Typically the control of alien species has focused on the use of chemical agents, such as herbicides and rotenone, or biological control agents such as insects that feed on a particular alien plant species. In response to growing concerns about chemical use, agencies and private landowners are beginning to rely more and more on biological control agents.[26] But using one exotic species to control another has its own risks. Biological control agents can become problems themselves by attacking native species or disrupting natu-ral communities in other ways. This is precisely what is happening with a Eurasian weevil, *Larinus planus,* introduced throughout much of the Great Plains and western states in an effort to control another exotic, Canada this-tle. Unfortunately, the weevil is feeding voraciously on native thistles as well. Researchers in Colorado found that the exotic weevil was feeding on a native, the Tracy's thistle, in preference over the target Canada thistle—and that seed viability of the native species had been reduced by 51 percent as a result.[27] In addition to Colorado, the exotic weevil has been introduced into Idaho, Nebraska, Oregon, South Dakota, and Wyoming with unknown impacts. Introduction sites include Badlands National Park, Buffalo Gap National Grassland, and Black Hills National Forest.

Other problems with biological control agents have been reported as well. Beetles brought in to control leafy spurge have also attacked rare native thistles. And *Gambusia,* or mosquitofish, a fish widely introduced to control mosquito larvae, also has a taste for Pacific treefrog tadpoles, juvenile native topminnows or almost anything small and wiggly.[28] In fact, so many problems exist with the *Gambusia* as a biological control agent that it has gar-nered the nickname "Damnbusia" among scientists and natural resource managers. Even proponents of biological control agents admit ignorance about the long-term fate of many of the species they are introducing. Mon-itoring is critical but often ignored. Most recent research efforts have focused on the development of more selective chemical treatments or on finding new biological control agents. In short, it has been easier to simply kill the invaders rather than understand the reasons for their success and how to reverse the trend.

An ecosystem-based approach focuses on understanding the ecological processes that confer advantages to alien species over native species. This is not to say that chemical treatments or biological control agents should not be used. But, they should be used in a more holistic context that seeks to redress the ecosystem changes that give a competitive advantage to the intro-duced species. Chemical agents, in fact, may be preferable to biological agents in many settings. Many conservation biologists correctly view biolog-ical control agents, because of all the unknowns, as a method of last resort.

We also need to change our research priorities. We need to find out what environmental variables are most critical to the spread of exotic species so we can focus management in the areas most susceptible to invasion and protect the remaining sites of biological diversity.[29] We need to find out the sub-tleties that make one habitat more vulnerable to invasion than another and understand why some introduced species will remain dormant for many years and then explode in abundance. Something has given a competitive advantage to the exotic species or a disadvantage to the native species. If an exotic species is favored by a habitat condition or a management scheme, chemical treatments or biological control agents may provide only a stopgap remedy. The root cause that allowed the alien species to become established in the first place must be treated.

The spread of alien species can occur as rapidly as the wind, the move-ments of all-terrain vehicles, or the flow of water. Administrative boundaries or changes in land ownership have little bearing on the dispersal abilities of alien species. Even habitat type has little meaning to some weedy species. Purple loosestrife, a plant from Europe and Asia, for instance, may dominate in wetland habitats as diverse as a small pond, drainage ditch, or large natural marsh. Control requires a collaborative effort. Well-coordinated management is needed among private landowners, state and federal agencies, counties, tribes, hikers, hunters and anglers, all-terrain-vehicle users, envi-ronmentalists, and many others. Not only collaboration is needed for suc-cessful control, but also public education so that more people will learn the damage that alien species cause, how to spot unwanted species, and how best to control them. Chances are that the first person on public land to see a new weed or catch a newly introduced fish will not be an agency scientist but a member of the public. The general public must become more aware of the threats that exotic species pose—threats to biological diversity, recreation, and the sustainability of natural resources.

Preventing the introduction and spread of alien species should be a goal of all land management. Controlling exotic species should be integrated across all programs rather than treated as a separate program unto itself. Too often the control of weeds, for example, is the task of a weed-prevention specialist or delegated to an agency suboffice such as range management. Controlling weeds should be integrated into all programs. Simply put, our land management actions can be part of the problem or part of the solution. Range managers, for example, can prevent the introduction and spread of weeds by requiring that livestock be given weed-free feed before being transferred from private pastures to public rangelands. Engineering staffs can make sure that contracts require road crews to use only weed-free sources of sand and gravel in road and trail construction and to reseed disturbed road edges only with native plant species. The public can be part of the solution, too. Hunters packing with horses, mules, or llamas should only use certified weed-free hay. All-terrain-vehicle users should clean their rigs between trips to ensure they do not spread weeds or seeds from one area to another. It is much easier to incorporate such practices into the daily activities of land management agencies and public land users than deal with the cost of control later.

Control efforts on the weed-infested Mormon Ridge of Montana's Lolo National Forest provide a good example of the problems that weeds cause and what an integrated control effort looks like. According to Forest Service staff, a combination of timber harvest, road building, livestock grazing, and wildfire suppression contributed to spotted knapweed and leafy spurge practically taking over the 900-acre Mormon Ridge from native bunchgrasses. Wildfire suppression allowed Douglas-fir to invade meadow areas. Livestock brought weeds onto the forest from weed-infested pastures, and roadwork created disturbed avenues for their spread. By 1996, approximately 56 percent of the vegetative biomass on the ridge was in weeds. Forbs and grass accounted for just 25 percent and 18 percent, respectively. Because of the critical value of the ridge as winter range for elk, an initiative was funded by the Rocky Mountain Elk Foundation and the Forest Service. An ambitious program—chemical treatments, prescribed fire, new procedures for road construction and maintenance, changes in livestock practices, replanting native species, and intensive monitoring—has transformed the area back into a bunchgrass community. By summer 1998, weed biomass in the ridge had been reduced to 2 percent while forb and grass production were 2 percent and 96 percent, respectively.[30]

The first step in controlling exotic species is to stop their introduction. Whether by authorized or unauthorized means, people continue to bring new species into this country or move introduced species from one spot to another. We already have enough problems dealing with alien species without adding more to the mix. Rather than banning the import of only those species that have proved to constitute a threat, our current practice, we should ban the import of any species that has not been proved safe.

In the long run, however, the general public must come to understand the problems inherent with exotic species—and then become advocates for their control. The need to address this growing problem should be a common interest among the agriculture, commerce, recreation, conservation, and health care communities.

Collaboration Works

The many restoration challenges we face today require a better understanding of ecosystem function and the desire not to degrade any further the quality of life for future generations. These set the stage for the reemergence of the true American spirit of innovation and entrepreneurship. Call it coordination, cooperation, or communication—simply people working together to restore the land—collaborative stewardship brings together people who love and depend on the land. The formation of local watershed councils and a variety of collaborative groups such as Oregon's Coquille Watershed Association, the Hiawassee River Action Team in the Appalachian Mountains, the Beaverkill-Willowemoc Watershed Initiative in New York's Catskill Mountains, and the Blackfoot Challenge in Montana are sprouting as a result of the grassroots desire to restore the health of the land.[31]

In the book *Making Collaboration Work*, Julie Wondolleck and Steven Yaffee cite four major uses of the collaborative process:

- Building understanding by fostering exchange of information and ideas.
- Providing a mechanism for effective decision making.
- Generating a means of getting necessary work done.
- Developing the capacity . . . to deal with challenges of the future.[32]

Landowners, environmentalists, industry and community leaders, and conservationists are increasingly coming together with the common goal of restoring the health and productivity of their watersheds.

Communities and Watersheds—An Inseparable Bond

Many people look with suspicion at community-based conservation and restoration, thinking perhaps that national interests will become "co-opted." They fear that community-based efforts represent an abdication of decision-making responsibility or, worse yet, portend the divestiture of public resources. These are honest concerns. But community-based collaborative efforts do not diminish federal or state mandates to clean our air and water, preserve endangered species, and protect public resources. Collaborative efforts can actually amplify the law's effectiveness by vesting communities with both interest in conservation and ownership in the health of the land.[33]

Collaborative watershed restoration is not a panacea for resolving tough resource issues. Three principles are critical to the creation of a successful community-based restoration project: balance among the diversity of interests, a shared vision for conserving or restoring an ecosystem, and a commitment to use the best available science. Collaboration is a process, not an outcome. It should never be used to avoid decision-making responsibilities—regardless of whether those responsibilities rest with federal, state, or even private landowners. The measure of success for any community-based approach is better decisions on the land and better working relationships among the communities of place and interest. Monitoring, both long-term and short-term, is essential.

Like the barn raisings of old, community-based restoration reunites and reconnects people to the land that sustains them. Such efforts demonstrate that we respect the gifts of our forebears and are committed to leaving the world a better place for future generations. This is the essence of community forestry and watershed restoration—and, as conservationist Aldo Leopold might have said, a basic requirement of membership in the land community. With human population growth demanding more and more natural resources, the need to restore the land has never been greater. Given popular support and the political will, society could fix what ails most watersheds. According to National Environmental Education and Training Foundation surveys, 74 percent of Americans polled either considered themselves environmental activists or sympathetic to environmental concerns.[34] Growing concern for the health of the land continues to bring diverse interests together to solve restoration challenges.

We must capitalize on this growing concern for land health. We must realize that technology cannot ensure our future. Indeed, our survival depends more on restoring the health of the land, the productivity of the soils, and the water quality of our rivers than on any technological fix. It is through the efforts of restoration that we can mobilize our community members and recapture our community spirit and thereby begin to build a sustainable relationship binding our society and the lands and waters that support us. If the task before us is enormous, so, too, are the rewards.

Chapter 7

Living within Limits:
Our Search for Sustainability

We need to let the western land shape us and stop trying to force the land to fit our ideals.

—Wallace Stegner, *American West as Living Space* (1987)

The concept of sustainability, in one form or another, has been a goal of public land management for more than a century. The Organic Act of 1897 provided early direction in management of forestland and called for "securing favorable conditions of water flows" and to "furnish continuous supply of timber" for the citizens of the United States. The concept has steadily evolved since that time. In present terms, the concept of sustainable natural resource management—or simply sustainability—means that land should be managed in a manner that does not lessen the ability of ecosystems to deliver ecological and economic services for present and future generations. The need for intergenerational equity can be traced from the American Indian belief in the need to leave enough resources for survival of the seventh generation to the most recent recommendations for natural resource management.[1]

Perhaps what is most important today is the recognition that our social and economic objectives cannot be met in the long run without first securing the health, diversity, and productivity of the land. Simply put: The land cannot provide the economic services we desire unless we maintain its ecological services.[2] "Ecological services" include, for example, the ability of watersheds to produce high-quality water, the ability of riparian habitats to moderate the effects of drought, ameliorate flood energy, and trap large amounts of silt in streamside vegetation, and the ability of trees to trap carbon, produce oxygen, and hold soil on steep hillsides. The implications of maintaining ecological services for management of our land, water, and air resources for future generations are profound.

Some contend that land should be managed to achieve a maximum sustained yield from forests, grasslands, or farmlands. Economic demands are their primary objective. Such management largely ignores long-term requirements for land health, diversity, and productivity. Not only are the broad needs of the land neglected, but management under the paradigm of maximum sustained yield focuses on those species that satisfy our immediate economic needs and ignores the overwhelming majority of species that have no obvious economic value. Under this paradigm, the biological diversity of those forests, grasslands, farms, and surrounding areas is compromised in the rush to maximize production of a select few species.[3]

Management for ecological sustainability, by contrast, focuses on meeting human needs without compromising land health and the composition, structure, and processes of ecological systems.[4] The land has limits on how many natural resources can be harvested, chemically treated, or otherwise modified without degrading the very land and water system that we depend on. It is this concept of living within the limits of the land that we will explore in this chapter.

The natural world imposes limits on management that must be considered if we are to live sustainably. First, the complexity and variability inherent in all ecosystems must be integrated into land management planning. Planning must not just allow for this complexity and variability—it must embrace it. Natural forces are constantly reshaping streams, grasslands, meadows, and forests. Second, solutions to problems must fit the broad ecosystem context. Too often our search for quick technological fixes is confounded by the complex interconnections of biological reality. Third, the distinct character of each piece of land must be recognized. When we monitor our actions and their impacts and employ adaptive management, we are listening to the land and learning what works on a site and what does not. Finally, our demand for resources must be reduced by controlling our consumption.

The Complexity of Natural Systems

John Muir often is credited with observing that every time we attempt to pick one thing out from the natural world we find it connected to everything else. Connectedness is a central tenet of ecosystems. It contributes to their complexity. Human disturbance, however, often interrupts this connectedness by fragmenting the landscape. For example, timber harvest may isolate one old-growth stand from another. Roads can become impenetrable barriers for everything from amphibians to grizzly bears trying to cross them.

Water connects the landscape. Flowing surface waters in streams and rivers connect headwaters to lower-elevation valley bottoms. Rainfall links upland terraces to streams as it flows downhill. Floodwaters may move in the opposite direction and link streams to floodplains. Water even links surface to subsurface areas through aquifers and hyporheic zones of saturated gravels below rivers. Watersheds are connected by flowing water in three spatial dimensions: longitudinal or altitudinal; lateral; and vertical. And these connections vary in time (the temporal dimension)—which adds even more complexity. (See Figure 7-1.)

Thinking in terms of water, it is easy to see how management activities disrupt the natural world. Dams and diversions interrupt longitudinal connections—not only blocking migratory fish pathways but also affecting downstream water temperature and sediment regimes. For major dams, such as Flaming Gorge on the Green River in Utah, these effects may manifest themselves for more than 100 miles downstream with damage to native fish populations such as the endangered Colorado pikeminnow and razorback sucker.[5] On a smaller scale, roads interrupt surface runoff and concentrate flows. Roads and railroads located in riparian areas restrict river channel movement, accelerate erosion, and increase the magnitude of floods.

Disturbances such as floods, drought, wildfire, diseases, and even volcanoes are a normal part of habitat and watershed rejuvenation and maintenance. Floods, for example, benefit healthy landscapes by depositing silt along floodplains—thus restoring soil productivity and kick-starting plant succession processes in riparian zones. Floods along the South Fork of the Snake River in Idaho are critical to stimulating recruitment of cottonwoods by providing new sediment beds along the river for seedling establishment.[6] Floods also scour deep pools and clean fish spawning gravels. Floods even help in the maintenance of native fish communities by eliminating nonnative species that thrive during periods of lower flows.[7] Without at least some

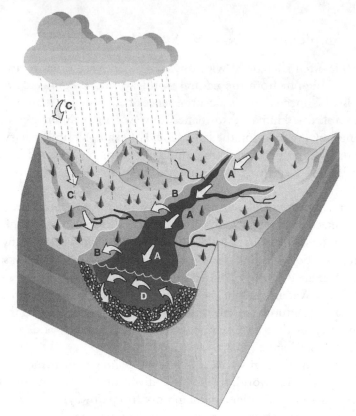

Figure 7-1. (A) In a healthy watershed, moving water interconnects the landscape in many dimensions. Streams connect headwaters to downstream valley bottoms. (B) During floods, rivers move laterally onto floodplains. (C) Rainfall percolates downhill and into groundwater. (D) Water moves between surface flows and subsurface hyporheic zones.

floods, the structure and composition of stream communities become degraded.

Intensive development in watersheds, by contrast, amplifies flood effects to the point where floods can do more harm than good. High road densities in forestlands speed runoff, which can result in accelerated rates of erosion.[8] Pavement, parking lots, and buildings have similar effects. Some of the best work on the effects of increasing urbanization on flood magnitudes and frequencies has been conducted by Luna Leopold (son of Aldo Leopold) and reported in his excellent treatise titled *A View of the River*.[9] In Seneca Creek, Maryland, a drainage of about 100 square miles, the mean annual flood increased from 2973 cubic feet per second (cfs) to

6014 cfs, an increase of more than 100 percent, following development and urbanization of the watershed. The capacity of Seneca Creek was exceeded thirty-five times (1.2 times a year) from 1931 to 1960—but following significant urbanization its banks overflowed 2.2 times a year during 1961–1991. Impacts on small drainages are even more pronounced. Leopold found that in a 3.7-square-mile subwatershed, the number of overbank flows was 1.4 times a year prior to urbanization but 7.3 times a year after.

Increased development of floodplains has caused economic as well as ecological hardship. According to data from the National Flood Insurance Program compiled by the National Wildlife Federation, flood damage in the United States has exceeded $8 billion annually in recent years. In response to the rising urban and residential damage claims, some communities have begun voluntary buyouts and relocation of homes away from floodplains. Some communities and homeowners however, particularly in Texas and Louisiana, fight logic and fate by failing to relocate buildings despite repeated flooding. In one extreme case in Houston, a home valued at $114,480 has received $806,591 in flood insurance payments for sixteen flood events over an eighteen-year period.[10]

Our typical response to flood problems is to remove riparian vegetation and channelize the river—effectively disconnecting the stream from its floodplain. But as stream channels are straightened and narrowed, the force of the stream flow increases with damaging consequences downstream. So the "solution" to one problem may create another problem elsewhere in the system. New problems multiply as floodplain development often follows river channelization—increasing the likelihood of river versus human conflicts in the future.

The key is to learn to live with disturbances rather than fighting them. One is reminded of the quote from a civil engineer: "I spent a year putting the bridge over the Missouri River. I've spent all my time ever since trying to keep the river under the bridge." The process of river meandering—the erosion and deposition associated with lateral movement of the channel—is critical to riparian plant succession and the overall health of the river and should be accommodated during land-use planning and development. This is true for rivers the size of the Mississippi or as small as a backwoods creek.

During the 1950s and 1960s, the U.S. government channelized many streams in the West to enable ranchers and farmers to mow hay meadows adjacent to streams. The idea was to replace natural spring flooding of hay meadows with channelized streams containing small diversion dams that could be used to irrigate fields. Unfortunately, the concept did not work as well in the real world as it did on paper. As the streams were channelized, their flows increased and flood energies eroded and downgraded the streams—lowering them below the elevation of the fields. The results included lower water tables (and drier meadows producing less hay) and eroded water diversion structures that became unworkable because the stream elevation during the irrigation season was below the field level. Jack Southworth, a cattle rancher near Seneca, Oregon, summed up the failed experiment on his own land:

> For almost the first 100 years of the ranch, we never thought of the ecosystem. We did everything we could to simplify it, to make it easier to understand, and therefore to manage. For example, in the 1950s, the Soil Conservation Service built a nifty plan to straighten the Silvies River where it runs through a couple of miles of our meadows. And we got rid of those obnoxious willows that got in our way during haying. . . . But then, we had to build riprap along the streambanks to stabilize them. . . . And the more we managed it, the worse it became.[11]

Wildfires, forest insects, and plant diseases have similar records of being desirable when functioning within their normal range of variability—but potentially damaging when functioning outside this range. At lower levels of disturbance, wildfires, forest insects, and diseases are desirable because they create diversity in habitats by opening up patches in the forest. For the dry forest types, such as the ponderosa pine habitats ranging from northern Arizona northward to central Idaho, low-intensity wildfires prevent the intense, high levels of wildfire, insects, and diseases that have plagued these forests over the past two decades. By selective harvest of large ponderosa pine and decades of wildfire suppression, forests over much of the Intermountain West are increasingly susceptible to broad-scale disturbances. Large expanses of forest have been homogenized into dense, single-age stands—which in turn provide dense fuel for unnaturally intense wildfire and breeding grounds for insect epidemics and plant diseases. William Gast and colleagues summed up the forest health problem in Oregon's Blue Mountains thusly: "Past management practices such as fire exclusion and selective timber harvesting, though carried out with the best of intentions and using the best information of the time, have led to potentially catastrophic [conditions]."[12] Nancy Langston's book on the history of forest management in the Blue Mountains presents an even more penetrating analysis:

> Attempts to engineer nature imply that the land is a predictable machine made up of disconnected parts. Any pieces we think are wasteful—insects, fires, vermin, dead wood, weed trees like alder—we just eliminate. A few years later, when the trees start dying, we wonder what went wrong. Only then do we notice that those wasteful parts had a critical function in the ecosystem.[13]

What is "good" and what is "bad" begins to take on a more subjective tone when one digs into the scientific underpinnings of disturbance. Although its negative effects on human communities that encroach on forest borders are undisputed, even large-scale wildfire may not be as bad as Smokey Bear would have us believe. In lodgepole pine forests, broad-scale stand-replacing fires are the normal method of forest regeneration and replacement. This is what happened after the 1988 fires in and around Yellowstone National Park. Such forests are adapted to large fires. In fact, the cones of lodgepole require the heat of wildfire to open and spread their seeds. In drier ponderosa pine forests, smaller undergrowth fires every ten to fifteen years are characteristic and large, intense wildfires occur much less frequently. But even when a large wildfire is intense, habitats and species can recover surprisingly quickly.

In the Boise National Forest, an uncharacteristically large wildfire burned more than 250,000 acres during the summer of 1992—resulting in direct mortality to native bull trout and redband trout, increased erosion, and debris torrents. Yet within one year, the native trout had returned and their numbers were approaching prefire levels within three years.[14] In some streams, juvenile trout densities were very high—suggesting that populations might even have benefited from the fire. Despite the severity of the 1992 fire, the disturbance was of short duration. And because not all areas burned with high intensity, local refuges were available for species from which they repopulated burned-out habitats. In at least some cases, recovery appears to be more readily achieved from a single high-intensity disturbance, whether it is a major flood or large-scale wildfire, than it is from smaller, human-induced disturbances (such as road building and logging) repeated over longer periods. Table 7-1 compares the effects of natural disturbances under varying levels of human impact.

Table 7-1. Generalized Comparison of Results of Disturbances in Intact vs. Developed Landscapes

DISTURBANCE	INTACT LANDSCAPE	DEVELOPED LANDSCAPE
Floods	Riparian areas ameliorate flows; larger floods spread onto floodplains where they lose energy and fine materials drop from suspension to replenish soils	Flood intensity and frequency are greater, resulting in increased erosion; flood energy intensifies as it moves downstream
Droughts	Rebuild stream channels; fish populations move downstream	Channels dry; because headwater fish populations are isolated from downstream habitats, they are extirpated
Wildfires in dry forest types	Fires remain at low intensities; undergrowth and smaller trees are killed; small patches of forest are cleared	Fire intensities often are high; small and large trees alike are killed; broad-scale fires may consume many thousands of acres
Forest insect pests	Insect outbreaks remain localized; small patches of forest are cleared	Insect outbreaks are of longer duration and cover large areas; large stands of trees may be killed

Note: Examples are drawn from dry forest types and associated valleys such as those common to northern Arizona, western Colorado, southern Idaho, northern New Mexico, eastern Oregon, Utah, and eastern Washington.

Complexity Confounds Management

Ecologists often say that "an ecosystem is not only more complex than we think it is, it is more complex than we can think it is." These words convey a cautionary note regarding land management. Too often society treats ecological systems as if they were predictable machines. Too often we think we understand these systems enough to fine-tune them to achieve the conditions we want. Too often natural resource managers think they can engineer their way out of biological problems.

Forest health problems in the Intermountain West demonstrate this sort of thinking. Despite our best intentions and the use of the best information available at the time, the overall health of many western forests declined steadily following World War II as a result of wildfire suppression, selective harvest of large pines, and a serious misunderstanding of the role of disturbance on the landscape. Once again, Nancy Langston puts the problems of Oregon's Blue Mountains into proper perspective:

> The more managers alter a forest, the less they can predict the paths that succession will take. Each road we build, each stand we cut and replant with another species, each application of herbicide and pesticide adds another confounding layer of possibility. This is startling, since the changes managers have made to forests have all been done with the goal of making succession more predictable, not less.[15]

Too often habitats and ecosystems are managed as if complexity and variability were either nonexistent or entirely predictable. Given this kind of thinking, forests, grasslands, and rivers are viewed as though they were simply commodities to be brought to market. This machine model suggests that with enough artificial inputs—such as application of fertilizers or introduction of new species—outputs from natural systems can be manipulated to any desired socioeconomic outcome. If ecosystems were well enough understood, theoretically they could be managed in such a way to maximize production while protecting water quality and recovering endangered species. Paul Hirt, a historian of land management from Washington State University, calls such thinking "a conspiracy of optimism." This is how he characterizes the management of our national forests from World War II through the late 1980s. The result was unsustainable levels of timber harvest, more forest roads than could be maintained, a growing number of endangered species, and a backlash from an expanding environmental constituency.[16]

Salmon and steelhead management in the Pacific Northwest offers similar insights into traditional approaches to natural resource problem solving. Because of complex life histories that involve migrations among freshwater, estuarine, and marine habitats, there are many reasons for the decline of salmon and steelhead. Each separate population or stock of salmon and steelhead has a unique habitat and a unique list of factors causing decline. Certainly for stocks in the middle and upper Columbia, Snake, and Salmon Rivers, dams are a huge problem. For some coastal Oregon and Washington stocks, overharvest by commercial fisheries is the main concern. Hatchery operations have been particularly hard on Oregon's coastal coho salmon stocks. But in reality, many factors affect declines. It is too easy to point at the other guy.

Here, for example, might be a typical finger-pointing session from somewhere in Idaho's Snake River drainage as Forest Service managers attempt to remove cows from meadows surrounding spawning habitats: "Why should we remove the cows when the dams on the lower Snake are the real problem—let's fix the dams. . . . Why should we fix the dams when most of the adults are being harvested before they ever get there—so let's reduce harvests. . . . Why should we reduce fishing harvests when terns (a fish-eating bird) take 10 million smolts from the river?" and so on. Most declining stocks, whether coastal or inland, have one thing in common: degradation of freshwater habitat. A 1991 report from the American Fisheries Society listed habitat decline as a serious cause in 91 percent of 214 stocks at risk of extinction in California, Idaho, Oregon, and Washington.[17]

Focus Essay

Reforestation: Recognizing the Ties that Bind*
DAVID A. PERRY†

In the mid-1970s, as a researcher for the Forest Service in the Rocky Mountains, I became interested in the poor recovery of high-elevation clearcuts, a problem that was cropping up in various places throughout the West. While clearcuts at mid and low elevations were usually reforested successfully, many at high elevations had been planted several times and still supported almost no living trees. What was going on? How could a site that once grew a

*For further reading on the complexities of forest soils and their roles in maintaining healthy forest ecosystems, I recommend the following: M. P. Amaranthus et al., "Soil Organisms, Root Growth, and Forest Regeneration," in *Forestry on the Frontier* (Washington, D.C.: Society of American Foresters, 1990); D. A. Perry et al., "Bootstrapping in Ecosystems," *BioScience* 39 (1989):230–237; and D. A. Perry et al., "Mycorrhizal Fungi in Mixed-Species Forests and Other Tales of Positive Feedback, Redundancy, and Stability," in M. G. R. Cannell et al., eds., *The Ecology of Mixed-Species Stands of Trees,* British Ecological Society, Special Publication 11 (London: Blackwell, 1992).

†David A. Perry is emeritus professor of ecosystem studies and ecosystem management, Oregon State University, and affiliate professor of tropical ecosystem and landscape management, University of Hawaii at Hilo.

healthy forest suddenly become unable to support trees at all? Even more puzzling, these were forest types with a history of wildfires from which they apparently recovered quite well. Clearly Mother Nature knew something we didn't, and the old idea that clearcutting mimicked a natural disturbance did not ring true.

My earliest work on the problem, on the high plateau bordering Yellowstone National Park in Montana, produced strong evidence that the key to the mystery lay somewhere in altered soil biology. The prime candidate in the puzzle was mycorrhizal fungi, a diverse group of fungi that often grow in a symbiotic, that is, a mutually benefiting, relationship with other plants.

In 1977, I joined the faculty at Oregon State University and gathered a team of students and other researchers to focus our efforts on the Siskiyou Mountains of southwestern Oregon and northern California. One of our sites, Cedar Camp, had been logged in the 1960s and by the end of the 1970s had been replanted four times but supported nothing more than exotic weeds. One of the team, Mike Amaranthus, performed a simple experiment with dramatic results. Recalling advice from his Italian grandfather about using soil from beneath older trees to inoculate young trees with truffles (the fruiting bodies of mycorrhizal fungi), he inoculated tree seedlings at Cedar Camp and other sites with small amounts (a half-cup) of soils from nearby healthy forests. While I expected some positive effect, the magnitude of the response at Cedar Camp amazed me. Despite a long history of reforestation failures, suddenly a high proportion of seedlings thrived when given a little soil from beneath living trees.

As we continued our studies, it became clear that the changes in the clearcut soil were much more complex than anyone had suspected. The mycorrhizal fungi were present after all. But the bacterial community, which was critical to the proper functioning of the fungi and tree root connection, was badly out of balance. Moreover, there were apparent negative impacts on the tiny invertebrate animals that, by feeding on microbes, play a keystone role in the nutrient cycle. The combined effect of these imbalances was to greatly reduce the ability of tree seedlings to gather resources and survive late-summer drought.

If the soil biology had been thrown out of balance by clearcuts, why didn't the same thing happen following fires? The answer was to be found in the forest hardwood trees and shrubs that accompanied conifer trees in natural forests of the region. The hardwoods play a vital role in forest recovery following disturbance. They sprout quickly from roots after their tops are killed—rapidly reestablishing a flow of photosynthetic energy into the soil ecosystem. Moreover, a number of hardwood species form symbiotic relationships with the same fungal species as do Douglas-fir and pines.

In a series of experiments, my students demonstrated that soils beneath several species of hardwoods commonly associated with conifer forests from southern Oregon to northern Mexico greatly benefited growth of Douglas fir seedlings. All the evidence indicated that hardwoods were actively creating biological and chemical conditions in the soil that favored at least some conifers. At Cedar Camp—and many other clearcuts across the West—sprouting hardwoods had been sprayed with herbicides after logging in a mistaken belief that it was necessary to eliminate competition between the hardwoods and conifers. No one recognized the complexity of soil communities or the critical role that hardwoods and soil invertebrates play in maintaining healthy forest conditions.

A radically new picture emerged from these studies. Soil is not a passive supporter of plants and a simple storehouse of nutrients and water—it is a complex ecosystem in intimate relationship with, and fundamentally shaped by, the plant community. We called this relationship "bootstrapping," a term used by physicists to describe systems whose character and integrity arise primarily from interactions within the system itself. In the final analysis, each organism depends on the integrity of the overall system in which it resides. It is not as simple as plants growing in soil. It is the whole plant/soil system in a dance of mutual creation.

How can we deal with all these problems? To date, technological approaches have dominated—building hatcheries to produce more fish, for example, and using fishways, bypass systems, and barges to move juvenile and adult fish around the dams. This has been the approach of a variety of government agencies over the past thirty years to restore salmon and steelhead in the Columbia River drainage. The results of these efforts have been less than encouraging: the continued decline or extinction of stocks and the listing of most remaining mid- and upper Columbia and all Snake River stocks as endangered or threatened.

In 1998, the Fish and Wildlife Service completed a review of the Lower Snake River Compensation Plan (LSRCP), which has been implemented since 1980 to mitigate for dam construction by producing fish from twelve major hatcheries and numerous satellite facilities. Despite releasing millions of young salmon, the survival of juvenile smolts to adults has been much less than anticipated. (See Figure 7-2.) The LSRCP goal for smolt-to-adult survival in the Grande Ronde basin, for example, was 0.65 percent but the actual survival was less than 0.05 percent in most years. Similarly, in the

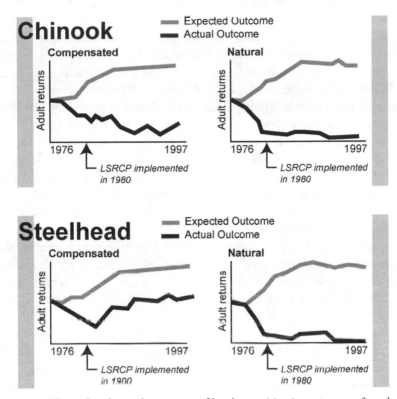

Figure 7-2. Planned and actual outcomes of hatchery mitigation programs for salmon and steelhead in the lower Snake River.

upper Salmon River the LSRCP goal for smolt-to-adult survival was 0.87 percent but the actual survival has been 0.10 percent or less since 1983.

The Fish and Wildlife Service review also uncovered a host of unanticipated problems associated with the hatchery program: a high straying rate of hatchery-produced fish (that failed to return to their natal stream); significant disease problems at hatcheries; high mortality of hatchery-produced smolts in some rivers with high velocities and steep gradients; and low reproductive output and size of hatchery-produced returning adults. The review concluded that hatcheries cannot solve the problem of declining salmon and steelhead on their own. Under present management strategies, it said many populations of salmon and steelhead in the Snake River basin will be extirpated by the year 2025.[18] Clearly a new approach to the salmon problem must be found, one that does not rely on novel technology or quick fixes.

In reviewing the efforts of hatcheries to replace natural production of salmon in the Pacific Northwest, Gary Meffe, a noted ecologist, summarized his findings as follows: "A management strategy that has as a centerpiece artificial propagation and restocking of a species that has declined as a result of environmental degradation and overexploitation, without facing the causes for decline, is not facing biological reality."[19] Somehow we always seem to find the money to build hatcheries, design "fish-friendly" turbines, or christen a new fish transport barge. But seldom do we find the will to transform reservoirs back into rivers despite convincing scientific studies that dams— Ice Harbor, Lower Monumental, Lower Granite, and Little Goose—are the primary culprit in the decline of upriver Columbia Basin salmon and steelhead stocks.[20] Not all dams should be removed. Scientists have focused on the four lower Snake River dams as the most significant problem for declining salmon and steelhead in Idaho.

David Orr of Oberlin College notes: "It is widely assumed that environmental problems will be solved by technology of one sort or another. Better technology can certainly help, but the crisis is not first and foremost one of technology. Rather, it is a crisis within the minds that develop and use technology."[21] To achieve sustainability, we would be better off focusing our technological efforts on discovering different ways to meet or reduce human demands for energy and water rather than trying to retrofit dams to meet the biological requirements of salmon. Efforts to retrofit, for the most part, have proved unsuccessful. Reducing our demand for energy, water, and other vital needs, however, has benefits beyond protecting streams and watersheds or reducing air pollution. It can save billions of dollars.

Management, Natural Disturbances, and Synergy: A Case Study

The effort to restore fish habitat on Fish Creek of Oregon's Mount Hood National Forest illustrates many of the complexities and pitfalls of how natural resource problems have been addressed in the past.[22] Fish Creek supports summer and winter steelhead and coho salmon. The watershed has been intensively managed with 41 percent of the watershed subjected to timber harvest and road-building activities that peaked during the 1980s. As a result, streams lost pool habitat due to siltation and removal of large woody debris from riparian areas. In an effort to recreate high-quality pool habitat, the Bonneville Power Administration and Forest Service constructed some five hundred instream structures consisting of logs tied into stream channels as well as boulders and root wads placed in the streams. This is a common approach to stream improvement and is widely practiced across the country.

In November 1995 and February 1996, large storms hit the drainage. The 1996 storm was considered to be a hundred-year flood event. The Forest Service inventoried 236 major landslides in the Fish Creek drainage after the storms: 42 percent of these landslides were attributed to timber harvest, 34 percent to roads, and 24 percent to nonmanagement causes. The devastation was overwhelming. Poor logging harvest and road-building practices, coupled with steep slopes, had set the stage for massive instability and soil loss. The resulting landslides and accelerated runoff led to destruction of most of the habitat improvement structures.

Perhaps the first lesson is that road building and timber harvest, at least the way they were practiced, were inappropriate for these steep slopes. Moreover, restoration might have focused not on the stream itself but on upslope damage caused by the extensive road network and past logging activities. If sustainability is our goal, we must treat the primary causes of habitat and ecosystem decline, not just the symptoms. At Fish Creek the symptoms were increased sedimentation and loss of pool habitat—but the primary cause was poor upland management. The instream fix failed to address the real problem. The cumulative effects of past management should have been analyzed and then addressed.

Using instream structures such as gabions, riprap, and logs to improve stream habitat is a common practice. When used as part of a watershed-scale restoration or management program that also addresses primary causes of problems, the structural approaches are perfectly acceptable. But when used alone they are increasingly disfavored by conservation biologists, as well as fisheries and hydrology professionals.[23]

The problem of an eroding streambank or loss of pool habitat must be viewed in its broad watershed context. Why is the stream eroding? Is the erosion at a natural rate or has it been accelerated? If so, what is the cause? Do adjacent riparian areas have sufficient vegetation to ameliorate high stream flow energy? What land management practices have occurred upslope or upstream that may have changed stream conditions?

Habitats within watersheds are interconnected. Our solution to problems must take into account the connectedness inherent in all natural systems. We need to reexamine our whole approach to natural resource problems.

The Art of Solving for Pattern

In a 1980 essay titled "Solving for Pattern," Wendell Berry wrote that the primary dilemma in agriculture is the damaging side effects of industrial and technological solutions to farm problems. Large feedlots can produce cattle at exceptional growth rates, but the side effects of crowding and manure disposal cause additional problems for animal health and water quality. It takes large doses of antibiotics to solve animal health problems, and injection wells send animal wastes into groundwater. New spinoff problems emerge that require additional solutions. Often the solutions to the secondary problems are cause for concern themselves.[24]

Natural resource management often suffers from the same shortsighted approach to problem solving. Sometimes the problem is defined so narrowly that the solutions are false. Natural resource problems are treated as if they comprised a series of disconnected concerns. But as we know, ecosystems are full of connections. In our attempt to deal with complex problems, we tend to isolate a piece of the puzzle and seek to resolve these smaller portions outside their context in the whole system. As Berry puts it: "The whole problem must be solved, not just some handily identifiable and simplifiable aspect of it."[25]

If, for example, the smolt-to-adult survival of salmon is declining, we build a hatchery to produce more smolts. If juvenile mortality of young salmon as they move downstream past a dam is too high, we simply barge juveniles around the dam. If an eroding streambank appears, we add riprap to stop the erosion. All of these approaches are well intended but wrongheaded. The larger pattern—the context—is conveniently ignored. We need to identify *why* the smolt-to-adult survival has declined, *why* juvenile mortality is high, *why* the streambank is eroding—and then fix the root problem, not fix a Band-Aid over the symptom. Incorrectly focused solutions create their own host of new problems. Those hatchery salmon compete with remaining wild fish for ocean food resources and scarce freshwater spawning and rearing habitat. Barges affect the homing ability of the smolts. Bypass systems funnel them through a pipe that eventually opens into the mouths of waiting predators. Riprap freezes one portion of the bank in place, but it also freezes out ecological processes that maintain the long-term health of the river.

Too often the root of the problem is misidentified or ignored altogether. In the case of streambank erosion, the real problem is not the erosion itself. The real problem is the cause of unnatural changes in the stream. What caused the higher flows and faster runoff? Often the answer may be found far upstream or upslope.

A "solution" is shortsighted if it acts in a harmful manner within the context of the whole system. A riprapped streambank may reduce erosion at the site of the riprap, but it increases stream energy and causes more erosion and flooding downstream. A juvenile bypass system may transport young salmon

past a dam, but predation may well increase when disoriented fish are concentrated at a release site. A good solution, by contrast, works in harmony
with the whole ecological system. No additional problems are created and
the root causes of dysfunction within the ecosystem are corrected. Here are
some characteristics of good natural resource solutions:

- Solve the problem without creating others.
- Solve for pattern—solutions must pay attention to broad context.
- Work harmoniously with the entire ecological system.
- Keep solutions at an appropriate and manageable scale.
- Minimize additional disturbances to the natural system.
- Work with—not against—natural processes.

If wildfire suppression and overharvest of large pine have created western
forests with high densities of young trees, building new roads to allow large-
scale clearcuts or even-age management is the wrong response. Even though
new roads and clearcuts reduce tree density and may temporarily lessen the
associated fire hazards, additional problems from road sediment will be cre
ated. And without the reintroduction of fire, how does this solution restore
natural forest function?

Sometimes the wrong solutions are applied because the overall goal of
land management was mistaken in the first place. If the goal is sys-
temwide—such as restoring the overall health of the watershed—then the
proper solution becomes more obvious. The forest with a high density of
young to middle-aged trees may need to be selectively thinned of those
small-diameter tree species and brush that are unnaturally high in abundance. Once they have been thinned, prescribed fire could be judiciously
reintroduced. The health of the forest may be restored when its habitats are
patchy and diverse (a mosaic of stand types of varying ages) and when
species composition is within the range of natural variability for site conditions. Forests that are patchy and composed of diverse species, age, and
structural components will be more resistant to broad-scale attack from fire,
insects, and disease. A healthy forest will absorb natural disturbances and
prevent them from amplifying to catastrophic scales and intensities.

Usually the goal of intensively managed forests is to produce wood fiber.
But the greatest structural and species diversity in forests typically occurs in
early shrub/forb/sapling stages and old-growth forests. Intensively managed
forests sacrifice diversity and complexity because they focus on middle-aged
trees of particular species of economic value. If your goal is a tree farm, this
may be acceptable. But it is wrong if your goal is a healthy and diverse forest. Resistance to insect and disease outbreaks, drought, and wildfire is great-

est in forests with diverse and complex habitats and tree stands that exhibit a wide range of age and species.[26] Diversity and complexity are critical for healthy grassland habitats, too. David Tilman and J. A. Downing, for instance, have demonstrated that drought resistance is greatest in grasslands with more species.[27]

Good solutions to natural resource problems work harmoniously with goals of ecosystem health, diversity, and resistance to disturbance. They solve problems without creating others. They solve for pattern. This is true whether solving problems on a farm in Kentucky, a river in Oregon, or a forest in Aldo Leopold's sand counties of southern Wisconsin. Perhaps Leopold said it best: "A thing is right when it tends to preserve the integrity, stability and beauty of the biotic community. It is wrong when it tends otherwise."[28]

Listen to the Land

In the spring of 1960, Paul Ehrlich began long-term studies of Bay checkerspot butterflies living on Jasper Ridge not far from San Francisco Bay. Over the past few decades, Dr. Ehrlich and hundreds of his students from Stanford University have studied the population dynamics, movements, mortality factors, and larval host plants associated with the butterfly.[29] Among their more striking discoveries was the periodic extinction of small satellite populations and their recolonization and subsequent reestablishment by a larger, more resilient nursery population. This concept, known as metapopulation theory, now is recognized as a central tenet of population dynamics for a wide range of species. Small headwater stream populations of bull trout may blink out of existence because of drought, for example, only to be reestablished by larger downstream populations once habitat conditions are restored. Long-term data gathering like that for the Bay checkerspot butterfly is extremely rare. But the power of observing nature and its change over time is clear.

Any scientist or natural resource manager is likely to agree that monitoring and data gathering are critical components of any management proposal, grazing plan, timber sale, or restoration project. Monitoring provides the data that allow us to determine the success of a project. Monitoring tells us whether we correctly implemented the project, whether the project attained our objectives, and whether our basic assumptions about how the ecological system works are correct. Unfortunately, the same scientist or resource manager will probably admit that monitoring is often neglected or done poorly. A recent review of livestock grazing on public lands, for example, found that "monitoring of land use activities is woefully lacking."[30] Monitoring is one

of the first items to disappear because of lack of funding, staff time, or commitment. Even if monitoring data are collected, they may not be analyzed
properly and conclusions may not be integrated into future decisions via the
learning process known as adaptive management.

Monitoring lets us know what is working, what is not working, and why.
As noted earlier in Chapter 6, two kinds of monitoring are essential to
understanding which management actions worked and why. *Implementation*
monitoring is the first essential. It asks whether the project was implemented
according to plan. Basically this type of monitoring answers the question:
Did we do what we said we would? Did we follow the plan? Did we, for
example, designate and abide by our 300-foot-wide riparian habitat conservation areas? *Effectiveness* monitoring is equally essential. This type of monitoring determines whether management prescriptions achieved the desired
results. Were those 300-foot wide riparian areas effective in buffering upslope activities from streams, for example, and thereby reducing sediment
delivery to the stream? This question is more complex than those posed by
implementation monitoring and demands a sound understanding of physical and biological processes in the area. Effectiveness monitoring must be
continued long enough for conclusions to be valid. If, for example, the concern is that road construction will lead to increased sediment during storm
events, then the time period for effectiveness monitoring must include
storms. Or if a new grazing prescription is being implemented to improve
stream channel function, then monitoring should include periods of both
drought and flood.

For monitoring to be fully successful, it must be an integral part of each
project. Monitoring must clearly relate to the goals of the project. Effectiveness monitoring must be able not only to detect change but to distinguish
change caused by natural variation from that caused by human actions and
account for the effect of human activity on natural variation. The effects of
each management action must be distinguishable from the effects of others.
We must be able to distinguish, for example, the increase in stream sedimentation caused by roads from that caused by livestock grazing.

Temporal components of monitoring are equally important. Monitoring
must be sufficiently long-term to detect changes, distinguish these changes
from natural variations caused by climate cycles, and establish cause-and-
effect relationships between management and changes observed on the
ground. Results from monitoring must be communicated widely and incor-
porated into changing goals, objectives, and procedures. This final component of making changes based on monitoring results is the heart of adaptive
management. Jeff Kershner, a Forest Service scientist at Utah State Univer-

sity, advises land managers about the key steps to understanding and implementing successful monitoring proposals.[31] The ten key steps are summarized here:

- Establish clear goals for monitoring related to the project's overall objectives.
- Develop a monitoring plan that includes implementation and effectiveness components.
- Fund adequately and commit to completion of monitoring.
- Design monitoring to detect change and be able to distinguish effects from other natural and artificial variables in your area.
- Establish a clear methodology so that different personnel can collect data consistently over time.
- Conduct baseline sampling to provide a benchmark for evaluating change over time relative to the conditions existing before the project began.
- Test whether an action has an effect by collecting data both where the action is present and where the action is absent (but all else is the same). This practice provides for a control sample.
- Take replicate (multiple) samples over space and time to ensure good results.
- Analyze monitoring data and report the results to partners and other interest groups.
- Modify the project's goals and implementation in response to the knowledge you gained from monitoring.

Thus there is more to monitoring than simple data collection and analysis. By gathering information on how the land reacts to management changes, we are in fact listening to the land. The land can tell us what management approach is most appropriate to the site given its template of soils, hydrology, and biology.

Wendell Berry argues that the proper approach to any kind of land use begins with two questions: What is the nature of the place? And what will nature permit here without damage to the soil, water, and biotic resources? By gaining a thorough knowledge of the land, we will come to know what nature will help us to do on any parcel. This is the knowledge Berry is seeking, and it is a key to living sustainably on the land.[32] Although Berry speaks about land management from his perspective of implementing sustainable agriculture on Kentucky farmland, his thoughts are just as relevant for management of the old-growth forests in the Pacific Northwest, the Southeast's longleaf pine forests, or elsewhere.

Land managers need to ask: "How can I make my objectives and actions harmonize with the local setting?" If livestock grazing is planned on western grasslands, for example, the following questions are relevant to achieving harmonious relationships. What kind of grazing occurred in the past? What was the amount and duration of grazing? What did the animals graze on? How much has the forage base changed in species and abundance compared to previous times? Were the animals migratory—and if so, where and when did they move? How does this activity compare to livestock that will graze the land? Discovering the historical context of how the land interacted with grazing is critical to finding the proper formula for livestock grazing in the future.

In her book on forest management in Oregon's Blue Mountains, Nancy Langston captures many of the subtle components of harmonizing land management to the local setting. She describes this process of monitoring and adaptive management—and the value of listening to the land—as follows:

> This process is never completely open-minded; initial ideas about how the world ought to work shape what we see, what we think is worth noting down. But there is an important ideal here, of allowing the natural world to shape our ideas, not just the other way around. . . . What [monitoring] means above all is people on the ground being responsive to what the land is telling them, and being responsible for acting on that knowledge.[33]

The Question of Greed

Perhaps the greatest gulf between our society and sustainability in the United States is our material greed and overconsumption. Use of wood products continues to grow unabated and is symptomatic of the never-ending demands. Although our population is about 5 percent of the world's total, the American people consume more than 25 percent of the industrial wood supply. From 1971 to 1996, the average size of new homes in the United States increased from 1520 to 2120 square feet despite a decrease in family size.[34] Is all that space—and the increased energy consumption required to heat and cool it—really necessary?

There is growing evidence that the rate of water use in the United States is unsustainable. The country's water consumption has doubled during the past forty years, and demands for agricultural and household water use continue to escalate. A typical family of four in the United States uses about

345 gallons of water per day compared to only 80 gallons a day for a family of four in developing countries. Only 3 percent of the American household use is for cooking and drinking. These water consumption rates are compounded by the pattern of population growth—especially in the West where already scarce water supplies are threatened by growth. Most western states are experiencing more than 4 percent annual population growth.[35]

Our growing demand for fresh water now presents a significant threat not only to freshwater ecosystems but to the integrity of public lands themselves. Dr. Catherine Pringle of the University of Georgia recently analyzed the cumulative effects of water use on public lands.[36] Her results paint a disturbing picture of how the growing demands for fresh water from farms and cities outside public land boundaries are affecting the integrity of lands and waters within the boundaries. This conflict occurs when demands increase for the water produced and stored in reservoirs on public lands. Water adjudications and other legal claims for water are a sign of this growing conflict. The Forest Service currently has more than five hundred legal claims concerning water in national forests. Of the 224 national wildlife refuges in the West, 150 of them report conflicts with water users located outside the refuges. The Forest Service predicts major water shortages in the upper and lower Colorado River basins as well as in California, the Rio Grande, the Great Basin, and the lower Mississippi River Valley by 2040.[37] Already, many western rivers are dry during substantial portions of the year because of unsustainable water use. Examples include Idaho's Snake River below Milner Dam, Arizona's Gila and Salt Rivers below Phoenix, Oregon's Powder River, California's San Joaquin River below Friant Dam, New Mexico's Rio Grande below Elephant Butte Reservoir, and the Arkansas River near the Colorado–Kansas border.

No matter how enlightened our land management policies are, there will be constant pressures to increase commodity production so long as the demand for water and other natural resources grows unabated. At the very least, we will look to exploiting other countries' resources even while recognizing the need to manage our own sustainably. Excessive individualism today threatens all of us tomorrow. As John Cairns Jr., Distinguished Professor at Virginia State University, has so clearly pointed out, the perceived rights so common to millions of Americans—for larger sport utility vehicles, larger homes, and more material goods—should not be tolerated when resources are being overutilized, when more than a billion people on this planet are malnourished, and when the gap between the poorest and the most affluent is the greatest in human history.[38]

Chapter 8

The Upshot: Conservation Challenges for a New Century

At first people refuse to believe that a strange new thing can be done, then they begin to hope it can be done, then they see it can be done—then it is done and all the world wonders why it was not done centuries ago.

—Frances Hodgson Burnett, *The Secret Garden* (1911)

Management of our public lands has evolved from the nineteenth-century frontier "conquer and tame" model, through the twentieth-century utilitarian "man manipulating nature" model, to the most recent conservation creed: ecological sustainability. Although the days of range wars and cut-and-run timber harvest are largely over, the debate over management of public lands, if anything, has intensified.

Today the citizen owners of the public lands are more involved in commenting on policies and helping shape management proposals than ever before. New information allows scientific studies to be aggregated and displayed in a meaningful way to people who might not otherwise understand how essential our large tracts of unfragmented lands are to maintaining water quality, wide-ranging wildlife, native fish species, and many other values.

The federal land management agencies struggle to keep pace with both social and technological changes. Some land managers resent public challenges to their decisions. Too often the prevailing sentiment within the agencies is "leave it to us, the experts that know best." From such a perspective public participation in land management planning can be viewed as either threatening or burdensome.[1] The days of the government biologist or forester spending a quiet career in the woods are over. Nearly every facet of their work is publicly scrutinized.

In an attempt to satisfy competing interests and comply with their multiple-use mandate and other laws, historically the Forest Service and BLM employed planning processes that dissect and partition the land. Special areas are set aside for timber production, for mining, for livestock grazing. Other areas are designated for wilderness, recreation, cultural, and other values. Layered over the top of this construct are ideological differences between the political parties that control powerful congressional committees and the White House. Upon taking office, the administration of George W. Bush, for example, made oil and gas development on public lands a top priority for the BLM and Forest Service.[2] Exploration and drilling in the Arctic National Wildlife Refuge was the centerpiece of their national energy policy. Contrast this emphasis with the focus of the interior secretary under President Bill Clinton, Bruce Babbitt, who much to the ire of many conservative western politicians created a National Landscape Conservation System to house the millions of acres of national monuments designated by the President. Although the successive political administrations maintain decidedly different objectives for public lands management, they share a common feature: both recognize the land as the wealth of the nation, one for material exploitation and economic opportunity, and the other as a legacy to pass on to future generations. Neither is "right" or "wrong," the question for all of us that own these lands is which best serves the interests of the nation in the long run?

Reflections on the Past

The notion that America's wealth and well-being come from the land is not new. On July 1, 1864, in the heat of the Civil War, President Lincoln signed a bill granting the Yosemite Valley and the Mariposa Grove of giant sequoias to California to be protected in their natural state. This became the core of today's Yosemite National Park. Even as the country was being torn apart by the Civil War, Lincoln recognized the importance of preserving the nation's natural wonders. Since Lincoln's time other presidents have followed his lead. Numerous laws and executive orders have protected millions of acres of our land. President Lyndon Johnson, for example, who like Lincoln is not well known for conservation policies, signed the Wilderness Act in 1964.

Almost forty years later, we have 104 million acres of federally designated wilderness as a memorial to our frontier heritage. This is an area larger than the state of California. Johnson and Lincoln understood that protecting this country and our way of life meant taking care of our lands and waters. President Carter protected more federal land, mostly in Alaska, than any other modern president. President Clinton, too, protected million of acres of land as national monuments and also established a vast marine reserve, the Northern Hawaiian Marine Protected Area.

The president most widely recognized as our greatest executive conservationist was focused on natural resource conservation when he became the nation's leader. On September 6, 1901, a shot fired by an assassin seriously wounded President William McKinley as he attended the Pan American Exhibition in Buffalo, New York. At the time, Vice-President Theodore Roosevelt was visiting members of the Vermont Fish and Game League at a luncheon on Lake Champlain. In eight days, he would become the nation's twenty-sixth president.

Roosevelt's rise appalled many of the leaders of his own political party. As the Republican governor of New York, Roosevelt had shown a troublesome interest in protecting natural resources and reining in corporate power. His initiatives flummoxed the high, mighty, and influential. They found a convenient solution to get this bull out of their china shop: draft Roosevelt for the vice-presidency. Six months later "that damned cowboy" was President. Roosevelt's White House tenure from 1901 to 1909 defined modern conservation. He understood and believed in science. Not since Thomas Jefferson had someone so well versed in the sciences occupied the White House. His conservation legacy is immense: more than 250 million acres of national forests, national monuments, national parks, and refuges.[3]

There are important lessons to be learned from the past, especially in land management, where we must always take the long view. Amid the strife in the Mideast, consider its natural resources. Today what in biblical times was called the "fertile crescent" belies its name. Once green valleys are brown, and most streams are dry. The land in the Mideast and many other parts of the world is simply used up and worn out from centuries of too many people pushing the land and water beyond their limits.

Increasing Our Ecological IQ

Although motivated by the best intentions, our efforts to manipulate nature often backfire. Repairing the long-term damage of the quick fix is often more expensive and socially disruptive than the original problem. After spending more than a billion dollars to mitigate the loss of salmon due to dams, we can now see that the effort has failed. Our effort now should turn to breaching the four lower Snake River dams in order to restore salmon habitat and populations.

After attempting to control the Missouri and Mississippi rivers, the government is breaching levees and spending hundreds of millions of dollars to buy out homeowners in floodplains. Millions more are being spent to put the meanders back into rivers, such as Florida's Kissimmee, that were straightened and channeled for flood control or navigation. In 2000, more than $2.5 billion was spent or appropriated to redress the legacy of past timber management practices and suppressing the rejuvenating role of fire in many western forests. There must be a better way.

Ecological destruction with all its economic costs and social disruption could be minimized through a more cautious approach to land management, but the utilarian-machine model remains deeply ingrained in our thinking. Some insist that federal statutes require federal land managers to concentrate on commodity production instead of land health. Others acknowledge the need for a broader approach but cloak their commercial interests in the guise of land health arguments. On the other end of the spectrum, some environmental interests refuse to accept anything other than wilderness-like management for all public lands.

Gradually, these old command and control philosophies are giving way to a more organic form of conservation. For almost a century, the utilitarian machine model ran its course. Faced with unprecedented forest and rangeland health crises and broad disagreement over how public lands should be used and managed, we need a new model for sustainable land management. One based less on technological quick fixes and more on approaches that bring people together to listen to the land and develop science-based collaborative solutions.

A greater proportion of citizens than ever before are living farther removed from the land. A few generations ago, more than 60 percent of our populace grew up in rural areas. Today 80 percent of the nation resides in urban or suburban areas. Rarely, if ever, has our nation undergone such dramatic and far-reaching demographic changes in so short a time. This may represent the most important and least understood threat to the future of public lands.

A well-educated and ecologically literate citizenry is the best defense against proposals to privatize or otherwise diminish the values of our public land legacy. Yet, most people give little thought to natural resources beyond food coming from supermarkets and energy from the light switch. Resource managers and scientists spend too much time talking to each other and too little time helping people understand the basic services provided by healthy functioning watersheds. Our task is to reconnect people with nature. We must learn to communicate in a way that connects peoples' hearts and minds with the land and the outdoors. This does not mean that people must live in the woods or out on the prairie. They just need to understand their roles and the effects of their daily actions and choices as consumers within the whole land community in order to better appreciate and understand our intrinsic connection to the lands and waters that surround us.

Grounding our politics and political debates in ecological common sense would not only protect wild landscapes but reduce the consumption, energy needs, and other demands that people place on nature. In addition to opening up the Arctic National Wildlife Refuge to energy development, a central component of George W. Bush's energy plan during his first few years in office was dramatically escalating coal-bed methane development from public lands in the lower 48. Stipulations protecting wildlife and fish habitats and water resources were described as "impediments." Predictably this position angered many environmentalists, hunters, and anglers.

Moreover, this policy ignored the fact that Americans consume 25 percent of the world's produced energy although only 3 percent of the world's energy supplies lie beneath our own soil. Oil and gas could be drilled from every wilderness area and national park, every sacred place and cultural site, and we still would fall dramatically short of meeting the nation's energy demands. A more informed and environmentally sensitive policy would be to rely less on the supply side of the equation and more on the gluttonous demand side.

Research done by Greg McPherson and his colleagues in California at the Center for Urban Forest Research reported there are some 177 million trees providing shade and conserving energy in that state. This saves California utilities an estimated $500 million annually in wholesale electricity purchase and generation costs. Moreover, these trees save consumers about $1 billion in air conditioning costs. McPherson's models predict that if Californians planted 50 million more shade trees in strategic locations, the energy saved would be equivalent to seven 100-megawatt power plants.[4] Trees produce the oxygen we breathe. They combat global warming by taking carbon from the air and providing shade. By intercepting precipitation, trees reduce storm-water runoff, which in turn saves money and improves water quality. Not only that, but trees improve the looks and livability of our cities and towns, increase property values, and help reconnect an urban society to nature.

Greening our cities and towns by energy efficient planning and by planting trees should be major elements of any national energy plan. Tree planting should be well ahead of drilling for oil and gas on sensitive lands or building more nuclear power plants. Rather than plundering our most remote treasures such as the Rocky Mountain Front for a few months' supply of oil and gas, given our high consumption levels, a more logical national energy plan would find ways to reduce energy demand, including harnessing the natural energy savings provided by trees and making community tree planting programs a priority.

Immediately following the events in New York City and at the Pentagon on September 11, 2001, America experienced an upwelling of patriotic sentiment. America's wealth is measured not only by its economic assets and military strength but also by the natural resources it passes on intact to future generations. A tangible expression of patriotism—the love and expression of that love for one's country—is learning to live sustainably on the land. At a minimum, protecting our national security includes living within the ecological limits of the land, and not allowing the hope of short-term economic gains to compromise the land legacy we bequeath to future generations. An ecologically literate constituency that demands reasonable and educated policies from its elected leaders is the key to maintaining our quality of life over the long haul.

Looking Toward a Sustainable Future

If multiple use is to continue as the governing axiom of public lands, their management must be guided by broadly supported principles. Chief among these is the overriding need to restore and protect land health and manage for basic ecological sustainability.

Ecological sustainability replaces the land-as-machine model's emphasis on commodity extraction with a broad multiple-use focus on all the benefits and values that healthy lands provide. Instead of trusting that soil and water conservation will emerge as a by-product of growing trees as crops, for example, ecological sustainability focuses on stabilizing soils, maintaining stream flows, and restoring the function, structure, and composition of watersheds. Then the trees that will then inevitably grow, including those removed and used for commercial purposes, will flow as the by-products of healthy forest ecosystems. The traditional timber sale contract, which establishes a private interest on public land, should be eliminated. The timber sale contract should be replaced with a new system that hires local people and companies to perform needed stewardship work. Merchantable timber could then be sold in the open market without the incentives to overcut that are built into traditional timber sales.

"The truth, as we are now beginning to realize," observed the novelist Aldous Huxley, "is that even things ought not to be treated as mere things. They should be treated as though they were parts of a vast living organism."[5] Sustainability is based on a land ethic—on forging a new relationship to the land. Living within the limits of the land is key. We offer the following six principles that we believe are critical to ensure sustainability of public lands in the future:

- *Learning and listening from the land.* Learning from the land means drawing conclusions about what the *land* needs. We should continually evaluate the effects of our management actions and modify our behavior accordingly. Listening to the land begins to treat the land as a community that we are a part of, not apart from.

- *Embrace complexity and natural disturbance on the land.* Wildfire, floods, forest insects and disease, and other disturbances are vital parts of the natural world that we must work with. When operating within their historic range of variability, they serve to increase habitat diversity and complexity. When human development interrupts ecological processes through decades of fire suppression, channelizing rivers, or draining wetlands, for example, it throws natural cycles of disturbance out of kilter—as the wildfires of 2000 and 2002 demonstrate—often with devastating effects on human communities. Management actions should solve for the broader pattern and functions of a dynamic landscape.

- *Managing the land in a conservative manner that maintains options for future generations.* Conservative use dictates that we protect remaining sensitive grasslands, roadless areas, and old-growth forests. Most important to this conservative perspective is the "precautionary principle" of land management, which dictates that we err on the side of doing no harm to the environment rather than harm it unintentionally or unexpectedly.

- *Respect people and place by integrating social, economic, and ecological components of sustainability into resource decisions.* As the writer Wendell Berry has said, "Our demands upon the earth are determined by our ways of living with one another; our regard for one another is brought to light in our ways of using the earth."[6] People are a part of the land; respect for the land must be based on respect for each other. Federal land managers have a moral and statutory obligation to invite and develop the broadest possible public involvement at every opportunity in land management planning, implementation, monitoring, and evaluation.

- *Collaborate across ownerships to address mutual problems.* Sooner or later, problems on our public lands become problems for neighboring landowners, and vice versa, as exotic species or land disturbances cascade downstream or downwind. An important task ahead for the American people will be to establish frameworks for collaborative planning across jurisdictional boundaries on multiple scales, from our smallest hollows in West Virginia to our mightiest river systems in the Northwest.
- *Incorporate sound science but commit to continuous learning.* Science, by its very nature, incorporates a principle of uncertainty that limits our knowledge and authority to act. The Committee of Scientists put it this way: "By approaching planning not as a 'cookbook' for making decisions, but as an opportunity to learn, to test new ideas, and to continuously evolve based on new understandings, the Forest Service will meet the expectations for 'conservation leadership' set forth in the National Forest Management Act."[7] We must be prepared to adapt when the land surprises us, when it tells us something didn't work as planned.

Focus Essay

Bringing People and Conservation Together: The Future Constituency for Public Lands
MARK VAN PUTTEN*

One of Aldo Leopold's more famous quotes comes from his essay "The Ecological Conscience." Leopold writes: "The practice of conservation must spring from a conviction of what is ethically and aesthetically right, as well as what is economically expedient. A thing is right only when it tends to preserve the integrity, stability and beauty of the community, and the community includes the soil, waters, fauna, and flora, as well as people."

*Mark Van Putten is president and CEO of the National Wildlife Federation.

Leopold recognized that people are an intrinsic and fundamental part of nature. Too often today, conservation is portrayed as a battle of progress versus preservation. Interest groups, elected leaders, and the media are all guilty of helping to perpetuate the myth that conservation and environmental protection are somehow divorced from human prosperity. Leopold understood that improvements in our nation's standard of living cannot take place without first securing the health of the lands and waters that sustain us all. Conversely, conservation efforts that do not take into account the well-being of people often lack the support needed to sustain them over the long haul.

Education is essential to creating an active constituency for conservation. The good news is that when presented with reliable scientific information, people will choose to support efforts to conserve and restore rare wildlife species and vanishing landscapes. Consider the case of the Florida Everglades. Once an 8-million-acre riverine wilderness, the fabled River of Grass was reduced to half its size by decades of urban sprawl and well-intentioned but ecologically damaging flood control and dredging. As a result, more than sixty-eight species that depend on the ecosystem are presently threatened or endangered and populations of wading birds have plummeted by 90 percent. Meanwhile 1.7 billion gallons of fresh water are dumped daily into the sea.

Local citizens understood that decades of manipulating the Everglades actually worsened flooding while devastating wildlife and fish species. They helped develop a twenty-year, $8 billion restoration plan that was overwhelmingly approved by Congress after the stakes were made clear. This plan provides a multiyear blueprint for restoring the ecological processes that allow the River of Grass to sustain both humans and wildlife.

The promise of the Everglades restoration offers hope—and an example to follow—for other conservation-minded citizens and communities who understand the inextricable link between conservation and prosperity. The environmental movement was spurred by incredible successes at the national level to pass laws and regulations that make our air and water cleaner and protect imperiled wildlife species. But it is likely that most future conservation gains will flow from local people working together to find what Republican President Theodore Roosevelt called "common sense solutions to common problems for the common good."

For example: A citizen management plan to reintroduce grizzly bears—only 1100 of which remain in the lower 48 states—to 15 million acres of wilderness in Idaho and Montana was the direct result of conservationists working in partnership with the timber industry and others. That the Bush administration in 2002 delayed the plan does not diminish the significance of these disparate interests coming together to restore North America's largest carnivore to the wild.

Taking care of the public lands and waters that sustain us is not an either/or proposition. Educating people about how conservation affects their lives in fundamentally important ways is the most effective method of building an active constituency for the protection and restoration of our public land legacy. For example: 25 percent of the nation's drinking water flows across our national forests. Not only do publicly owned rivers and streams provide habitat for native fish and wildlife, they provide downstream communities with clean drinking water while saving hundreds of millions of dollars in reduced filtration costs. The value of saving an obscure fish species may not always resonate with every citizen. But few other issues are as important to them as the quality of their drinking water.

Every environmentalist is keenly aware of how land development and urbanization threaten wildlife and fish habitats. Yet we must strive to explain how healthy public lands translate to improved standards of living and quality of life for millions of citizens.

America's public lands are the envy of the world. No other nation possesses the comprehensive system of public parks, refuges, forests, and rangelands that are every American's birthright. But as so many patriots have warned, freedom is not free. Proposals to develop, privatize, sell, or otherwise remove public lands from public hands are entertained by Congress and state legislatures every year.

Whether people support public lands because they make their living from them, use them for recreation, or just take solace in knowing that they still exist in an increasingly urbanized and developed landscape is less important than the fact that we must not become complacent. Public lands are our gift to our children's children. Our active involvement helps sustain and strengthen this incredible land legacy.

Conservation Challenges

The challenge for policymakers, land managers, and interested citizens is not to predict the annual flow of wood fiber, forage, or energy produced from public lands. Nor is it to anticipate shifting political winds and act accordingly. The role of the resource manager is to state what is in the best long-term interest of the land and explain what services the land can provide in an ecologically sustainable manner based on the best science of the day. Elected leaders and political appointees typically shape these policies to fit their political agenda. As controversies over the spotted owl in the Pacific Northwest and more recent efforts to drill in the Arctic National Wildlife Refuge and exploit coal bed methane energy resources in the Rocky Mountains demonstrate, in the end it is the citizens that own these lands who speak loudest and last. Every citizen has the power to tell the agencies how they want their lands managed and, if that fails, to seek recourse in the court system or redress through the ballot box.

Stewardship of the public lands means managing with an eye to the future. What are the values that make our network of public lands so unique? What will we want from this land in fifty years? If public land managers and the people they serve are not continually asking these questions, they need not worry about the answers. Because odds are that the public land network we now enjoy will cease to exist, either through privatization or other political dismemberment. This long-term perspective is often confounded by election cycles of two to six years that impel some political leaders to demand more from the public lands and waters than they can sustain over the long term, the values and characteristics of public lands that will provide for what Gifford Pinchot called "the greatest good for the greatest number for the longest time."[8]

Below we identify the significant conservation challenges for multiple-use public lands now and in the future. Resolving these issues will require a confluence of scientific information, citizen activism, ecological understanding, agency leadership, and political will.

Our public lands—over 500 million acres—are a uniquely American heritage. Other cultures have their great edifices or works of art. England and Spain have their great sea captains, Rome and Athens their temples, and Egypt its pyramids. We in the United States have our public lands—what remains of the frontier that shaped our character as a people and a nation.

At one time public lands were viewed as a vast storehouse of inexhaustible resources. Whoever was capable of exploiting those resources for personal profit, in the name of progress and growth, could do so. Too often the result was environmental destruction and, along with it, social and economic disruption. The tragedy of the commons is a very real part of our history and a central motive behind the creation of the Forest Service and BLM. Without thoughtful conservation leadership over such vexing issues, to intone Plato's overused but seldom heeded prediction, the past may very well serve as prologue to the future.

Protect Our Waters

Past wars were fought over land and religion. Without forethought and planning, the wars of the future will center on water. Water demands tripled worldwide between 1950 and 1990. According to a recent report of the United Nations Economic Commission, two-thirds of the world's population will face water shortages within the next twenty-five years. In California, where national forests supply half of the surface runoff in the state, water has always been the volatile issue. In the arid Southwest, new battles are brewing and old battles continue to be fought over the badly depleted waters of the Colorado River basin. The Great Plains states, from the Dakotas to Texas, depend on the Ogallala Aquifer. The Ogallala is being depleted faster than it is being replenished and is now 10 to 100 feet below historic levels.

The cleanest water in the country flows from our forests and wildlands. Collectively our public lands are the largest and most important water provider in the United States. Drinking water for some 60 million Americans living in 3400 communities in thirty-three states, for example, flows across the 192-million-acre National Forest System. Yet local politicians fight efforts to secure federal water rights for fish and wildlife, not to mention drinking water, at every opportunity.

The federal agencies measure hundreds of thousands of data points annually to predict timber and forage production, wildlife populations, and other resource values. We know that the marginal value of water alone from national forests exceeds $3.7 billion per year.[9] Yet we possess no systematic and consistent methodology to evaluate the most important measure of all: the health of our watersheds. Watershed function is the interaction of soil, water, and vegetation. Keeping water on the land longer reduces soil erosion and allows more time for percolation into groundwater aquifers. Given the fundamental importance of water to all life, watershed health and water quality should be the basic measure of success for all of our public land managers.

Protect Remaining Wildlands from Fragmentation

National forest roadless areas contain all or portions of 354 municipal watersheds contributing drinking water to millions of citizens. Maintaining these and other forested areas in an undisturbed condition saves downstream communities millions of dollars in water filtration costs.[10] Moreover, 25 percent of endangered and threatened animal species and 13 percent of listed plant species are likely to have habitat within national forest roadless areas. In other words: About 2 percent of America's land base affects or provides habitat to 25 percent of the nation's listed species.[11]

The implications of the excessive loss of large unfragmented tracts of land are too often lost on those who call themselves "conservative." Facing an $8.4 billion road maintenance backlog growing exponentially through neglect, the effort to protect roadless areas described in Chapter 5 are not a bold action for the Forest Service so much as a first step to reducing a multibillion-dollar taxpayer liability. Similarly, prohibiting the harvest of the few remaining old-growth forests is not "liberal"; rather, it is the height of conservatism when so little old-growth forest remains. A true conservative does not use up a diminishing resource. Similarly, designating wilderness areas is not radical; it is one of the most conservative actions the government can take regarding the present and future use of public lands.[12]

Maintaining large open spaces and tracts of public land is an increasingly important task given the fragmentation and sprawl occurring on private lands. For example: An average of 3.2 million acres per year of private forest, wetland, farmland, and open space—an area about twice the size of Delaware or over 8700 acres per day—were converted to urban uses between 1992 and 1997.[13] This is more than double the rate of development of the previous decade, though the population growth remained relatively constant.

Today's rate of sprawl and development brings real meaning to Will Rogers' advice: "Buy land, they ain't making it any more." Even though Congress has designated 104 million acres within the National Wilderness Preservation System, more is needed. Much of the presently designated wilderness is rock and ice, while some of the most biologically important ecosystems—bottomland hardwoods and tall-grass prairie, for example—are dramatically underrepresented.

The continued development and sprawl on private land adjacent to public land and the fragmentation of public land have an indirect effect of increasing recreation pressure on the remaining large tracts of public land. Recreation use of public lands continues to grow rapidly. Recreation visitor-days in national forests have increased from under 20 million per year immediately after World War II to well over 200 million fifty years later.[14] This trend will surely continue as private land is increasingly posted with "no trespassing" signs. The recreational, aesthetic, and ecological values of public lands far outstrip their commodity values. But recreational use, or any use, should not be allowed to destroy the long-term health, diversity, and productivity of the land.

Consider one of the downsides of motorized off-road recreational vehicles. Advances in technology enable more people to reach more remote and higher elevations on land, snow, and water than ever before, causing fragmentation of wildlife and fish habitat, degradation of water and air quality, user conflicts, and increased noise levels. For example: Snowmobiles in Yellowstone Park so diminish air quality that park rangers are now forced to wear air masks. Off-road vehicles are a legitimate use of some public lands, but their use must take place within the ecological and social limits of the land. Off-road vehicle use should be limited to designated roads and trails, not allowed to degrade remote and untrammeled landscapes. By working with communities of interest and communities of place to set limits in open and public forums, off-road vehicle users and public-land agencies can achieve mutually agreeable policies that protect the land.

Focus Essay

Enduring Values of Our Public Lands: Peace, Wildness, and Beauty

GAYLORD NELSON*

America has a special love affair with its public lands—the only large, wide-open spaces left that still resemble the lands our ancestors viewed when they came here. This huge estate totals 623 million acres or almost a million square miles. It is a remarkable mosaic of forests, plains, mountains, valleys, rivers, lakes, seashores, deserts, and marshlands.

While we properly fuss and worry about endangered species, we tend to forget that perhaps the most important "endangered species" of all is America's unique heritage of wildlands, wilderness, and natural landscapes. Let's take a quick look at where we were, where we are, and where we are going. A few numbers will tell the story—a story that will alarm everyone who is concerned about the legacy we leave to our children and the generations that follow.

Back in 1930, there were about 3 million recreation visits to the national

*Gaylord Nelson is a former Wisconsin governor and United States senator and the founder of Earth Day.

parks; in 1950, there were 30 million; by 1999, there were about 300 million—a hundredfold increase in seventy years. At the current rate, many of our national parks, national forests, national wildlife refuges, and BLM public lands soon will resemble little more than noisy, crowded theme parks. If we try to duplicate on the public lands every activity permitted on the private lands we will quickly destroy the special quality of these natural landscapes.

Most people are attracted to the public lands for their scenic beauty and peace and quiet. They go there for sightseeing, camping, picnicking, cross-country skiing and snowshoeing, bird watching, hunting, fishing, hiking, photography, and other light-impact activities. Unfortunately, the proliferation of off-road vehicles (ORVs) is rapidly destroying the natural qualities that we hold dear. The all-terrain vehicles, motorcycles, jet skis, and snowmobiles are heavy-impact and noise-intrusive vehicles. The Forest Service estimates that ORV use will increase from 5.3 million visitor-days annually twenty years ago to a projected 118 million visitor-days per year by 2020—just in the national forests!

More than fifty-two years of active involvement in conservation matters leads me to the conviction that a large majority of our citizens would support whatever measures may be necessary to maintain the integrity of our last great natural landscapes. By this standard, only those activities that are sustainable without environmental deterioration would be permitted on public lands. What a difference it would have made had we listened to the words of wisdom about our public lands by observers of another era.

In 1912, James Bryce, British ambassador to the United States, had this to say about Yosemite National Park: "What Europe is now, is that toward which you in America are tending. Presently, steam cars stop some 12 miles away from the entrance of Yosemite. . . . Surely development should come no closer. . . . If you were to realize what the result of the automobile will be in that wonderful, that incomparable valley, you would keep it out." No one paid any attention to Mr. Bryce. So now that "wonderful, that incomparable valley" has traffic jams during the day and evening accommodations for 7500 people. The night scene has been described as looking like downtown Los Angeles. Surely this is not what we want for our national parks or other public lands.

Over sixty years ago, Interior Secretary Harold Ickes warned against permitting airplane flights over our parks: "If we encourage the airplane business, we will see Glacier, Yellowstone and Yosemite from the air at 100 miles an hour. . . . I don't see any reason for catering to that sort of thing."

In 1985, Governor Bruce Babbitt testified at a congressional hearing that the airplane noise in the Grand Canyon is "equivalent to being downtown in Phoenix at rush hour." That's a far cry from Zane Grey's description of the Grand Canyon in 1906 when he wrote: "One feature of this ever-changing spectacle never changes, its eternal silence."

In the 1920s, Charles Russell, the great cowboy painter, described his view of what we are doing to the land and what we should do about it in the rough and ready language of the cowboy West. After listening to a long run of self-congratulatory, windy bombast by boosters from Great Falls, Montana, he finally got his chance: "In my book, a pioneer is a man who turned all the grass upside down, strung barb-wire over the dust that was left, poisoned the water and cut down the trees, killed the Indian who owned the land, and called it progress. If I had my way, the land here would be like God made it, and none of you sons of bitches would be here at all."

The bottom line comes to this—in the next few decades when total recreation visits to the public lands expand to one and one-half billion or more and the off-road vehicular mix expands by a factor of four or more then, sad to say, our rare heritage of natural lands could be history. The only way to save these special lands is to change the current management practices dramatically—and soon. This will mean significantly reducing all activities that degrade the land or water, impact on critical habitats, or intrude upon the tranquility and enjoyment of these lands. This is the critical imperative if we are serious about preserving the last large natural landscapes left within our boundaries.

No other nation has undertaken to set aside such a large and magnificent portion of its landscape as a commons for the use and enjoyment of its citizens and to provide such a varied habitat for its wild creatures. If a significant slice of natural America is to be preserved for this and future generations, it must be here on these lands. There is no other place.

Learn to Live with Wildfires

Smokey Bear represents perhaps the most successful public education campaign in our history. Today the challenge is to help people understand that although fire is always dangerous, not all fire is bad. Like wind and water, fire is an agent of change that can rejuvenate the land.

Many forests are unhealthy, as we have seen because of a combination of past logging and grazing practices and the cumulative effects of decades of fire suppression within fire-dependent ecological systems. Scientists widely acknowledge the healthy and rejuvenating role played by fire in fire adapted ecosystems. The recognition of what ails our forests and grasslands is slow to translate to changes in policy, however. For half of the year there is talk about the need to reintroduce, or otherwise allow, fire in fire-adapted ecosystems; in the other half we spend hundreds of millions of dollars to suppress it. In 2000 and 2002, for example, federal agencies sought to suppress well over 95 percent of all fire starts. More than $1 billion in each of those years was spent fighting fires on public lands.

The Kalmiopsis region of Oregon's Siskiyou National Forest illustrates this complex dilemma. On September 15, 2001, lightning started the Craggie Fire in the Kalmiopsis Wilderness. The fire was in extremely rugged terrain and posed no threat to structures. The 96,240-acre Silver Fire had burned the same area in 1987 and other large fires were known from the same area in 1938 and the summers of 1917 and 1918. Rather than allowing the Craggie Fire to burn, it was immediately attacked by aerial tankers and helicopters. By the time the Craggie Fire was controlled, 275 acres had burned with a suppression cost of $2.2 million. Forest Service policy dictated that the fire be attacked and controlled because of dry conditions and high fuel loads despite the shorter days of mid-September and the onset of cooler and moister weather. To some, allowing the Craggie Fire to burn might seem risky. But the alternative is a fire in some future year that occurs in the middle of summer with even more fuel present.

This is precisely what happened in 2002. On July 13 of that year, during a hot dry summer, lightning started a series of fires in Oregon, including several in and around the Kalmiopsis Wilderness. Because of the number of fires burning at that time, no firefighters were available for the initial four days to fight the Kalmiopsis fires. In the dry rugged terrain and hot weather, the wildfires exploded. By August 7, several fires around the Kalmiopsis combined into the Biscuit Fire and spread to 286,000 acres with more than 2,000 firefighters on the lines. By August 13, an army of more than six thousand firefighters battled the fire, which had spread to more than 375,000 acres. By the time the Biscuit Fire was contained in early September, fire had swept across nearly five hundred thousand acres with firefighting costs approaching $150 million, making this the most expensive fire fought in the Forest Service's nearly 100-year history.

Contrary to media reports, the Biscuit Fire did not "destroy" the landscape. The fire burned at various intensities, leaving some patches of forest scorched but other areas completely untouched. The result was a classic mosaic pattern of burning on the landscape, which benefits many ecosystem functions and restores habitat diversity. According to Forest Service estimates, approximately 15 percent of the area burned at high severity, 24 percent at moderate, 61 percent at low severity or was unburned.[15] The costs of such massive firefighting efforts are not just high in terms of dollars, but also in terms of firefighter safety, damage caused by bulldozers to fragile soils and sensitive botanical areas, and the potential for spread of exotic organisms with firefighting equipment. In the long run, restoration of fire will occur in one form or another. *How* fire returns to these fire-adapted ecosystems is the question.

The federal fire bureaucracy spends hundreds of millions annually, over a billion dollars in a bad fire year, in fire suppression with little oversight or accountability. Meanwhile, costs continue to escalate and the tragic loss of young firefighters is now all too common. Federal wildland fire agencies need to rethink their whole approach to fires. The general approach should be that remote wilderness and roadless area fires will be closely monitored but generally allowed to burn, provided they do not threaten human communities. Meanwhile the fire programs of the federal agencies should focus the overwhelming majority of their hazardous fuels reduction and suppression efforts on protecting lives and property in the areas where forests and communities meet, including efforts to help landowners reduce fire risk in the immediate vicinity of their homes. Such an approach would help restore natural fire cycles in remote places, save tens of millions of dollars, and above all, minimize risks to firefighter safety.

This is not to say that a "let it burn" philosophy should prevail. The challenge is to put fire back on the land in a way that minimizes the risk to people and communities while mimicking natural fire regimes to the extent possible. Many forests evolved with fire and indeed need fire for their healthy development. The complicating factor is people. The sprawl of housing developments in rural areas, foothills and even up mountainsides is occurring all over the country, especially in fire-prone areas such as California and the Intermountain West. Making matters worse, many homeowners fail to take steps to protect their homes and lives such as avoiding wood roofs and cedar siding, keeping woodpiles away from the home, clearing vegetation adjacent to the house, and other common-sense precautions.

The wildland/urban interface now extends across millions of acres. In the year 2000, the Forest Service received its largest budget increase ever, mostly to rebuild its firefighting capability and reduce fire risk on the land. In the aftermath of the 2002 fire season, congressional and executive branch proposals to limit public involvement, eliminate environmental analysis requirements, and severely curtail judicial review of thinning projects were rampant. Judicious use of prescribed fire, along with efforts to thin brush, small trees, and other fine fuels are part of the solution. But cutting people and scientific analyses out of the process is shortsighted at best and will likely lead to further confrontation and polarization between the public and government. Without significant investments in research to determine which treatments reduce fire risks while restoring landscapes, the agencies are unlikely to overcome the distrust of a populace that has begun to question all timber harvest.

Fire, like floods, drought, and hurricanes, are natural events that are largely uncontrollable. Rachel Carson once said: "The control of nature is a phrase conceived in arrogance."[16] Perhaps what we need most is the humility to accept that we cannot control all natural forces.

Recover Rare Species

We are losing species at an alarming rate and the trend must be reversed. The world-renowned biodiversity expert, E. O. Wilson warns: "Species of plants and animals are disappearing a hundred or more times faster than before the coming of humanity, and as many as half may be gone by the end of this century."[17] The development that gives us homes in the woods, strip malls, and harvest of old-growth forests simultaneously dismantles our genetic library piece by piece. Once extinct, these species and the role they play in the whole community of life are gone forever. Aldo Leopold put it this way: "To keep every cog and wheel is the first precaution of intelligent tinkering."[18]

Public lands serve as a biological refuge for many native species. National forests and grasslands, for example, contain 181 of the 327 watersheds identified by The Nature Conservancy as critical for the conservation of biodiversity in the United States.[19] High biodiversity enhances ecosystem stability, resistance to invasion by nonnative species, and resilience to both natural and human-caused disturbances.[20]

That public lands harbor such a large percentage of our remaining wild heritage is of significant value, something to be nurtured rather than a problem to be worked around or viewed as an impediment to the extraction of natural resources. Restoring biodiversity, like other forms of public land and water conservation, is the mark of a mature and forward-looking nation. Congress should make clear that the conservation of biodiversity and water quality are the central objectives of all public land management. Such a focus would help to dispel the debate and confusion within multiple-use agencies about their primary mission. Restoration of public lands could lead to tens of thousands of jobs in rural communities across the United States repairing damaged rangelands, cleaning up abandoned mines, healing forests, reducing fire risk to human communities, and obliterating unneeded roads. This would be a legacy to be proud of. The social and economic benefits would be enormous.

Reform the 1872 Mining Law

The 1872 Mining Law is without question the most outdated natural resource law in the United States. It should either be jettisoned or updated to meet the needs of the twenty-first century. The statute is a product of an era when women and most minorities could not vote, the nation was struggling through Civil War reconstruction, and St. Louis represented the western frontier. Its antiquated approach to royalties is well known and for good reason—none exist. The result is a blatant giveaway of public resources. Since its inception, the law has allowed public lands as large as the state of Connecticut to be privatized for as little as $2.50 per acre.

The Environmental Protection Agency estimates that 40 percent of all headwater rivers and streams in the western United States are polluted because of hard-rock mining.[21] Every other use of natural resources on public land—timber, grazing, oil and gas, recreation—is subject to approval or rejection by field managers for environmental or safety reasons. Hard-rock mining is not. Anyone who stakes a claim and can prove the economic value of underlying hard-rock minerals maintains a right to mine. As with every other multiple use, federal managers need the latitude to place lands off limits or to allow mining through the broad public-land planning process. When a site-specific analysis determines that mining is detrimental to other multiple uses, a local manager must have the power to say no.

New legislation should clearly define bonding provisions sufficient to mitigate watershed damage and minimize the long-term risk to taxpayers of mine failure. Finally, a fund financed by mining royalties should be established to address reclamation of abandoned mines on public lands that threaten human health, drinking water supplies, or fish and wildlife habitat. Mining Law reform should be at the top of the list of conservation priorities for congressional and executive action.

Control Exotic Species

The EPA's *State of the Great Lakes Ecosystem Report* suggests that biological pollution is a more substantial threat than chemical pollution.[22] Some scientists believe that only deforestation during the lumbering era was as ecologically damaging as the spread of invasive species. In the western United States, the Interior Department estimates that noxious weeds spread at a rate of 1.7 million acres annually. This is more than 4600 acres per day. Leafy spurge has infested over 5 million acres in twenty-three states, causing economic losses of some $100 million annually.[23] Yellow starthistle has spread to eight states and has infested over 12 million acres in California alone. So many acres are infested with yellow starthistle in California that it had to be removed from the state's noxious weed list because by law all noxious weeds on the state's official list must be controllable. Many believe that starthistle has long surpassed the treatable stage.[24]

The exotic species problem is an explosion in slow motion. Dutch elm disease wiped out the majestic elms and changed the look of hundreds of American cities and towns. Chestnut blight was discovered in the early 1900s and in fifty years had devastated the species that once accounted for one in every four trees in many eastern hardwood forests.[25] White pine blister rust, kudzu, melaleuca in the Everglades, and the long and growing list of species displacing native rangeland plants foreshadow other lasting social and ecological impacts. New invaders such as the Asian longhorn beetle made their way into North America via the ports of New York and Chicago.

Modern transportation systems and international travel to every continent of the world make the transport of millions of organisms, bacteria, seeds, insects, and others around the world commonplace. We are mixing plant and animal species and homogenizing our biological landscape with largely unknown but likely dire consequences. Pangaea, the supercontinent from billions of years ago, is being recreated at least in the biological sense. Weedy species are taking over the land and water with resulting ecosystem instability and reduced productivity.

Managing exotic species is difficult because many of them thrive in disturbed habitats. Our best defense against exotics is protecting our remaining undisturbed habitats and landscapes and maintaining native biodiversity. Effective import inspections and standards are essential. So too is a science-based approach that is proactive and predictive as opposed to the typical reactive approach of trying to corral the horse after it is out of the barn.

Control efforts should take an ecosystem approach that spreads across ownerships and land jurisdictions. Similar to programs within the Farm Bill that encourage conservation, the federal government should create incentives for private landowners who eradicate exotic invasive species from their lands. Methods of spread and establishment should be identified and then halted. Biological control agents, when they are called for, should be rigorously screened for unwanted impacts on native species.

Stop Cutting Old-Growth Forests on Public Lands

Commercial logging of old-growth forests on public lands should end. Today's forestry practices are far superior to those of just a generation ago.

Yet, there is no policy, practical, or economic reason to harvest our few surviving old-growth forests so that they can be made into lumber for homes.

More than any other issue, the old-growth forest debate symbolizes the conflict and controversy that has plagued the Forest Service and BLM for the past thirty years.[26] Some attribute this controversy to "analysis paralysis," the inability of federal land management agencies to complete projects on the ground.[27] But the length of time it takes to complete a project as well as the many administrative hurdles placed before the federal agencies are a direct reflection of the fact that some Forest Service and BLM proposals are anathema to the majority of the citizen owners of public lands. The requirements for study, review, and then more study are a direct reflection of widespread distrust of certain policies and activities. No issue demonstrates this point more clearly than the debate over old-growth forests. The multitude of lawsuits in a democratic society is often a direct expression of public dissatisfaction. Yet the bureaucracies and the internal incentive systems that impel cutting valuable big, old trees refuse to change.

Presently there are about 4.5 million acres of multistoried late-successional and old-growth forests on public lands within the range of the northern spotted owl. This represents a fivefold loss from historic conditions. Not long ago, old-growth forests were viewed as decadent or "overmature." Old-growth forests provide a host of ecosystem services and functions, including:

- Buffering microclimate changes and stresses during seasonal weather extremes.
- Producing food for old-growth-adapted species.
- Storing carbon, which can act as a buffer to broad-scale climate change.
- Retaining high amounts of nutrients and water per acre.
- Providing sources of arthropod predators and organisms beneficial to other successional forest stages.
- Maintaining low soil erosion.

It is time, past time, that policymakers catch up with the public and the science and recognize the ecological and social values of these few remaining old-growth forests and preserve them for the use and benefit of future generations.

Practice Watershed-Scale Restoration

Restoration and maintenance of watershed function should be a central premise for public land management, but it is vital for private land as well.

Few prospects offer more promise for the future of conservation than cooperative efforts to restore hundreds of millions of acres of privately owned land in the United States. About two-thirds of the forests in the United States—some 490 million acres—are in nonfederal ownership. This includes over 9 million woodland owners who own tracts of land less than 100 acres. Of these, only a small percentage have science-based management plans. According to a 1998 National Research Council report, more than 20 million acres of forest are classified as urban and community forests.[28] And over 70 million acres of cities and towns now sprawl over what once was forest.[29]

Restoration literally means to bring back to a former state. Watershed restoration is the reestablishment of the original structure, function, and ecological processes of a watershed, including its natural diversity. Successful restoration means that the characteristics and function (such as, plant productivity and hydrology) of a watershed have been recreated or repaired and that natural processes can occur.

Ecologists and conservation biologists often become obsessed by terms such as "historic" or "presettlement conditions" to define the goals of restoration.[30] We have affected, and will continue to affect, our lands and waters. Aiming for some presettlement condition as the goal of restoration may belie reality, and worse, distance people whose support is essential. Working with people to emphasize the restoration of an ecological system ensures that watersheds can continue to provide the goods and services upon which we all depend.

Perhaps a more practical objective is to take steps to manage the landscape toward a condition that is more self-sustaining than at present. The key is to work together across all ownerships to address the primary causes of degradation such as too many roads, riparian logging, and land fragmentation through energy development—not simply focusing on the obvious symptoms such as site erosion.

The benefits of a healthy watershed include:

- High-quality and dependable water supplies.
- Moderation of the effects of climate change, flooding, and drought.
- Recharge of stream systems and groundwater aquifers.
- Maintenance of healthy riparian areas that reduce erosion, buffer the effects of flooding, and moderate stream temperatures.
- Resilience to natural events such as fire and drought and the ability to recover rapidly from management activities and other disturbances.
- High biological diversity and habitat complexity for native species.
- Long-term soil productivity and assurance that overall soil and nutrient loss does not exceed soil formation.

Watershed councils and citizen groups that represent the full array of socio-economic and environmental interests help public land managers decide on priorities and strategies for restoration. Engaging communities of place and communities of interest in restoration projects helps to create a personal interest in the successful outcome of restoration.

Protecting roadless areas and old-growth forests alone will not heal what ails our watersheds. Although roadless areas represent some of our most important remaining habitat for fish and wildlife, these areas are often among the least biologically productive portions of the landscape. Roadless areas and old-growth forests are often found at harder-to-reach high elevations with steep-gradient streams and highly erosive soils. The more biologically productive lands are often at lower elevations on private land, in valley bottoms, and along main-stem rivers. Our challenge is to protect the best of what remains while working across ownerships to knit disconnected patches of the land into a healthy functioning landscape.

The Upshot

Despite a general acceptance of their causes, we have only just begun to redress our forest, river, and grassland health problems. It took decades of fire suppression and timber and grazing management practices, for example, to build up the fuels that today endanger our communities and forests. It will take more than a few years to restore wildfire to its natural role and make communities safer. What we need now are not quick fixes determined through short-term election cycles but a sustained commitment by the citizen-owners of the public lands. It is long and hard work. But it is worth it. By working together with an eye toward restoring the ecological processes and reconnecting our communities to the watersheds that deliver their most vital services, we can make our planet a better place.

Many decades ago, Aldo Leopold ventured a prediction: "Fifty years from now, the acquisition of public game lands may be recognized as a milestone in the evolution of democratic government."[31] Leopold's prophecy came true. Americans cherish their public wildlands as a crowning achievement. Fifty years from now, our shared commitment to live within the limits of the land will be recognized as a milestone in the evolution of our public land management. It remains for us to translate our need for sustainability into on-the-ground results that Americans will cherish in fifty, a hundred, a thousand years: healthy watersheds supporting vibrant communities living in harmony with the lands and waters that sustain us all.

Notes

Chapter 1

1. J. Muhn and H. R. Stuart, eds., *Opportunity and Challenge: The Story of BLM* (Washington, D. C.: GPO, 1988).
2. C. A. Wood, "The Lands Everybody Wants," *Environmental Forum* 12(4) (1995): 14–21.
3. P. W. Gates, *History of Public Land Law Development* (Washington, D.C.: GPO, 1968).
4. M. Conover, *The General Land Office: Its History, Activities, and Organization*, Institute for Government Research, Service Monographs of the U.S. Government, no. 13 (Baltimore: Johns Hopkins University Press, 1923).
5. Muhn and Stuart, *Story of BLM*, p. 9.
6. Muhn and Stuart, *Story of BLM*.
7. Gates, *History*.
8. S. T. Dana, *Forest and Range Policy—Its Development in the United States* (New York: McGraw-Hill, 1956).
9. Gates, *History*, p. 710.
10. Ibid., p. 723.
11. Ibid., p. 418.
12. Dana, *Forest and Range Policy*.
13. John Wesley Powell's 1878 "A Report on the Land of Arid Region of the United States" was considered by historian Bernard De Voto to be one of the most revolutionary books on land use ever written by an American. The report not only set forth the initial surveys of the West but fundamentally attacked the whole body of law on which the West was being developed.
14. Gates, *History*.

15. S. J. Pyne, *Fire in America: A Cultural History of Wildland and Rural Fire* (Princeton: Princeton University Press, 1982).

16. P. N. Limerick, *Legacy of Conquest: The Unbroken Past of the American West* (New York: Norton, 1987).

17. T. Ewing, *Annual Report of the Secretary of the Interior,* House Executive Document, 31st Congress, 1st Session, vol. III, no. 5, pt. 2 (serial no. 570), U.S. Congress, House of Representatives, Washington, D.C., 1850.

18. G. P. Marsh, *Man and Nature; or, Physical Geography as Modified by Human Action,* ed. D. Lowenthal (Cambridge, Mass.: Belknap Press of Harvard University Press, 1965).

19. H. D. Thoreau, *The Maine Wood.* (Boston: Ticknor & Fields, 1864).

20. G. W. Williams, "Chronology of Events and People in the Development of the American Conservation/Environmental Movement, 1799–2000," USDA Forest Service, unpublished manuscript.

21. H. K. Steen, *The Beginning of the National Forest System,* Publication FS-488 (Washington, D.C.: USDA Forest Service, 1991).

22. H. K. Steen, *The U.S. Forest Service: A History* (Seattle: University of Washington Press, 1976).

23. Gates, *History.*

24. C. F. Wilkinson, *Crossing the Next Meridian: Land, Water, and the Future of the West* (Washington, D.C.: Island Press, 1992).

25. G. Pinchot, *Breaking New Ground* (New York: Harcourt, Brace, 1947).

26. D. H. Smith, *The Forest Service: Its History, Activities, and Organization* (Washington, D.C.: The Brookings Institution, 1930).

27. S. Fox, *John Muir and His Legacy: The American Conservation Movement* (Boston: Little, Brown, 1981).

28. J. A. Salmond, *The Civilian Conservation Corps, 1933–1942* (Durham: Duke University Press, 1967).

29. J. B. Loomis, *Integrated Public Lands Management: Principles and Applications to National Forests, Parks, Wildlife Refuges, and BLM Lands* (New York: Columbia University Press, 1993).

30. G. W. Williams, *The USDA Forest Service: The First Century,* Publication FS-650 (Washington, D.C.: USDA Forest Service, 2000).

Chapter 2

1. A. Leopold, "The Ecological Conscience," *Bulletin of the Garden Club of America* (September 1947):45–53.

2. Rachel Carson's revolutionary book *Silent Spring* (Boston: Houghton Mifflin, 1962) would change the way people viewed their lives and the impact of these lives on our planet. In spite of feeling ill with breast cancer, Carson appeared in a CBS documentary in March 1963 and concluded her remarks by saying: "We still talk in terms of conquest. We still haven't become mature enough to think

of ourselves as only a tiny part of a vast and incredible universe. Man's attitude toward nature is today critically important simply because we have now acquired a fateful power to alter and destroy nature. But man is a part of nature and his war against nature is inevitably a war against himself."

3. "History of Earth Day," speech given by former Senator Gaylord Nelson to the Catalyst Conference in Illinois in 1980. Nelson served both as U.S. senator and as governor of Wisconsin. He is also the founder of Earth Day.

4. H. K. Steen, *The U.S. Forest Service: A History* (Seattle: University of Washington Press, 1976).

5. R. McArdle, "National Forest Timber Sale Problems," U.S. Senate Committee on Interior and Insular Affairs, statement to Subcommittee on Legislative Oversight Function, February 21, 1956.

6. R. F. Kennedy, 42 Opinion of the Office of the Attorney General 127; 1962 US AG LEXIS 4.

7. USDA Forest Service, unpublished information. A recreation visitor-day is the equivalent of one person engaged in recreation for twelve hours, or two people for six hours, and so on.

8. Steen, *History,* p. 302.

9. See for example, H. Kaufman, *The Forest Ranger: A Study in Administrative Behavior* (Baltimore: Johns Hopkins University Press, 1960).

10. C. J. Buck, memo to Forest Supervisors, October 16, 1934, in "Controversy over Clear-Cutting," Gerald Williams, USDA Forest Service, October 22, 1998.

11. Gifford Pinchot, pers. comm. with C. J. Buck, September 9, 1937, in Williams, "Controversy," http://www.lib.duke.edu/forest/USFScoll/policy/Forest_Management/Clearcutting/Pinchot_to_Buck.doc.

12. Robert Wolf, pers. comm., August 2000.

13. "A University View of the Forest Service," prepared for the U.S. Senate Committee on Interior and Insular Affairs, University of Montana, 91st Congress, 2nd Session, December 1, 1970, Senate Document 91-115.

14. Ibid.

15. D. LeMaster, *Decade of Change: The Remaking of Forest Service Statutory Authority During the 1970s* (Westport, Conn: Greenwood Press, 1984).

16. From Senate Select Committee on Small Business, Timber Management Polices, Hearing Before Subcommittee on Retailing, Distribution, and Marketing Practices, 90th Congress, 2nd Session, 1969; cited in LeMaster, *Decade of Change,* pp. 241–242.

17. LeMaster, *Decade of Change.*

18. *Izaak Walton League v. Butz,* 367 F. Supp. 422 (N. D. West Virginia 1973).

19. *Izaak Walton League v. Butz,* 522 F. 2d 945 (4th Circuit 1975).

20. John Crowell; quoted in T. Egan, *The Good Rain: Across Time and Terrain in the Pacific Northwest* (New York: Vintage Departures, 1991).

21. Memorandum from Chief R. Max Peterson to Regional Foresters (January 12,

1987) and letter from Chief F. Dale Robertson to Congressman Peter DeFazio (April 13, 1987).

22. USDA Forest Service, Feedback to the Chief from the Forest Supervisors of Regions 1, 2, 3, and 4, in *Sunbird Proceedings* (Washington, D.C.: USDA Forest Service, 1989).

23. Steve Yaffee provides an excellent chronology of the northern spotted owl conflict in his 1994 book *The Wisdom of the Spotted Owl: Policy Lessons for a New Century* (Washington, D.C.: Island Press, 1994).

24. John R. McGuire, letter to Spencer Smith, director of the U.S. Fish and Wildlife Service; quoted in J. W. Thomas et al., *Viability Assessments and Management Considerations for Species Associated with Late Successional and Old-Growth Forests of the Pacific Northwest* (Portland: USDA Forest Service, 1993).

25. Oregon Endangered Species Task Force, minutes, First Meeting, June 29, 1973; cited in Yaffee, *Wisdom,* p. 21.

26. Yaffee, *Wisdom,* p. 36.

27. Ibid., p. 103. Yaffee quotes Forest Service biologist Dick Holthausen, who worked on the supplemental EIS, as follows: "One of the hard decision criteria was that the decision should not trade off more than five percent of the timber harvest. . . . That was very much a Chief's and Regional Forester's decision."

28. C. Wilkinson, *Crossing the Next Meridian: Land, Water, and the Future of the West* (Washington, D.C.: Island Press, 1992).

29. In January 2001, the chief of the Forest Service, Mike Dombeck, announced that the Forest Service would develop agency policy to inventory and map remaining old-growth forests; to protect, sustain, and enhance existing old-growth forests as an element of ecosystem diversity; to plan for old growth within a landscape context extending beyond forest boundaries; to determine the extent, pattern, and character of old growth in the past (prior to European contact and, potentially, at the time the area entered the National Forest System); and to project forward in time the amount, location, and pattern of old growth envisioned under alternative management options.

30. José Ortega y Gasset, *The Revolt of the Masses* (New York: Norton, 1993).

31. W. deBuys, "Los Alamos Fire Offers a Lesson in Humility," *High Country News,* July 3, 2000.

32. The Secure Rural Schools and Community Self-Determination Act of 2000.

33. J. W. Gardner, "Uncritical Lovers, Unloving Critics," commencement address to Cornell University, June 1, 1968.

34. R. N. Sampson, "Federal Investment in Natural Resources and the Environment (NRE)," *Wildlife Forever* (October–November 1998): 19–21.

Chapter 3

1. The following reports are perhaps the most comprehensive regarding the north-

ern spotted owl and management of its late-successional and old-growth habitat: J. W. Thomas et al., *A Conservation Strategy for the Northern Spotted Owl: A Report of the Interagency Scientific Committee to Address the Conservation of the Northern Spotted Owl* (Portland: USDA Forest Service, USDI Bureau of Land Management, U.S. Fish and Wildlife Service, and National Park Service, 1990); J. W. Thomas et al., *Viability Assessments and Management Considerations for Species Associated with Late-Successional and Old-Growth Forests of the Pacific Northwest* (Portland: USDA Forest Service, 1993).

2. W. Nehlsen, J. E. Williams, and J. A. Lichatowich, "Pacific Salmon at the Crossroads: Stocks at Risk from California, Oregon, Idaho, and Washington," *Fisheries* 16(2) (1991):4–21.

3. Forest Ecosystem Management Assessment Team (FEMAT), *Forest Ecosystem Management: An Ecological, Economic, and Social Assessment* (Portland: USDA Forest Service, USDC National Marine Fisheries Service, USDI Bureau of Land Management, Fish and Wildlife Service, National Park Service, and U.S. Environmental Protection Agency, 1993). FEMAT was headed by Jack Ward Thomas as the principal author.

4. Ibid.

5. U.S. General Accounting Office, *Western National Forests: A Cohesive Strategy Is Needed to Address Catastrophic Wildland Fire Threats,* Report GAO/RCED-99-65 (Washington, D.C.: GAO, 1999).

6. W. R. Gast et al., *Blue Mountains Forest Health Report: New Perspectives in Forest Health* (Portland: USDA Forest Service, 1991). N. Langston. *Forest Dreams, Forest Nightmares: The Paradox of Old Growth in the Inland West* (Seattle: University of Washington Press, 1995), p. 299.

7. W. J. Hann et al., "Landscape Dynamics of the Basin," in T. M. Quigley and S. J. Arbelbide, tech. eds., *An Assessment of Ecosystem Components in the Interior Columbia Basin and Portions of the Klamath and Great Basins,* General Technical Report PNW-GTR 405 (Washington, D.C.: USDA Forest Service, 1997).

8. T. M. Quigley and S. J. Arbelbide, tech. eds., *An Assessment of Ecosystem Components in the Interior Columbia Basin and Portions of the Klamath and Great Basins,* 4 vols., General Technical Report PNW-GTR-405 (Washington, D.C.: USDA Forest Service, 1997). Comparisons of ecological integrity between federal and nonfederal lands appear in various sections of the report. The specific figures quoted here are from *Status of the Interior Columbia Basin: Summary of Scientific Findings,* General Technical Report PNW-GTR-385 (Washington, D.C.: USDA Forest Service, 1996).

9. J. O'Laughlin et al., *Forest Health Conditions in Idaho* (Moscow: Idaho Forest, Wildlife, and Range Policy Analysis Group, University of Idaho, 1993).

10. The assessment analyzed ten resource conditions of which only four are discussed in the text. Other resource models include watershed vulnerability, watershed condition, fire occurrence, Canada lynx, pileated woodpecker, and white-headed woodpecker. See L. Tippin, et al., *A Forest-Wide Risk Assessment*

for Management of the Boise National Forest (Boise: USDA Forest Service, 2000).

11. For Aldo Leopold's "Conservationist in Mexico" (1937) see S. L. Flader and J. B. Callicott, eds., *The River of the Mother of God and Other Essays by Aldo Leopold* (Madison: University of Wisconsin Press, 1991), p. 240.

12. Reports of rangeland health problems began as early as 1936. See U.S. Department of Agriculture, *The Western Range: A Great But Neglected Natural Resource,* report from the secretary of agriculture to the U.S. Senate, Senate Document 199 (Washington, D.C.: GPO, 1936). More recent reviews have been provided by the U.S. Comptroller General, *Public Rangelands Continue to Deteriorate,* report to Congress by the comptroller general of the United States, Report CED-77-88, 1977, and by the U.S. General Accounting Office, *Rangeland Management: More Emphasis Needed on Declining and Overstocked Grazing Allotments,* Report GAO/RCED-88-80, 1998.

13. These data are provided in J. E. Mitchell, *Rangeland Resource Trends in the United States: A Technical Document Supporting the 2000 USDA Forest Service RPA Assessment* (USDA Forest Service, Rocky Mountain Research Station General Technical Report RMRS-GTR-68, 2000), table 3, and include data for Arizona, Colorado, Idaho, Montana, Nevada, New Mexico, Oregon, Utah, Washington, and Wyoming. Data for California were lacking for 1992, but the report showed 2 percent as excellent, 31 percent as good, 40 percent as fair, and 28 percent as poor in 1982.

14. D. W. Sada et al., *A Guide to Managing, Restoring, and Conserving Springs in the Western United States,* Technical Reference 1737-17 (Washington, D.C.: UDSI Bureau of Land Management, 2001).

15. A. Y. Cooperrider and D. S. Wilcove, *Defending the Desert: Conserving Biodiversity on BLM Lands in the Southwest* (New York: Environmental Defense Fund, 1995).

16. Bureau of Land Management, *Partners Against Weeds: An Action Plan for the Bureau of Land Management* (Billings: U.S. Bureau of Land Management, 1996).

17. P. S. White et al., "Southeast," in M. J. Mac et al., eds., *Status and Trends of the Nation's Biological Resources,* vol. 1 (Reston: U.S. Department of the Interior, Geological Survey, 1998).

18. An excellent summary of the history of longleaf pine forests has been written by K. W. Outcalt: "The Longleaf Pine Ecosystem of the South," *Native Plants Journal,* 1(1) (2000): 54–58.

19. Ibid., pp. 42–44 and 47–53. See also K. W. Outcalt, "Status of the Longleaf Pine Forests of the West Gulf Coastal Plain," *Texas Journal of Science* 49(3) suppl. (1997):5–12.

20. Ibid.

21. From M. Van Doren, *Travels of William Bartram* (New York: Dover, 1928) quoted in Outcalt, "Longleaf Pine," p. 186–187.

22. K. W. Outcalt and R. M. Sheffield, *The Longleaf Pine Forest: Trends and Current Conditions,* Resource Bulletin SRS-9 (Washington, D.C.: USDA Forest Service, 1996).

23. The Southern Forest Resource Assessment was completed in November 2001 and is available online from the USDA Forest Service's Southern Research Station and Southern Region Website.

24. *Sacramento Bee* editorial, August 30, 1999, "Killer Weeds: Foreign Intruders Taking over California's Landscape."

25. M. J. Mac et al., *Status and Trends of the Nation's Biological Resources,* vol. 1 (Reston, Va.: U.S. Department of the Interior, Geological Survey, 1998).

26. D. Pimentel et al., "Environmental and Economic Costs of Nonindigenous Species in the United States," *BioScience* 50 (2000):53–65.

27. S. Pimm and M. Gilipin, "Theoretical Issues in Conservation Biology" in J. Roughgarden, R. May, and S. Leven, eds., *Perspectives in Ecological Theory* (Princeton: Princeton University Press, 1989); J. Randall, "Weed Control for the Preservation of Biological Diversity," *Weed Technology* 10 (1996):370–383.

28. D. G. Thompson, R. L. Stuckey, and E. B. Thompson, *Spread, Impact, and Control of Purple Loosestrife (Lythrum salicaria) in North American Wetlands,* Fish and Wildlife Research Report 2 (Washington, D.C.: U.S. Fish and Wildlife Service, 1987).

29. C. Goold, "The High Cost of Weeds," in *Noxious Weeds: Changing the Face of Southwestern Colorado* (Durango, Colo.: San Juan National Forest Association, 1994). Because of the impacts on wildlife populations from leafy spurge, the Rocky Mountain Elk Foundation helps fund numerous weed control efforts with the USDA Forest Service, BLM, and others. See M. Fegely, "Leafy Spurge: Biting Back in North Dakota," *Bugle* (July–August 2000):5–6.

30. J. Brotherson and D. Field, "*Tamarix:* Impacts of a Successful Weed," *Rangelands* 9 (1987):110–112.

31. *Invasive Plants: Changing the Landscape of America,* a Fact Book prepared by Randy Westbrooks of the U.S. Department of Agriculture, was published in 1998 by the Federal Interagency Committee for the Management of Noxious and Exotic Weeds. Available commonly from federal agencies, it is a good summary of exotic plant introduction problems, causes, and solutions.

32. USDA Forest Service and USDI Bureau of Land Management, *A Range-Wide Assessment of Port-Orford-Cedar (*Chamaecyparis lawsoniana*)* (2000). A Port Orford cedar root disease brochure printed by USDA Forest Service (September 1988) contains a good summary of the disease problem.

33. R. G. Krebill and R. J. Hoff, "Update on *Cronartium ribicola* in *Pinus albicaulis* in the Rocky Mountains, USA," *Proceedings of the 4th IUFRO Rusts of Pines Working Party Conference,* Tsukuba, Japan (1995):119–126.

34. R. E. Keane and S. F. Arno, "Rapid Decline of Whitebark Pine in Western Montana: Evidence from 20-year Remeasurements," *Western Journal of Applied Forestry* 8(2) (1993):44–47.

35. See various publications and Internet information written by Sandra Anagnostakis of the Connecticut Agricultural Experiment Station in New Haven for details on the spread of chestnut blight.

36. P. A. Opler, "The Parade of Passing Species: A Survey of Extinctions in the United States," *Science Teacher* 43 (1976):30–34.

37. S. L. Anagnostakis, "Chestnuts and the Introduction of Chestnut Blight," Plant Pathology Fact Sheet No. 08. (New Haven: Connecticut Agricultural Experiment Station, 1997), p. 2.

38. See also a report by the American Fisheries Society documenting large-scale declines in freshwater mussels: J. D. Williams et al., "Conservation Status of Freshwater Mussels of the United States and Canada," *Fisheries* 18(9) (1993):6–22.

39. The Nature Conservancy's 1997 Species Report Card.

40. G. W. Williams, *The USDA Forest Service: The First Century,* Publication FS-650 (Washington, D.C.: USDA Forest Service, 2000), p. 145.

Chapter 4

1. L. L. Master, S. R. Flack, and B. A. Stein, *Rivers of Life: Critical Watersheds for Protecting Freshwater Biodiversity* (Arlington, Va.: The Nature Conservancy, 1998).

2. See the *Idaho Statesman* article titled "Biologists Find Marsh Creek Salmon Nests: Chinook Cheat Extinction, for Now, as Researchers Find 29 Live Fish and 27 Clusters of Eggs," August 21, 2000.

3. T. Burton et al., *Five-Year Monitoring Report for Bear Valley Streams and Riparian Habitats* (Boise: Boise National Forest, 1998). See also T. Burton, *Bank Stability Monitoring in Bear Valley Basin: An Overview* (Boise: Boise National Forest, 1999).

4. Much has been written about the Snake River and the effects of dams. Tim Palmer's *The Snake River: Window to the West* (Washington, D.C.: Island Press, 1991) is excellent. For an overview of the effects of dams we recommend M. Collier, R. H. Webb, and John C. Schmidt, *Dams and Rivers: Primer on the Downstream Effects of Dams,* Circular 1126 (Tucson: USGS, 1996).

5. C. N. Peters and D. R. Marmored, eds., *PATH Preliminary Evaluation of the Learning Opportunities and Biological Consequences of Monitoring and Experimental Management Actions* (Vancouver: ESSA Technologies, 2000).

6. Testimony of R. F. Thurow presented November 20, 2000, in Boise, Idaho, at the U.S. Senate Committee on Environment and Public Works Subcommittee on Fisheries, Wildlife, and Water.

7. In addition to FEMAT, *Forest Ecosystem Assessment: An Ecological, Economic, and Social Assessment* (Portland: USDA Forest Service et al., 1993), see F. J. Swanson and C. T. Dryness, "Impact of Clear-Cutting and Road Construction on Soil Erosion by Landslides in the Western Cascade Range, Oregon," *Geology* 3

(1975):393–396), and M. J. Furniss, T. D. Roelofs, and C. S. Yee, "Road Construction and Maintenance," in W. R. Mechan, ed., *Influences of Forest and Rangeland Management on Salmonid Fishes and Their Habitats,* Special Publication 19 (Bethesda, Md.: American Fisheries Society, 1991).

8. FEMAT, *Assessment.*

9. B. A. McIntosh et al., *Management History of Eastside Ecosystems: Changes in Fish Habitat over 50 years, 1935 to 1992,* Technical Report PNW-GTR-321 (Portland: USDA Forest Service, 1994).

10. USDA Forest Service and USDI Bureau of Land Management, *Environmental Assessment for the Implementation of Interim Strategies for Managing Anadromous Fish Producing Watersheds on Federal Lands in Eastern Oregon and Washington, Idaho, and Portions of California* (Washington, D.C., 1994).

11. For recent discussions of the stock concept and its importance to fishery conservation see E. E. Knudsen et al., eds., *Sustainable Fisheries Management: Pacific Salmon* (Boca Raton, Fl.: Lewis, 2000).

12. W. Nehlsen, J. E. Williams, and J. A. Lichatowich, "Pacific Salmon at the Crossroads: Stocks at Risk from California, Oregon, Idaho and Washington," *Fisheries* 16(2) (1991):4–21.

13. FEMAT, *Assessment.* Strategies described in this report would become the basis for the Northwest Forest Plan.

14. J. E. Williams and C. D. Williams, "An Ecosystem-Based Approach to Management of Salmon and Steelhead Habitat," in D. J. Stouder, P. A. Bisson, and R. J. Naiman, eds., *Pacific Salmon and Their Ecosystems: Status and Future Options* (New York: Chapman and Hall, 1997).

15. D. C. Lee et al., "Broadscale Assessment of Aquatic Species and Habitats," in T. M. Quigley and S. J. Arbelbide, tech. eds., *An Assessment of Ecosystem Components in the Interior Columbia Basin and Portions of the Klamath and Great Basins,* vol. 3, General Technical Report PNW-GTR-405 (Portland: USDA Forest Service, 1997), demonstrates the high value of roadless areas to remaining strongholds of salmon and steelhead in the interior Columbia River Basin.

16. See W. L. Minckley, *Fishes of Arizona* (Phoenix: Sim, 1973), and H. W. Robison and T. M. Buchanan, *Fishes of Arkansas* (Fayetteville: University of Arkansas Press, 1988) for excellent accounts of native and introduced fishes.

17. W. L. Minckley, "Status of the Razorback Sucker, *Xyrauchen texanus* (Abbott), in the Lower Colorado River Basin," *Southwestern Naturalist* 28 (1983):165–187.

18. W. L. Minckley and J. E. Deacon, *Battle Against Extinction: Native Fish Management in the American West* (Tucson: University of Arizona Press, 1991), provides an excellent summary of the plight of desert fishes and the battles of those trying to understand and save them. The nonprofit Desert Fishes Council (Bishop, California; Austin, Texas) publishes annual proceedings and hosts a detailed Website devoted to saving desert fishes and their habitats.

19. The fight to save the San Pedro is described in the "Riverkeeper" chapter of Todd Wilkinson's *Science Under Siege* (Boulder: Johnson Books, 1998).

20. Two publications are of special importance in identifying desert fishes and their habitats: J. N. Rinne and W. L. Minckley, *Native Fishes of Arid Lands: A Dwindling Resource of the Desert Southwest*, General Technical Report RM-206 (Ft. Collins: USDA Forest Service, Rocky Mountain Forest and Range Experiment Station, 1991), and J. E. Williams et al., "Endangered Aquatic Ecosystems in North American Deserts with a List of Vanishing Fishes of the Region," *Journal of the Arizona-Nevada Academy of Science* 20 (1985):1–62.

21. The initial publication from the Great Basin survey resulted in fifty-eight new species and more are to follow. See R. Hershler, "A Systematic Review of the Hydrobiid Snails (Gastropods: Rissooidae) of the Great Basin, Western United States, Part I, Genus *Pyrgulopsis*," *Veliger* 41(1) (1998):1–132.

22. The saga of the Devils Hole pupfish is chronicled in J. E. Deacon and C. D. Williams, "Ash Meadows and the Legacy of the Devils Hole Pupfish," in W. L. Minckley and J. E. Deacon, eds., *Battle Against Extinction: Native Fish Management in the American West* (Tucson: University of Arizona Press, 1991).

23. U.S. Fish and Wildlife Service, *Arizona Trout (Apache Trout) Recovery Plan* (Albuquerque: U.S. Fish and Wildlife Service, 1983).

24. Information on fishes of Alabama is from M. F. Mettee et al., *Fishes of Alabama and the Mobile Basin* (Birmingham, Ala.: Oxmoor House, 1996); for fishes of Tennessee see D. A. Etnier and W. C. Starnes, *The Fishes of Tennessee* (Knoxville: University of Tennessee Press, 1993); for mussels see J. D. Williams et al., "Conservation Status of Freshwater Mussels of the United States and Canada," *Fisheries* 18(9) (1993):6–22.

25. Numbers of freshwater mussels were taken from Williams et al., "Freshwater Mussels."

26. In addition to Williams et al., "Freshwater Mussels," see also C. A. Taylor et al., "Conservation Status of Crayfishes of the United States and Canada," *Fisheries* 21(4) (1996):25–38) and M. L. Warren Jr. et al., "Diversity, Distribution and Conservation Status of the Native Freshwater Fishes of the Southern United States," *Fisheries* 25(10) (2000):7–31.).

27. B. A. Stein, L. S. Kutner, and J. S. Adams, eds., *Precious Heritage: The Status of Biodiversity in the United States* (New York: Oxford University Press, 2000).

28. Warren et al., "Native Freshwater Fishes."

29. J. D. Williams and G. K. Meffe, "Nonindigenous species," in M. J. Mac et al., eds., *Status and Trends of the Nation's Biological Resources*, vol. 1 (Reston, Va.: Department of the Interior, Geological Survey, 1998).

30. P. L. Fuller, L. G. Nico, and J. D. Williams, *Nonindigenous Fishes Introduced into Inland Waters of the United States*, Special Publication 27 (Bethesda, Md.: American Fisheries Society, 1999).

31. R. J. Behnke, *Native Trout of Western North America*, Monograph 6 (Bethesda, Md.: American Fisheries Society, 1992); Fuller et al., *Nonindigenous Fishes.*

32. D. C. Lee et al., "Broadscale Assessment of Aquatic Species and Habitats," in T. M. Quigley and S. J. Arbelbide, eds., *An Assessment of Ecosystem Components in the Interior Columbia Basin and Portions of the Klamath and Great Basins,* vol. 3, General Technical Report PNW-GTR-405 (Washington, D.C.: USDA Forest Service, 1997).

33. W. J. Liss and G. L. Larson, "Complex Interactions of Introduced Trout and Native Biota in High-Elevation Lakes," in M. J. Mac et al., eds., *Status and Trends of the Nation's Biological Resources,* vol. 1 (Reston, Va.: U.S. Department of the Interior, Geological Survey, 1998).

34. The June 2001 issue of the journal *Ecosystems* was devoted to the legal, ethical, and scientific problems associated with fish stocking in wilderness lakes. Information on the Frank Church–River of No Return Wilderness can be found in D. S. Pilliod and C. R. Peterson, "Local and Landscape Effects of Introduced Trout on Amphibians in Historically Fishless Watersheds," *Ecosystems* 4 (2001):322–333.

35. E. P. Pister, "Wilderness Fish Stocking: History and Perspective," *Ecosystems* 4 (2001):285.

36. J. E. Williams and D. W. Sada, "Status of Two Endangered Fishes, *Cyprinodon nevadensis mionectes* and *Rhinichthys osculus nevadensis,* from Two Springs in Ash Meadows, Nevada," *Southwestern Naturalist* 30 (1985):475–484.

37. Fuller et al., *Nonindigenous Fishes.*

38. W. R. Courtenay Jr. and C. R. Robins, "Exotic Aquatic Organisms in Florida with Emphasis on Fishes: A Review and Recommendations," *Transactions of the American Fisheries Society* (1973):102–112.

39. P. B. Moyle, H. W. Li, and B. A. Barton, "The Frankenstein Effect: Impact of Introduced Fishes on Native Fishes in North America," in R. H. Stroud, ed., *Fish Culture in Fisheries Management* (Bethesda, Md.: American Fisheries Society, 1986).

40. P. B. Moyle et al., *Fish Species of Special Concern in California,* 2nd ed. (Sacramento: California Department of Fish and Game, 1995).

41. Moyle et al., "Frankenstein Effect."

42. C. N. Spencer, B. R. McClelland, and J. A. Stanford, "Shrimp Stocking, Salmon Collapse, and Eagle Displacement," *BioScience* 41(1) (1991):14–21.

43. Ibid.

44. Stein et al., *Precious Heritage.* Federally listed species are those officially listed as threatened or endangered pursuant to the Endangered Species Act. Rare/Imperiled species include a broader list of rare species as recognized by The Nature Conservancy.

45. Ibid.

46. J. M. Scott, R. J. F. Abbitt, and C. R. Groves, "What Are We Protecting?" *Conservation Biology in Practice* 2(1) (2001):18–19.

47. Several good examples of integrating conservation efforts on public and private lands are presented in the case studies section of J. E. Williams et al., eds.,

Watershed Restoration: Principles and Practices (Bethesda, Md.: American Fisheries Society, 1997).

48. A. C. Benke, "A Perspective on America's Vanishing Streams," *Journal of the North American Benthological Society* 9 (1990):77–88.

Chapter 5

1. The Roadless Area Conservation Rule was published in the *Federal Register,* January 12, 2001, vol. 66(9):3243–3273. Much of the background for this chapter is taken from the Roadless Rule and final environmental impact statement.

2. See USDA Forest Service, "Common Interest Classifications by State," EIS Content Analysis Team, Salt Lake City, Utah, March 20, 2001.

3. Roadless Area Conservation Rule, chap. 3, pp. 3–216. Moreover, all the new roads are planned within portions of inventoried roadless areas that were already developed with classified roads, recreation sites, and other constructed features. These developed portions of inventoried roadless areas may have lost their roadless character and would likely have been exempt from the Roadless Rule, thereby allowing the 33 miles to be constructed regardless of the rule.

4. The region in Minnesota was later designated as the Boundary Waters Canoe Area Wilderness.

5. G. W. Williams, *National Forest Service History: Wilderness Act and the Roadless Area Reviews* (Washington, D.C.: USDA Forest Service, 2000).

6. USDA Forest Service, "RARE II Final Environmental Impact Statement, Roadless Area Review and Evaluation," USDA Forest Service, FS 325, January 1979.

7. See, for example, the Southern Forest Resource Assessment. The assessment was completed in November 2001 and is available online from the USDA Forest Service's Southern Research Station and Southern Region Website.

8. J. W. Thomas, pers. comm., 2000.

9. T. W. Birch, *Private Forestland Owners of the United States, 1994,* Resource Bulletin NE-134 (Radnor, Pa.: USDA Forest Service, Northeastern Experiment Station, 1996).

10. USDA Natural Resource Conservation Service, *NRI Inventory, 1982–1997.*

11. H. K. Cordell, *Outdoor Recreation in American Life: A National Assessment of Demand and Supply Trends* (Champaign, Ill.: Sagamore, 1999).

12. Environmental Protection Agency, *Drinking Water Infrastructure Needs Survey: First Report to Congress* (Washington, D.C.: U.S. Environmental Protection Agency, Office of Water, 1997).

13. See, for example, Western Native Trout Campaign, "Imperiled Western Trout and the Importance of Roadless Areas: A Report by the Western Native Trout Campaign," November 2001.

14. D. C. Lee et al., "Broadscale Assessment of Aquatic Species and Habitats," in T. M. Quigley and S. J. Arbelbide, tech. eds., *An Assessment of Ecosystem Components in the Interior Columbia Basin and Portions of the Klamath and Great*

Basins, vol. 3, General Technical Report PNW-GTR-405 (Portland: USDA Forest Service, 1997).

15. T. M. Quigley, R. W. Haynes, and R. T. Graham, tech. eds., *Integrated Scientific Assessment for Ecosystem Management in the Interior Columbia River Basin,* General Technical Report PNW-GTR-382 (Portland: USDA Forest Service and USDI Bureau of Land Management, 1996).

16. USDA Forest Service, *Roadless Area Conservation, Final Environmental Impact Statement* (Washington, D.C.: USDA Forest Service, 2000).

17. C. A. Wood, "Forest Service Roads and Roadless Policies: Options and Rationale"; C. A. Frissell, "Consequences of Roads for Aquatic Biota"; both published in C. W. Slaughter, ed., *Proceedings of the Seventh Biennial Watershed Management Conference,* Water Resources Center Report 98 (Davis: University of California, 1999).

18. For a thorough discussion of the ecological effects of roads, see *Conservation Biology* 14(1) (February 2000); see also H. Gucinski et al., eds., *Forest Roads: A Synthesis of Scientific Information,* General Technical Report PNW-GTR-509 (Portland: Pacific Northwest Research Station, 2001).

19. R. W. Gorte, *Forest Roads: Construction and Financing,* 97-706 (Washington, D.C.: Congressional Research Service, 1997).

20. Ibid.

21. USDA Forest Service, Timber Sale Program and Reporting System, 1992–1998

22. Congress determines annual spending caps for each of the departments in the federal government.

23. USDA Forest Service, *Public Forest Service Roads* (Washington, D.C.: USDA Forest Service, 2000).

24. Ibid.

25. Ibid.

26. M. Dombeck, testimony before the Energy and Natural Resources Management Committee, U.S. Senate February 25, 1997.

27. B. T. Hill, "Forest Service Decision-Making: Greater Clarity Needed on Mission Priorities," testimony before the Subcommittee on Forests and Public Lands Management, Committee on Energy and Natural Resources, U.S. Senate, GAO/T-RCED-97-81.

28. M. Dombeck, speech to Forest Service employees, "A Gradual Unfolding of a National Purpose: A Natural Resource Agenda for the 21st Century," Missoula, Montana, March 2, 1998.

29. For example, the House Agriculture, Resources, and Budget committees held a rare joint oversight hearing on the lack of accountability in the Forest Service on March 26, 1998. Although these hearings focused on fiscal issues, GAO testimony at the hearing pointed out that accountability extends to management as well.

30. USDA Forest Service, "Administration of the Forest Development Transportation System: Temporary Suspension of Road Construction and Reconstruction

in Unroaded Areas," Interim Rule; 36 CFR Part 212; 64 *Federal Register* 7290; February 12, 1999.

31. See, for example, *Missoulian* editorial, "Road Moratorium's Impact Would Be Slight," March 8, 1998; *New York Times* editorial, "The Forest Service's New Deal," February 16, 1999.

32. F. Murkowski, et al., letter to Mike Dombeck, chief of the Forest Service, February 20, 1998. Ironically, two years later Congress would appropriate the largest budget increase in Forest Service history.

33. *Los Angeles Times* editorial, "Chopping the Forest Service," March 13, 1998.

34. *Washington Post* editorial, "Forest Fire," March 13, 1998.

35. In July 1999, for example, a survey by Republican pollster Frank Luntz claimed that 88 percent of Americans worry that "many of the nation's natural treasures will be lost" unless the government acts to protect them. In June 1999, a national poll conducted by the Mellman Group, a Democratic polling firm, claimed that 63 percent of Americans favor protecting all "wild national forest" areas of 1000 acres or more.

36. J. Porter, letter to the secretary of agriculture, Dan Glickman, January 13, 1998.

37. M. Dombeck, letter to Forest Service employees, July 1, 1998.

38. Seven House and Senate oversight hearings were held on the roadless area issue. See, for example, U.S. Senate, Hearing Transcript, Committee on Energy and Natural Resources, Subcommittee on Forests and Public Land Management, February 22, 2000.

39. F. D. Robertson, excerpt of August 12–14, 1999, interview by Harold K. Steen, in "Traditional Forestry Hits the Wall," *Forest History Today* (Spring 2000):40.

40. Complete membership of this group is found in USDA Forest Service, *Roadless Area Conservation FEIS,* vol. 1, pp. 4–13 and 4–14.

41. W. J. Clinton, memorandum to the secretary of agriculture, October 13, 1999.

42. B. Supulski, "NEPA and the Challenge of Objectivity for Administration Policies," in *Proceedings of the 2001 National Association of Environmental Professionals Conference,* Crystal City, Virginia.

43. See USDA Forest Service, "Common Interest Classifications by State," EIS Content Analysis Enterprise Team, Salt Lake City, Utah, March 20, 2001.

44. USDA Forest Service, *Roadless Area Conservation FEIS,* vol. 4, pp. 573, 579, 583–588.

45. For example, a January 2000 survey by Republican pollster Linda DiVall claimed that 76 percent of Americans (including 62 percent of Republicans) supported a policy to "permanently protect the remaining wild areas in America's National Forests from development, and preserve them as an important legacy for future generations." A January 2000 poll conducted by Responsive Management for the Teddy Roosevelt Conservation Alliance found that 86 percent of anglers and 83 percent of hunters support protections for remaining wild areas in national forests.

46. L. S. Flanders and J. Cariello, *Tongass Road Condition Survey Report,* Technical Report 00-7 (Anchorage: Alaska Department of Game and Fish, 2000).

47. USDA Forest Service, *National Summary Forest Management Program Annual Report*, app. D (Washington, D.C.; USDA Forest Service, 2001).

48. M. Dombeck, letter to the secretary of agriculture, Ann Veneman, March 23, 2001.

49. Statement of James R. Lyons before the Subcommittee on Forests and Public Lands Management, Committee on Energy and Natural Resources, U.S. Senate, February 22, 2000.

50. I. McTaggert Cowan, "Science and the Wilderness," in *The Meaning of Wilderness to Science*; cited by George Marshall, *Alaska Wilderness*, 2nd ed. (Berkeley: University of California Press, 1970), p. ix.

Chapter 6

1. J. Cairns Jr., "Eco-societal Restoration: Creating a Harmonious Future Between Human Society and Natural Systems," in J. E. Williams, C. A. Wood, and M. P. Dombeck, eds., *Watershed Restoration: Principles and Practices* (Bethesda, Md.: American Fisheries Society, 1997).

2. J. Abramovitz, "Nature's 'free' services," in L. R. Brown and E. Ayres, eds., *The Worldwatch Reader on Global Environmental Issues* (New York, Norton, 1998); W. E. Westman, "How Much Are Nature's Services Worth?" *Science* 197 (1978):960–964.

3. Y. Baskin, ed., "Ecosystem Services: Benefits Supplied to Human Societies by Natural Ecosystems," *Issues in Ecology* 2 (Spring 1997):1–16.

4. Abramovitz, "Free Services."

5. J. Sedell et al., *Water and the Forest Service*, Publication FS-660 (Washington, D.C.: USDA Forest Service, 2000).

6. E. G. McPherson et al., *Tree Guidelines for the San Joaquin Valley Communities* (Sacramento: Local Government Commission, 1999).

7. L. Anderson and K. Cordell, "Residential Property Values Improved by Landscaping with Trees," *Southern Journal of Forestry* 9 (1988):162–166.

8. A. Leopold, *For the Health of the Land*, ed. J. B. Callicott and E. T. Freyfogle (Washington, D.C.: Island Press, 1999), p. 219.

9. Abramovitz, "Free Services," p. 153.

10. N. Johnson and J. Kenna, "Ecological Restoration," in N. C. Johnson et al., eds., *Ecological Stewardship*, vol. 1: *Key Findings* (Oxford: Elsevier Science, 1999).

11. National Research Council, *Restoration of Aquatic Ecosystems: Science, Technology, and Public Policy,* (Washington, D.C.: National Academy Press, 1992).

12. A. D. Bradshaw, "Ecological Principles and Land Reclamation Practice," *Landscape Planning* 11 (1984):35–84.

13. C. Maser and J. Sedell, *From the Forest to the Sea: The Ecology of Wood in Streams, Rivers, Estuaries, and Oceans* (Delray Beach, Fla.: St Lucie Press, 1994).

14. J. R. Sedell, G. H. Reeves, and P. A. Bisson, "Habitat Policy for Salmon in the Pacific Northwest," in D. J. Stouder, P. A. Bisson, and R. J. Naiman, eds.,

Pacific Salmon and Their Ecosystems: Status and Future Options (New York: Chapman & Hall, 1997).

15. Williams et al., *Watershed Restoration,* p. 4.
16. P. Pernin, *The Great Peshtigo Fire: An Eyewitness Account,* 2nd ed. (Madison: Wisconsin Historical Society, 1999).
17. S. J. Pyne, *Fire in America: A Cultural History of Wildland and Rural Fire* (Princeton: Princeton University Press, 1982).
18. Ibid.
19. USDA Forest Service, *Protecting People and Sustaining Resources in Fire-Adapted Ecosystems* (Washington, D.C.: 2000).
20. W. J. Hann et al., "Landscape Dynamics of the Basin," in T. M. Quigley and S. J. Arbelbide, tech. eds., *An Assessment of Ecosystem Components in the Interior Columbia Basin and Portions of the Klamath and Great Basins,* General Technical Report PNW-GTR-405 (Portland: USDA Forest Service 1997).
21. *Wall Street Journal,* "Review and Outlook" (editorial), June 21, 2002.
22. *New York Times,* "Scorched-Earth Politics" (editorial page), June 30, 2002.
23. The principles of restoration are summarized from Williams et al., *Watershed Restoration,* and C. A. Wood et al., "The Art and Science of Stream Restoration," *Trout* 4(1) (Winter 1998):30–36.
24. Cairns, "Eco-societal Restoration."
25. R. W. Van Kirk and C. B. Griffin, "Building a Collaborative Process for Restoration: Henrys Fork in Idaho and Wyoming," in J. E. Williams, C. A. Wood, and M. P. Dombeck, eds., *Watershed Restoration: Principles and Practices* (Bethesda, Md.: American Fisheries Society, 1997).
26. Most biological control agents are flies, beetles, or other insects imported from the home country of the weed because they feed on or parasitize that species in its homeland.
27. S. M. Louda and C. W. O'Brien, "Unexpected Ecological Effects of Distributing the Exotic Weevil *Larinus planus* (F.) for the Biological Control of Canada Thistle," *Conservation Biology* 16(3) (2002):717–727.
28. The September 17, 1999, issue of *Science* has a series of articles on biological invaders. See especially D. Malakoff, "Fighting Fire with Fire," in that issue for a discussion of problems associated with biological control efforts.
29. Recent studies in South Africa may be valuable in this regard. See D. C. Le Maitre et al., "Invasive Plants and Water Resources in the Western Cape Province, South Africa: Modeling the Consequences of a Lack of Management," *Journal of Applied Ecology* 33 (1996):161–172. See also S. I. Higgins et al., "Predicting the Landscape-Scale Distribution of Alien Plants and Their Threat to Plant Diversity," *Journal of Conservation Biology* 13 (1999):303–313.
30. D. Stalling, *Weeds: An Exotic Invasion of Elk Country* (Missoula: Rocky Mountain Elk Foundation, n.d.); Andy Kulla, pers. comm., Lolo National Forest, Missoula.
31. Williams et al., *Watershed Restoration.*
32. J. M. Wondolleck and S. L. Yaffee, *Making Collaboration Work: Lessons from*

Innovation in Natural Resource Management (Washington, D.C.: Island Press, 2000).

33. M. P. Dombeck, C. A. Wood, and J. E. Williams, "Restoring Watersheds, Rebuilding Communities," *American Forests* 103(4) (1998):26; M. P. Dombeck, J. E. Williams, and C. A. Wood, "Watershed Restoration: Social and Scientific Challenges for Fish Biologists," *Fisheries* 22(5) (1997):26–27.

34. National Environmental Education and Training Foundation, *National Report Card on Environmental Knowledge, Attitudes, and Behaviors. The Fifth Survey of Adult Americans* (New York: Roper Storch, 1996).

Chapter 7

1. Committee of Scientists, *Sustaining the People's Lands: Recommendations for Stewardship of the National Forests and Grasslands into the Next Century* (Washington, D.C.: U.S. Department of Agriculture, 1999).

2. C. A. Wood, "Ecosystem Management: Achieving the New Land Ethic" *Renewable Resources Journal* 12(1) (1994):6–12.

3. P. R. Ehrlich, "The Loss of Diversity: Causes and Consequences," in E. O. Wilson, ed., *Biodiversity* (Washington, D.C.: National Academy Press, 1988).

4. See J. B. Callicott and K. Mumford, "Ecological Sustainability as a Conservation Concept," *Conservation Biology* 11(1) (1997):32–40. See also Committee of Scientists, *Sustaining*, chap. 3, for definitions of composition, structure, and processes.

5. H. M. Tyus, "Ecology and Management of Colorado Squawfish," pp. 379–402 in W. L. Minckley and J. E. Deacon, eds., *Battle Against Extinction: Native Fish Management in the American West* (Tucson: University of Arizona Press, 1991).

6. M. F. Merigliano, *Ecology and Management of the South Fork Snake River Cottonwood Forest*, BLM Technical Bulletin 96-9, U.S. Bureau of Land Management, Idaho. Note that successful cottonwood reproduction usually requires a flood event.

7. W. L. Minckley and G. K. Mcffe, "Differential Selection by Flooding in Stream-Fish Communities of the Arid Southwest," in W. J. Matthews and D. C. Heins, eds., *Community and Evolutionary Ecology of North American Stream Fishes* (Norman: University of Oklahoma Press, 1987).

8. M. J. Furniss, T. D. Roelofs, and C. S. Yee, "Road Construction and Maintenance," in W. R. Meehan, ed., *Influences of Forest and Rangeland Management on Salmonid Fishes and Their Habitats*, Special Publication 19 (Bethesda, Md.: American Fisheries Society, 1991).

9. L. B. Leopold, *A View of the River* (Cambridge, Mass.: Harvard University Press, 1994).

10. National Wildlife Federation, *Higher Ground: A Report on Voluntary Property Buyouts in the Nation's Floodplains* (Vienna, Va.: National Wildlife Federation, 1999).

11. N. Langston, *Forest Dreams, Forest Nightmares: The Paradox of Old Growth in the Inland West* (Seattle: University of Washington Press, 1995), p. 305.

12. W. R. Gast et al., *Blue Mountains Forest Health Report: New Perspectives in Forest Health* (Portland: USDA Forest Service, 1991), p. 299.

13. Langston, *Forest Dreams*, p. 274.

14. B. Rieman et al., "Does Wildfire Threaten Extinction for Salmonids? Responses of Redband Trout and Bull Trout Following Recent Large Fires on the Boise National Forest," in J. Greenlee, ed., *Proceedings of the Conference on Wildfire and Threatened and Endangered Species and Habitats, November 13–15, 1995, Coeur d'Alene, Idaho* (Fairfield, Wash.: International Association of Wildland Fire, 1997).

15. Langston, *Forest Dreams*, p. 277.

16. P. W. Hirt, *A Conspiracy of Optimism: Management of the National Forests Since World War Two* (Lincoln: University of Nebraska Press, 1994).

17. W. Nehlsen, J. E. Williams, and J. A. Lichatowich, "Pacific Salmon at the Crossroads: Stocks at Risk from California, Oregon, Idaho, and Washington," *Fisheries* 16(2) (1991):4–21.

18. U.S. Fish and Wildlife Service, "Lower Snake River Compensation Plan Status Review," Boise, Idaho, 1998.

19. G. K. Meffe, "Techno-Arrogance and Halfway Technologies: Salmon Hatcheries on the Pacific Coast of North America," *Conservation Biology* 6(3) (1992):351.

20. Numerous studies and reviews conducted during the 1990s demonstrated that a consensus among scientists in the Pacific Northwest had emerged regarding the need to breach the lower four dams on the Snake River as a prerequisite for survival and recovery of steelhead and salmon stocks in the river's drainage. See Independent Science Group, *Return to the River: Restoration of Salmonid Fishes in the Columbia River Ecosystem* (Portland: Northwest Power Planning Council, 1996), and H. A. Schaller et al., "Contrasting Patterns of Productivity and Survival Rates for Stream-Type Chinook Salmon (*Oncorhynchus tshawytscha*) Populations of the Snake and Columbia rivers," *Canadian Journal of Fish and Aquatic Science* 56 (1999):1031–1045). Moreover, 92 percent of the more than two hundred fish biologists attending the 1999 Idaho chapter of the American Fisheries Society annual meeting in Boise agreed that breaching the four dams offered the best hope for recovery of these endangered stocks.

21. D. W. Orr, *Earth in Mind: On Education, Environment, and the Human Prospect* (Washington, D.C.: Island Press, 1994), p. 2.

22. G. H. Reeves et al., "Fish Habitat Restoration in the Pacific Northwest: Fish Creek of Oregon," in J. E. Williams, C. A. Wood, and M. P. Dombeck, eds., *Watershed Restoration: Principles and Practices* (Bethesda, Md.: American Fisheries Society, 1997).

23. C. A. Frissell and R. K. Nawa, "Incidence and Causes of Physical Failure of Artificial Habitat Structures in Streams of Western Oregon and Washington," *North American Journal of Fisheries Management* 12 (1992):182–197. See also B. B. Roper, J. J. Dose, and J. E. Williams, "Stream Restoration: Is Fisheries Biology Enough?" *Fisheries* 22(5) (1997):6–11.

24. W. Berry, *The Gift of Good Land: Further Essays Cultural and Agricultural* (New York: North Point Press, 1981).

25. Ibid, p. 136.

26. D. A. Perry, *Forest Ecosystems* (Baltimore: Johns Hopkins University Press, 1994).

27. D. Tilman and J. A. Downing, "Biodiversity and Stability in Grasslands," *Nature* 367 (1994):363–365.

28. A. Leopold, *A Sand County Almanac and Sketches Here and There* (New York: Oxford University Press, 1949), pp. 224–225.

29. P. R. Ehrlich, *The Machinery of Nature* (New York: Simon & Schuster, 1986).

30. J. N. Rinne, "Fish and Grazing Relationships: The Facts and Some Pleas," *Fisheries* 24(8) (1999):19.

31. J. L. Kershner, "Monitoring and Adaptive Management," in J. E. Williams, C. A. Wood, and M. P. Dombeck, eds., *Watershed Restoration: Principles and Practices* (Bethesda, Md.: American Fisheries Society, 1997).

32. For a further discussion on Wendell Berry's philosophy of "listening to the land," we recommend his 1981 book *The Gift of Good Land* as well as a 1993 interview with Berry by J. Fisher-Smith, "Field Observations: An Interview with Wendell Berry," *Orion* 12(4) (1993): 50–59.

33. Langston, *Forest Dreams,* p. 286.

34. D. MacCleery, "Aldo Leopold's Land Ethic: Is It Only Half a Loaf Unless a Consumption Ethic Accompanies It?" paper presented at the Building on Leopold's Legacy conference, October 4–7, 1999, Madison, Wisconsin. See also C. A. Wood, "The Next Decade of the Forest Service: Does the Past Hold the Key to the Future?" in R. A. Sedjo, ed., *A Vision for the U.S. Forest Service: Goals for Its Next Century* (Washington, D.C.: Resources for the Future, 2000).

35. R. J. Naiman and M. G. Turner, "A Future Perspective on North America's Freshwater Ecosystems," *Ecological Applications* 10(4) (2000):958–970.

36. C. M. Pringle, "Threats to U.S. Public Lands from Cumulative Hydrologic Alterations Outside of Their Boundaries," *Ecological Applications* 10(4) (2000):971–989.

37. U.S. Forest Service, *An Analysis of the Water Situation in the United States: 1989–2040,* General Technical Report GTR-RM-177, U.S. Forest Service Rocky Mountain Forest and Range Experiment Station, 1989.

38. J. Cairns Jr., "Excessive Individualism Today Threatens Liberty Tomorrow: Sustainable Use of the Planet," *Population and Environment* 19 (1998):397–409.

Chapter 8

1. J. J. Kennedy and M. P. Dombeck, "The Evolution of Public Agency Beliefs and Behavior Toward Ecosystem-Based Stewardship," in W. T. Sexton et al., eds., *Ecological Stewardship,* vol. 3 (Oxford: Elsevier Science, 1998).

2. In December 2001, the BLM interpreted Executive Order 13212 (which instructed the agencies to expedite permitting of oil and gas development) to

require preparation of a "Statement of Adverse Energy Impact" for any decisions that might otherwise slow energy production on public lands. Many observers cried foul, arguing that such an extraordinary action shifts oil and gas development to a dominant use against which all other uses are impediments or constraints.

3. Summarized from C. Meine, "Roosevelt, Conservation, and the Revival of Democracy," *Conservation Biology* 15(4) (2001):829–831.

4. E. G. McPherson and J. R. Simpson, *Effects of California's Urban Forests on Energy Use and Potential Savings from Large-Scale Tree Planting* (Davis, Calif.: Center for Urban Forests Research, Pacific Southwest Research Station, USDA Forest Service).

5. A. Huxley, "The Politics of Ecology: The Question of Survival." Quoted in *Documentary History of Conservation in America*. Edited by Robert A. McHenry (New York: Praeger, 1972), 349.

6. W. Berry, *The Unsettling of America: Culture and Agriculture.* (San Francisco: Sierra Club Books, 1977), p. 131.

7. Committee of Scientists, *Sustaining the People's Lands: Recommendations for Stewardship of the National Forests and Grasslands into the Next Century* (Washington, D.C.: U.S. Department of Agriculture, 1999).

8. G. Pinchot, *Breaking New Ground* (New York: Harcourt, Brace, 1947).

9. J. Sedell et al., *Water and the Forest Service,* Publication FS-660 (Washington, D.C.: USDA Forest Service, 2000).

10. Environmental Protection Agency, *Drinking Water Infrastructure Needs Survey: First Report to Congress* (Washington, D.C.: U.S. Environmental Protection Agency, Office of Water, 1997).

11. USDA Forest Service, *Roadless Area Conservation: Final Environmental Impact Statement,* November 9, 2000, pp. 3–179.

12. C. A. Wood, "The Struggle to Protect Roadless and Wilderness Areas," *Wild Oregon* 28(3) (2001):4–6.

13. T. W. Birch, *Private Forestland Owners of the United States, 1994,* Resource Bulletin NE-134 (Radnor, Pa.: USDA Forest Service, Northeastern Experiment Station, 1996).

14. USDA Forest Service, *National Forest Recreation Use, 1924–1996* (Washington, D.C.: USDA Forest Service, Recreation, Heritage, and Wilderness Resources Staff, 1997).

15. Biscuit Fire burn severity estimates provided by Jon Brazier, Burn Area Emergency Rehabilitation Team Leader, Biscuit Fire, U.S. Forest Service, personal communication, October 2002.

16. R. Carson, *Silent Spring* (Boston: Houghton Mifflin, 1962), p. 297.

17. E. O. Wilson, *The Future of Life* (New York: Knopf, 2002), p. xxiii.

18. A. Leopold, *Round River* (New York: Oxford University Press, 1953), p. 177.

19. B. A. Stein, L. S. Kutner, and J. S. Adams, eds., *Precious Heritage: The Status of Biodiversity in the United States* (New York: Oxford University Press, 2000).

20. D. Tilman, "The Ecological Consequences of Changes in Biodiversity: A Search for General Principles," *Ecology* 80(5) (1999):1455–1474.

21. According to the EPA, *Liquid Assets 2000: America's Water Resources at a Turning Point* (Office of Water EPA-840-B-00-001), mining in the western United States has contaminated stream reaches in the headwaters of more than 40 percent of the watersheds in the West. The EPA is spending $30,000 a day to treat contaminated mine drainage at the Summitville mine in Colorado, which will eventually cost an estimated $179 million to clean up. Remediation of the half a million abandoned mines in thirty-two states may cost up to $35 billion more.

22. *Great Lakes Ecosystem Report 2000,* EPA-9050R-01-001 (Chicago: U.S. Environmental Protection Agency, Great Lakes Program Office, 2000).

23. Bureau of Land Management, *Partners Against Weeds: An Action Plan for the Bureau of Land Management* (Billings, Mont.: BLM, 1996).

24. *Sacramento Bee* editorial, August 30, 1999, "Killer Weeds: Foreign Intruders Taking over California's Landscape."

25. J. Van Driesche and R. Van Driesche, *Nature Out of Place* (Washington, D.C.: Island Press, 2001).

26. For a thorough discussion of old-growth forests and values see B. G. Marcot, "Biodiversity of Old Growth Forests in the West: A Lesson from Our Elders," in *Creating a Forestry for the 21st Century: The Science of Ecosystem Management* (Washington, D.C.: Island Press, 1997).

27. Statement of Dale Bosworth, chief, USDA Forest Service, to Subcommittee on Forests and Forest Health, Committee on Resources, U.S. House of Representatives, Washington, D.C. (2001).

28. National Research Council, *Forested Landscapes in Perspective: Prospects and Opportunities for Sustainable Management of America's Non-Federal Forests* (Washington, D.C.: National Academy Press, 1998).

29. G. Moll, "The State of Our City Forests," *American Forests,* May/June 1987; cited in National Research Council, *Forested Landscapes.*

30. This question—whether the goal of restoring ecological sustainability entails mimicking pre-European conditions in North America—was a subject of intense debate among the Committee of Scientists (1999).

31. A. Leopold, "The Forester's Role in Game Management," *Journal of Forestry* 29(1) (1931):25–31.

About the Authors

Michael P. Dombeck currently is the Pioneer Professor of Global Environmental Management at the University of Wisconsin–Stevens Point and University of Wisconsin System Fellow for Global Conservation. He completed his undergraduate and graduate education at the University of Wisconsin–Stevens Point and the University of Minnesota prior to receiving his doctorate from Iowa State University. After his retirement from public service he returned to the woods and lakes of Wisconsin, not too far from where he began his career as a fishing guide and zoology instructor.

Christopher A. Wood currently is vice president for conservation programs at Trout Unlimited in their national office in Arlington, Virginia. He completed his undergraduate work at Middlebury College in Vermont. When not chasing fish with a flyrod or working to restore streams and watersheds for TU, he is busy stalking gophers and restoring his own part of the Back 40 at his farm near Points, West Virginia.

Jack E. Williams presently is senior fellow at the AuCoin Institute for Ecological, Economic, and Civic Studies at Southern Oregon University in Ashland. He completed his undergraduate and graduate education at Arizona State University and the University of Nevada at Las Vegas prior to receiving his doctorate from Oregon State University. He resides in the Oregon's Rogue River Valley where he works to eliminate alien weeds and promote native fish.

Collectively, Mike Dombeck, Chris Wood, and Jack Williams have worked for over five decades for the Bureau of Land Management, Fish and Wildlife Service, and U.S. Forest Service. **Mike Dombeck** joined the Forest Service in 1978 as a biological technician in Michigan's Hiawatha National Forest and would eventually become the agency's chief in Washington, D.C. (1997–2001). He also served the Forest Service as fisheries biologist in Michigan and Wisconsin, regional fisheries program manager in California, and national fisheries program manager in Washington, D.C. Mike served as acting assistant secretary of the interior for lands and mineral management and at the BLM as acting director (1994–1997), and special assistant and science adviser to the director. **Chris Wood** started his federal career as a seasonal employee for the Forest Service in Boise, Idaho, in1991 before moving on to American Rivers in Washington, D.C. He returned to federal service as a program analyst for the BLM in Washington, D.C., before rejoining the Forest Service as senior policy and communications adviser to the chief in 1997. **Jack Williams** began his federal career with the U.S. Fish and Wildlife Service in 1980 before joining the BLM in 1989 as national fisheries program manager and, later, science adviser to the director. He also served the Forest Service as deputy forest supervisor at the Boise National Forest in Idaho and forest supervisor for the Rogue River and Siskiyou National Forests in Oregon. Jack, Mike, and Chris edited *Watershed Restoration: Principles and Practices,* which was published by the American Fisheries Society in 1997.

About the Illustrator

Award-winning artist **William Millonig** is an avid outdoorsman and science and math teacher who lives in Wisconsin's Kettle Moraine near Campbellsport.

Index